The Pursuit of Ruins

Diálogos Series

KRIS LANE, SERIES EDITOR

Understanding Latin America demands dialogue, deep exploration, and frank discussion of key topics. Founded by Lyman L. Johnson in 1992 and edited since 2013 by Kris Lane, the Diálogos Series focuses on innovative scholarship in Latin American history and related fields. The series, the most successful of its type, includes specialist works accessible to a wide readership and a variety of thematic titles, all ideally suited for classroom adoption by university and college teachers.

Also available in the Diálogos Series:

Creating Charismatic Bonds in Argentina: Letters to Juan and Eva Perón
by Donna J. Guy

Gendered Crossings: Women and Migration in the Spanish Empire
by Allyson M. Poska

From Shipmates to Soldiers: Emerging Black Identities in the Río de la Plata
by Alex Borucki

Women Drug Traffickers: Mules, Bosses, and Organized Crime by Elaine Carey

Searching for Madre Matiana: Prophecy and Popular Culture in Modern Mexico
by Edward Wright-Rios

Africans into Creoles: Slavery, Ethnicity, and Identity in Colonial Costa Rica
by Russell Lohse

Native Brazil: Beyond the Convert and the Cannibal, 1500-1900 edited by Hal Langfur

Emotions and Daily Life in Colonial Mexico edited by Javier Villa-Flores
and Sonya Lipsett-Rivera

The Course of Andean History by Peter V. N. Henderson

Masculinity and Sexuality in Modern Mexico edited by Anne Rubenstein
and Víctor M. Macías-González

For additional titles in the Diálogos Series, please visit unmpress.com.

The Pursuit of Ruins

Archaeology, History, and the Making of Modern Mexico

CHRISTINA BUENO

University of New Mexico Press ❖ Albuquerque

Names: Bueno, Christina, 1966–
Title: The pursuit of ruins : archaeology, history, and the making of modern Mexico /
Christina Bueno.
Description: Albuquerque : University of New Mexico Press, 2016. |
Series: Diálogos Series | Includes bibliographical references and index.
Identifiers: LCCN 2015049831 (print) | LCCN 2016009414 (ebook) |
ISBN 9780826357311 (cloth : alkaline paper) |
ISBN 9780826357328 (paperback : alkaline paper) | ISBN 9780826357335 (electronic)
Subjects: LCSH: Indians of Mexico—Antiquities. | Archaeology and history—
Mexico. | Mexico—Antiquities. | Archaeology and state—Mexico—History. |
Cultural property—Political aspects—Mexico—History. | Material culture—Political
aspects—Mexico—History. | Nationalism—Mexico—History. | Díaz, Porfirio,
1830–1915—Influence. | Mexico—Politics and government—1867–1910. |
Mexico—Cultural policy.
Classification: LCC F1219 .B918 2016 (print) | LCC F1219 (ebook) |
DDC 972/.01—dc23
LC record available at http://lccn.loc.gov/2015049831

Cover photograph: Porfirio Díaz poses with the Aztec Calendar in the National
Museum, 1910 (photograph courtesy of INAH). The plaque under the calendar
focuses on the history of the object's location rather than its meaning, explaining
that "in December of the year 1790 while the new pavement was being installed in
the Plaza Mayor in this capital, this monument was discovered and then hung at
the foot of the west tower of the cathedral on its west-facing side and from there it
was transferred to the museum in August 1885."

Designed by Lila Sanchez
Composed in Minion Pro 10.25/13.5
Display type is Minion Pro

To Patricio.

And to Nico, who promised to never read this.

Contents

◄◊

Acknowledgments

⚜ I CAME TO THIS BOOK BY WAY OF THE BERING STRAIT. SEVERAL years ago, I had the good fortune of reading Yuri Slezkine's magnificent *Arctic Mirrors*, a history of the encounter between the Russians and the indigenous people of Siberia. Much of Slezkine's book examines the anthropologists who worked for the Soviet government. The topic sparked my interest, and I decided to explore something similar in Mexico. Once I got to the archives I discovered that the Mexican government's relationship with anthropologists took root during the reign of Porfirio Díaz, the era known as the Porfiriato (1876–1910). I also learned that the branch of anthropology the government emphasized at the time was not ethnography or any other field dealing with live people. Instead, it emphasized archaeology.

Since those first days in the archives, I have benefited from the intellectual and emotional support of many teachers and friends who made the writing of this book a much easier journey, I imagine, than actually crossing the Bering Strait. I am deeply indebted to all of them. Some of the first were my mentors, Arnold Bauer, Andrés Reséndez, and Charles Walker. I thank them for their guidance over the years, not to mention the countless letters of support they've written on my behalf. I am also grateful to three very generous institutions: the Ford Foundation supported this project in its earliest stages. Once I became a professor, fellowships from the American Council of Learned Societies and the National Endowment for the Humanities gave me the breaks I needed from a busy teaching schedule to finish this book.

Of course, none of this would have been possible without the help of librarians and archivists. Special thanks go to María Trinidad Lahirigoyen at Mexico's Archivo Histórico del Museo Nacional de Antropología, Teresa Serrano Espinosa at the Biblioteca Nacional de Antropología e Historia, the entire staff at the Archivo General de la Nación, Mai Reitmeyer at the American Museum of Natural History, and Debbie Siegel in Northeastern

Illinois University's interlibrary loan department. Elvira Pruneda also shared with me her vast knowledge of her great-grandfather, the archaeologist Leopoldo Batres, the central figure in this book. Spencer Burke was equally generous with his many insights into the life of American archaeologist Edward Thompson.

I also profited immensely from the help of other friends and colleagues who commented on this work at different stages, offered me guidance, made me laugh, or all of the above. These include Bill Beezley, Dina Berger, Julie Cottle, Mira Marinova, Erin McGinty, Julia Medina, Alexandra Puerto, Frances Ramos, Santi and Patrick Rizzo, Lia Schraeder, Gabriela Soto Laveaga, and Yanna Yannakakis. I owe tremendous debt to Alec Dawson, who has pushed me in my thinking over the years and has helped me more than he probably realizes. I am also grateful to the earlier mentors who shaped my life: Julyana Peard, Barbara Loomis, Mary Felstiner, and the violinist Teresa DiTullio.

At Northeastern Illinois University I found the friendliest, most supportive community of scholars I could ask for. Heartfelt thanks go to all the members of the history department. Conversations with Christina Gomez, Patrick Miller, Francesca Morgan, Zach Schiffman, and the late Susan Rosa, in particular, found their way into these pages. Jon Hageman answered my innumerable questions about archaeology with infinite patience. Cris Joe helped me with my computer problems with her typical good cheer. I am also grateful to the students at Northeastern Illinois University who, among other things, have taught me the importance of "talking straight." I hope this lesson has translated into an accessible book. As luck would have it, I found another group of brilliant folks at the University of New Mexico Press. Clark Whitehorn, Marie Landau, Lisa Tremaine, and Lila Sanchez helped me at every step. Kris Lane offered keen insights and suggestions as Diálogos editor, making this a much better book. Others also made it much prettier: photography editor Rebecca Robertson worked her magic hunting down images. Cartographer Nat Case crafted the beautiful maps, which were paid for by Northeastern Illinois University. I am also indebted to MJ Devaney for her marvelous editing.

Finally, I must thank my family, whom I have dragged along on this journey for too many years to count. My relatives in Mexico, especially Eloisa, Montse, and María de Lourdes Bueno, opened their hearts and homes to me. Roxy Rizzo and the late Don Garibaldi were wonderful companions. My sisters Monica and Rebecca Bueno have been my constant confidants;

I thank them for simply being who they are. I have also been blessed with wonderful parents, Juan and Donna Bueno, who have shown me nothing but love and support. My father served as the perfect sounding board over the years, reading this book several times—a true test of love! He also did much of the legwork involved in accessing some of the images. Last but certainly not least I must give the biggest of "shout-outs" to my compañero, Patricio Rizzo, and my beloved son, Nico, who have walked beside me from beginning to end and who've made this as well as every other journey worthwhile. Thank you.

INTRODUCTION

The Allure of Antiquity

✦ MEXICO'S FIRST INHABITANTS LEFT THE LANDSCAPE FULL OF TRACES
of their existence: countless weapons, tools, and statues—over a staggering
ten thousand archaeological sites at last count. The most sophisticated of
these civilizations built spectacular cities with wide avenues, apartment
complexes, and many other features associated with urban living today.
They built towering pyramids so that their altars might be as close to the sky
as possible. Over time, great cities like these flourished and fell. One of the
last was the Aztec capital of Tenochtitlán in present-day Mexico City,
brought down by the Spanish conquest in 1521. A much earlier city was
Teotihuacán. What began as a cluster of villages in the Valley of Mexico
sometime around 200 BC grew to become one of the world's largest cities at
the time, with magnificent temples, the enormous Pyramid of the Sun, and
perhaps as many as two hundred thousand inhabitants.[1] It must have been
a spectacular sight: the city would have been teeming with people, with rulers decked out in full regalia and pyramids painted in vivid colors, especially bright red. And then, mysteriously, disaster struck. At some point in
the seventh century—we're not exactly sure when or why—the city was set
on fire and its altars and temples shattered. Archaeologists continue to
search for clues, but what is clear is that the assault was especially fierce, as
if the attackers wanted to destroy not only the city itself but every trace of
the Teotihuacano civilization. The civilization did, in fact, perish, but the
ruins of the city remained.

Soon, nature began to invade. Layer upon layer of soil settled, turning temples into mounds of dirt and the Pyramid of the Sun into a gigantic hill. Plants began to sprout. The cacti, mesquite, and maguey, the flora of that dry, stark region, dug roots deep into the structures, loosening the blocks of stone. Rainy seasons came and went and earthquakes struck, eroding the pyramids even further. All of Mexico's ancient cities suffered this same fate. In Uxmal, Yucatán, it was the tropical lushness, the creepers and vines, that consumed the ruins of the ancient Maya. In Palenque, Chiapas, even the birds and bats got involved. They smothered the Temple of the Inscriptions with guano, the layer becoming so thick that in 1838, when the French explorer Jean Frédéric de Waldeck tried to copy the temple's hieroglyphics, he could barely make them out and resorted to inventing what he could not see. Waldeck was not the only one who sought out these ancient places. Many others continued to visit and even occupy the pre-Hispanic cities long after they had fallen. Teotihuacán, to take just one example, was never really abandoned. Soon after its destruction, settlers began to arrive, making their homes in its ancient apartments.

Today, Teotihuacán's Pyramid of the Sun is no longer covered in dirt, and the temples of Palenque are generally free of creepers and vines. The ruins look picture perfect. Throngs of tourists visit them each year. Countless Mexicans and foreigners endure the stifling heat of Palenque and climb the nearly 250 steps to reach the top of the Pyramid of the Sun. Even the most die-hard "spring breaker" in Cancún will most likely spend an afternoon in nearby Chichén Itzá. The Mexican government has gone to great lengths to rebuild the fallen cities; it has pieced together block after block of stone, creating a landscape full of pristine showcases of an ancient past. It has turned the objects of the ancient Indians into patrimony or property of the nation, a process, this book argues, that took off in the late nineteenth century during the dictatorship of Porfirio Díaz, the period known as the Porfiriato (1876–1910). The Díaz regime worked harder than any of Mexico's previous governments to bring the ancient objects under state control; it placed guards at ruins, strengthened federal legislation so as to give the state more power over monuments, and in 1885 established the first agency exclusively to protect them, the General Inspectorate of Archaeological Monuments of the Republic. It gave unprecedented support to the National Museum in Mexico City, filling it with relics. It peeled away the centuries of sediment along with the cacti, mesquite, and maguey that enveloped the Pyramid of the Sun, turning Teotihuacán into the nation's first official archaeological site in 1910. Antiquity had taken on a heightened ideological importance for Mexico's political and intellectual elites. It had become inseparable from their nationalist sentiment and their efforts to build the nation.

This does not mean Mexican leaders had ignored antiquity before the age of Díaz. The Indian past had long served as an ideological resource; in fact, even the ancient Indians used it. We know that the Olmecs, Maya, and Aztecs collected objects from earlier cultures that they admired and wished to emulate. The Aztecs excelled at this practice. In their efforts to associate themselves with the Teotihuacanos and the Toltecs, they gathered relics from the cities of both people, leaving the Toltec city of Tula so bare that several contemporary scholars have suggested it "is not spectacular enough to have been the Toltec capital!"[2]

Over the course of the rest of Mexican history, this interest in antiquity would wax and wane. One of the high points was the late colonial period, when Charles III and Charles IV of Spain, two Bourbon rulers influenced by the Enlightenment and the scientific revolution, sponsored excavations at several of Mexico's ruins. The viceroys under both these monarchs also began accumulating artifacts in the Royal and Pontifical University in Mexico City, initiating the collection that would later serve as the basis of the National Museum. By that time, antiquity had become an important source of inspiration for another group known as the creoles, people born in Mexico of Spanish descent. The creoles no longer identified with Spain but considered Mexico, their place of birth, as their fatherland, or patria. In the eyes of the creoles, Mexico's origins lay in the Indian past, a period that they believed gave the nation deep and prestigious roots, much like those of the Old World. As the main actors in the struggle to break free from Spain, the creoles used this past to justify Mexico's independence. They argued that a Mexican nation had existed since long before the conquest and that it was entitled to recover its freedom. For the creoles, though, not all of the ancient Indians were equal; they glorified the Aztecs as the nation's founding culture, the people of Mexico City, the historical seat of power.

Soon after independence, Mexico took steps to conserve the relics and ruins. The government established the National Museum in Mexico City in 1825 and, two years later, passed the nation's first law prohibiting the exportation of antiquities. Mexican scholars, especially those belonging to the liberal faction, not only devoted themselves to the study of the Indian past but continued the well-established trend of glorifying the Aztecs. Much like the creoles, the liberals embraced antiquity out of a sense of nationalism and pride, feelings that became all the more intense during the middle of the century, when Mexico lost over half its territory to its neighbor to the north. Nineteenth-century Mexico was a chaotic place, a land of coups, invasions, and civil wars. This turmoil had an impact on the ruins. As one journalist explained, the "scandals of our government" kept it from tending to the monuments.[3] The legislation outlawing the exportation of antiquities went unenforced, leading to a steady hemorrhaging of artifacts from the country. The National Museum, Mexico's most important center of archaeological conservation and study, was also plagued with problems. The institution suffered from sparse and sporadic funding, was frequently moved and shut down, and was even used to quarter soldiers—rowdy ones, to boot. In 1860 one of these men went berserk and began to break the antiquities; "so great was his speed and drunken state" that no one was able to stop him.[4] (He was fined a paltry 15 pesos.) No wonder an exasperated José Fernando Ramírez, the museum director in the early 1850s, could be found complaining that scholars of antiquity like himself had not enjoyed the "support of the national government."[5]

Ironically, support eventually came by way of a foreign invader, the Austrian archduke Ferdinand Maximilian. Installed as emperor of Mexico by the French, Maximilian's brief reign lasted from 1864 to 1867. In an effort to appear patriotic and to legitimize his rule, the emperor put an end to the nomadic wanderings of the museum. In 1865 he gave the museum a permanent home at 13 Moneda Street in a building that made up part of the National Palace. The institution would remain there, just a few steps from Mexico City's famous Zócalo, or main plaza, for nearly a century, until it was transferred to Chapultepec Park in 1964. Mexico's next leader, Benito Juárez, the president who defeated Maximilian and made the word "hapless" almost a prefix to the emperor's name, similarly supported the museum, raising its budget to an all-time high of 500 pesos a month. Juárez also passed a decree prohibiting anyone from carrying out archaeological excavations in the country without a permit from the federal government. But the enforcement of this and other laws was inconsistent. What is more, the museum would continue to go "unnoticed," according to Manuel Orozco y Berra, one of the leading historians of the day.[6] It had not received the support it needed to make the "patria shine," claimed the writer Manuel Rivera Cambas.[7]

This brief overview is not meant to be exhaustive but to simply serve as a reminder of Mexico's long-standing interest in the pre-Hispanic past. Despite this interest, by the time Porfirio Díaz came to power in 1876, a series of viceroys, presidents, and rulers had done little to take charge of the nation's ruins. This lack of action would begin to be addressed under Díaz. His regime made a more concerted effort to control and display the archaeological remains, an effort that was embedded in the larger process of late nineteenth-century nation building.

Nation Building and the Ancient Past

Nations, as many scholars have shown, are historical constructions. They arose largely in the nineteenth century, replacing more traditional forms of government, such as empires and dynastic states. But nations are not some sort of "natural" product of history. Instead, they have been actively created, a process referred to, not surprisingly, as nation building. The process of nation building is ongoing—there is no such thing as a "finished" nation. It also involves a wide range of phenomena and developments such as the consolidation of a state of national dimensions, a state that is capable of dominating the national territory and establishing a uniform system of institutions, activities, and laws.

In Mexico, the Porfiriato intensified this process. The Díaz regime brought greater control over the national territory. Using the so-called *pan o palo* (bread or the stick) strategy, it concentrated power in the hands of federal authorities by suppressing the interests of state and local governments, co-opting some people and coercing others, and lashing out violently at dissenters. By the end of the period even the nation's most peripheral regions had been subjugated by the capital, a process that saw wars against the Yaqui Indians far north in Sonora and the Maya in Yucatán. The Díaz regime was a dictatorship notorious for its brutality, but it put an end to the country's many years of chaos, ushering in a period of stability (this false sense of peace came at great cost to most Mexicans, as the 1910 revolution would attest). The motto of the regime was "Order and Progress." To bring about order, the government shored up the *rurales*, the special rural police force in charge of quelling dissent. To bring about progress, it pursued a modernizing agenda based on promoting technology and courting capital from abroad. Money flowed in, unleashing a spectacular economic boom, one that made the rich much richer and that allowed the government to construct the trappings of modernity: paved streets, electric lights, trolleys and trams. It supported huge public works projects, too, like

the railroad, which came to crisscross the entire nation by the time Díaz
fell from power, and a drainage system for Mexico City, which was under-
taken by a British company that installed miles of tunnels to extract the
water that constantly flooded a capital built on an ancient city located on
an island in the middle of a lake. Mexico's newfound stability and economic boom also sparked the expansion of the federal bureaucracy—the
government payroll swelled an astounding 900 percent between 1876 and
1910.[8] This growth translated into more funding and employees for the
Inspectorate of Monuments and the National Museum, the two institutions
in charge of tending to the remains of the past. As one observer explained,
once the difficult task of "national reconstruction" was resolved and "the
coffers of the Treasury allowed," the government set out to "restore some
of the buildings most important to our pre-history."[9]

But nation building is not just about politics and economics. It is a cultural process as well, one aimed at endowing a country's diverse population
with a common national culture. Mexico, for instance, is often thought to
be not one but "many Mexicos," to use Lesley Byrd Simpson's much-quoted
phrase, a land of disparate regions and of peoples divided along lines of
race, ethnicity, gender, and class. During the age of Díaz most of these people would have considered themselves members of a village or town rather
than citizens of a nation. They identified with their local surroundings
instead of the more abstract concept of the Mexican nation. The creation of
a common culture helps diminish these sorts of divisions. It forges a sense
of belonging to the nation, making Mexicans, say, out of people who had
seen themselves as Chiapanecos, Tampiqueños, or Chatinos. It helps impart
a sense of unity to the population; all nations, as Benedict Anderson
explains, are made up of members who "will never know most of their
fellow-members, meet them, or even hear of them, yet in the minds of each
lives the image of their communion." According to Anderson, this sense of
unity or communion is generated through certain "institutions of power,"
things like maps, museums, and censuses, that allow a government to imagine its domain.[10]

Central to this sense of unity is the invention of a national past, a history
that gives the population a shared heritage and origin. The key word here is
"invention." National histories are inventions. They are elite interpretations
of the past, histories constructed by statesmen and intellectuals who have
been remembered as "nation builders." Often, these leaders base such histories in antiquity or a remote past in an attempt to give the nation a sense of

timelessness along with prestigious, ancient roots. Even though nations are relatively new, points out Anderson, they are usually portrayed as having origins that go way back in time.

For a nation like Mexico that was born of a former colony and wracked by generations of oppression and invasions, antiquity can also provide a past prior to foreign domination, a history of autonomy before colonialism. It can provide a nation with an "authentic past of its own." At the same time, the making of this past is far from simple. As postcolonial theorists have shown, nations that have freed themselves from colonial rule face certain challenges when constructing their histories. If they focus on the colonial era, they risk appearing as if they have no past of their own. If they emphasize antiquity or the period before colonialism, on the other hand, their national culture may appear "obsolete or trapped in bygone times and therefore backward."[11] Nevertheless, the embrace of a preconquest or ancient past has served as a strategy of decolonization in many parts of the world. Nations have used antiquity to showcase their "genuine" culture, to counter a history of colonialism and the hegemony of Western values.

Porfirian elites turned to antiquity for these very reasons. Mexico had a long history of foreign exploitation. It was a nation deemed inferior by the dominant Eurocentric racist thinking of the day, a nation considered so backward and inept that its artifacts were ripe for the taking. Porfirian elites sought to change this image, a desire that was driven by their concerns with attracting foreign immigration and investment but that was also a matter of pride. The elites longed for Mexico to be considered among the civilized, developed countries of the globe. They not only promoted all things thought to be modern—like the train—but held fast to the consumption patterns of the West, especially those of France, importing everything from European political theories to pianos and perfume.[12] Their embrace of an Indian past grew out of this same concern with asserting and defending the nation's image. They turned to antiquity to present Mexico as a unified nation with a sophisticated ancient past. For them, as for their creole and liberal predecessors, antiquity was a source of pride, a way to counter Mexico's inferior image and place the country on a more equal footing with the world's dominant powers. In fact, it was under Díaz that Mexico's official history became more firmly rooted in the Indian past. A telltale sign was *Mexico through the Centuries* (1887–1889), the nation's first comprehensive historical narrative, a work that forged a single story out of the different phases in the Mexican past, beginning with antiquity.[13]

But again, this was not a simple process. Although Mexican elites sought to craft an "authentic" ancient past for their nation, they were operating in a world dominated by the West. The antiquity they created did not break free from the hegemony of Western values. Instead, it took shape in response to the cultural standards and racial hierarchies of the West, with the many contradictions, as we'll see, that this entailed. While scholars continue to debate whether Mexico, along with the rest of the countries in Latin America, are postcolonial nations (a term typically assigned to countries that gained independence in the second half of the twentieth century), the insights of postcolonial theorists about the problems of constructing a national past do resonate with Mexico's experience.[14] As in other postcolonial nations, the making of Mexico's official history would be a contradictory, tricky process.

Histories, of course, do not exist only in texts. "Memory takes root in the concrete, in spaces, gestures, images, and objects."[15] Mexico's pre-Hispanic past was thought to take tangible, material form in the antiquities found scattered throughout the land, objects that were perceived as the nation's patrimony, although the word "patrimony" was hardly ever used at the time. Instead, Mexicans spoke about these objects in more poetic ways, as "the mute witnesses of the past" or "the delicate pages" of our history books.[16] Much like national histories, national patrimony is thought to unify a population under a common culture. The objects are believed to capture a nation's essence or brilliance and are thus celebrated and protected. One only needs to think of the Eiffel Tower in France or the Star-Spangled Banner, the flag of Betsy Ross, found hanging in the Smithsonian Institution. Theorists today have many definitions of patrimony. Néstor García Canclini, for instance, describes it as "a fixed repertory of traditions condensed in objects." Canclini also reminds us that patrimony extends beyond material objects and includes "invisible cultural goods," such as customs and language.[17] In Mexico, however, the government has tended to favor material objects, especially those from history but above all those from the pre-Hispanic past. This was clearly the case during the Porfiriato. As antiquity became the basis of Mexico's official history and image, the government sought to take control of its remains. And it did so through the science of archaeology, a discipline that, much like antiquity, had come to take on special meaning.

For the wealthy and educated elites, the very act of studying and controlling the past gave Mexico the coveted aura of a scientific, cosmopolitan, and modern nation. Taking charge of the past also proved that Mexico was sovereign. Foreigners had been exploiting the ruins for centuries. Explorers like Waldeck had come and gone, carting off trunks full of relics, quite often with the aid of the local residents. Porfirian elites hoped to put an end to this profiteering and demonstrate that Mexico was not only the master of its history but also of its territory and the objects within it. Their turn to archaeology was driven by this same concern with defending the country's image. And here, of course, they were not alone. Nations throughout the world have embraced archaeology as a form of resistance to imperialism. Places as diverse as China and Greece began their own archaeological traditions in response to the relic-hunting expeditions of Western powers.

Not surprisingly, Mexican archaeology developed as a *national* archaeology—that is, it focused almost exclusively on the study of the archaeological record within its own borders. It was in Mexico that "one of the earliest, most successful, and internationally influential" national traditions came into being, the roots of which are clearly visible in the Porfiriato.[18] But the science would also develop as a *nationalist* archaeology—that is, the discipline was used for the purpose of nation building. Archaeology helped construct an official past in Mexico. And it was characterized by the "culture-historical approach," a type of archaeology that emphasizes the achievements of earlier civilizations in order to boost national pride and morale.[19] The government channeled the science to the making of showcases to exalt the ancient past, and it focused especially on two of them: the National Museum and the ruins of Teotihuacán.

National museums are one of the fundamental institutions of nation building. They are, quite literally, the warehouses of the nation, places that hold a country's patrimony, everything from art to coins to specimens from the natural world. The exhibits they contain can be read much like texts, with objects put on display in ways that cast certain interpretations of the nation and its past. The ruins, too, are places "where nationalism may be embodied and made visible." They are sites where foreigners can witness a country's ancient splendor and where citizens can rekindle their "faith and belief in the national ideal."[20] Although the Díaz regime would try to control as many ruins as possible, none were as important as Teotihuacán. The government carried out a major reconstruction of the site in preparation for the *centenario* of 1910, Mexico's centennial celebration of independence from Spain, which drew thousands of visitors from around the world. For a regime fond of big state projects like the drainage works and railroad, Teotihuacán was its tour de force in the realm of archaeology.

This book, then, is essentially about objects. It examines how the ruins of the ancient Indians—monuments overtaken by nature and used by foreigners and local people for centuries—were transformed into museum pieces and official sites. It looks at the making of patrimony, how the pots and statues of the Toltecs, Aztecs, and many other ancient cultures became *Mexican* objects. It does not pretend to be an intellectual or institutional history of archaeology, nor a comprehensive history of the science. Instead, it focuses on archaeology's role in nation building during one of Mexico's pivotal regimes, a dictatorship that is often thought to have turned Mexico into a modern state. It explores the process of constructing an ancient patrimony and past—the Porfirian government's effort to cast a net over the pre-Hispanic remains and draw them into the fold of the state.

The book is divided into three parts. Part 1, "Ruins and Meaning," looks at the significance of the ancient monuments to a variety of people. The first chapter in this section, "A Day at the Ruins," explores what the monuments had come to mean to the locals and foreigners who used them. Chapter 2, "Ruins and the State," turns to Mexico's political and intellectual elites. It addresses their reasons for placing the monuments under state control and how the objects were intertwined with leaders' nationalist sentiments. Part 2, "The Archaeologists," consists of two chapters devoted to Mexico's archaeologists, the principal actors in the government project. Chapter 3, "The Museum Men," examines the scientists who worked in the National Museum, while the next chapter, "El Inspector," looks at Leopoldo Batres, the official archaeologist who oversaw much of the government project in his role as the head of the Inspectorate of Monuments. Comprised of four chapters, the next part of the book, "Making Patrimony," focuses on the mechanisms the government established to take control of the ancient remains. These included the Inspectorate of Monuments, archaeological legislation, a network of guards, as well as the transfer of artifacts to the museum, and the reconstruction of Teotihuacán.

Much like the making of the official past, the construction of Mexico's ancient patrimony was a difficult process. It led to many disagreements among the elites. And it occurred through fits and starts, unevenly throughout the country, sometimes successfully, sometimes not, as the net the government would cast over the nation's antiquities proved to be tenuous and fragile. Still, it brought an unprecedented degree of control over the monuments, one that intensified over time and that gradually, after some tinkering, established the patterns and infrastructure that are still in place to this day. It set the foundation for contemporary institutions like the massive National Museum of Anthropology in Chapultepec Park, which has more than three miles of corridors full of artifacts (not counting the enormous basement storage) that leave visitors completely overwhelmed.

On the one hand, then, this is the story of how a poor, peripheral country sought to take charge of its past in order to shape and defend its image, of how one nation's desire to contest its inferior place within the global order drove it to construct an official patrimony and past. But it is also the story of how this same effort proved to be exclusionary in several ways. The antiquity the elites created was a selective reconstruction of the past. It celebrated certain cultures and omitted others. Not all peoples and their material remains were deemed worthy of preservation. Herein lies what Guillermo Bonfil Batalla calls "the poverty of the national project." The nation, he writes, is "an artificial construction, an undertaking, an impossible desire."[21] Rather than a reflection of the population, some sort of "real" fusion of its different peoples, the national culture is essentially an imposed culture. This means that just as Mexico's official past served to counter the nation's history of imperialism, it also reinforced patterns of domination. It was exclusionary in its own right. What was chosen to be part of the official narrative reflected the views of the elites and interests of the state. The government focused on the dominant groups of antiquity, people like the Mixtecs and Maya. But it especially emphasized the Aztecs. Like the creoles and liberals of years before, Porfirian elites depicted the Aztec civilization as the nation's founding culture, a portrayal, scholars have noted, that forged a symbolic link between the ancient rulers, who had been based in the modern capital, and the contemporary state. The Díaz dictatorship, then, did not rely on armed force and electoral fraud alone "for its legitimacy and survival" but also on the making of memory.[22]

Just as the official history ignored many pasts and peoples, the making of patrimony negated other uses for the ancient objects. Artifacts, like all other objects, have no absolute value, no meanings "apart from those that human transactions, attributions, and motivations endow them with."[23] Their value is created. It is also flexible, shifting from one context to the next. Even the words "antiquity" and "artifact" that I use throughout this book are loaded with meaning. I resort to them knowing full well that they are not neutral terms. They come out of the fields of archaeology and collecting and endow the objects with scientific, historical, and monetary value. But Mexico's ruins had other uses and meanings. Local people farmed on them.

They hammered away at the sites, turning them into quarries for the making of new structures. They combed through them for relics to sell to visitors and antiquities traffickers. Some locals even lived in the crumbling palaces and temples. The artifacts were part of people's "material universe," things they "felt and lived" as their own, objects they passed daily, say, on the way to work their fields or milpas.²⁴ The locals often had strong connections to the pieces of the past, and there is no doubt that for many they were objects to cherish, links to traditional rites and rituals and to local histories and identities.

At the same time, the success of Mexico's archaeological project often depended on these very people. When possible, I have tried to examine how the government's efforts impacted them, especially the Indians who lived near the ruins. I realize that there are limits to my approach, as the archival record reflects the views of those in power. The voices of the Indians are usually absent, muted, distorted. But there are moments when they can be more easily heard, and I have tried to highlight them. Some locals cooperated and even aided the state, serving as guards at the sites and carrying out the digging and heavy lifting involved in the archaeological excavations and reconstructions. But others resisted, protesting as the government stripped them of ancient objects they held dear and ran roughshod over their desires. The making of patrimony often came about through sheer force. Rather than a national unifier, patrimony can thus be seen as "a space of material and symbolic struggle," one that both reflects and reinforces the inequalities inherent in a population.²⁵

While Mexican archaeology developed in defense of the nation, as a national and nationalist science, its practitioners, especially Inspector Batres, often operated like colonizers in their own land. The government forced Indian peasants off the ruins of Teotihuacán, and it made the guards—local men—abandon their traditional dress and adopt European clothing. It camouflaged them, in other words. Mexico's archaeological project was not only authoritarian at times but had an anti-Indian streak woven through it, a fact that should come as no surprise, as the elites saw the nation's diverse indigenous population as backward and uncivilized. Mexican leaders expressed a range of complex and often contradictory views about the "Indian problem," the idea that native peoples hindered the nation's progress. If they struggled over the Indian past, their debates about the Indian present were even more contentious as they grappled with the possibility and ways of integrating the indigenous population into national life. Some, like the journalist Francisco Cosmes, found the Indians hope-lessly barbaric and beyond redemption. Others, like the celebrated states-man and intellectual Justo Sierra, believed they had potential. Sierra blamed the condition of the Indians on Spanish colonialism, which he thought had kept them in a state of "incurable passivity."[26] And while he advocated edu-cation as a way to integrate the Indians into the larger population, he still believed they needed to be Westernized or changed. Even Sierra, one of the most sympathetic commentators, thought the native peoples were degraded.

Still, while Sierra and others debated these issues, the government's poli-cies were decidedly anti-Indian. It was a regime, writes Alan Knight, with "quasi-colonial attitudes and methods," one that hunted down and enslaved the Yaqui and Maya in full-scale Indian wars, a regime that pushed a model of development that consolidated wealth in the hands of the few, robbing Indians of their land on a scale not seen before, leaving them to eke out a liv-ing as peons on the haciendas, or landed estates, that were burgeoning throughout the country.[27] Ironically though, it was through the labor of the Indians, through the toil of the people considered lowly and vile, that the government took possession of the objects of the celebrated ancient cultures. Mexico's archaeological project would have been impossible without the con-temporary Indians; they were the state's main source of labor. They not only served as the guards and workers at the sites but also hauled monoliths to the museum. The making of Mexico's ancient patrimony, then, was carried out on the backs of people who were considered a degraded reflection of their glorious ancestors—in a project full of contradictions, this was, perhaps, the greatest of them all.

No wonder the Porfiriato has been ignored in the studies on *indigen-ismo*, the multifaceted trend in Latin America aimed at exalting and protect-ing the Indian. The Porfirian regime went down in history as a regime that "denigrated the national heritage," a consequence not only of its outright hostility toward native peoples but of scholars' tendency to associate indigen-ismo with the successive revolutionary state that was touted as pro-Indian.[28] Historians have characterized Porfirian leaders as Europhiles, as men enam-ored with all things European, dismissing their interest in the ancient past as simply "pallid, cerebral and arty."[29] Recent scholarship, however, has begun to delve more deeply into the indigenismo of the times, an indigen-ismo that was confined to glorifying antiquity rather than promoting the well-being of the Indians. It has focused on elite constructions of the ancient past, paying particular attention to cultural expressions such as statues, paintings, and architecture.[30] And it has shown that the disdain for the contemporary peoples and veneration for the ancients existed side by side, pointing to the disconnect between the ways in which the Indians of the past and present were treated and perceived.

But this disconnect did not just magically appear. Instead, it was constructed and reinforced through actions, policies, and words. And it was constituted in the field, in the very archaeological projects that negated the contemporary Indians, that stripped them of artifacts and removed them from sites, rejecting them while relying on their labor. And it was constituted, too, in the sheer act of focusing on the past. Thinking about history forces us to make a distinction between the present and past, writes historian Zachary Schiffman. When we "focus on the past as an object of thought" we tend to conflate the idea that "the past is, quite simply, the time before the present" with the idea that "the past is not simply *prior* to the present but *different* from it."[31] The Indian past was thought to be everything the Indian present was not. It was a space where the Indians could be imagined in ways that gave the nation prestige; it provided a refuge from the loathsome natives, a way out of the dominant racist thinking that held indigenous people to be inherently inferior. The glorification of antiquity did not simply sit alongside the hostility toward the Indians. Instead, it gave shape to the notion that the Indians were lesser beings, nothing like the builders of the fabulous civilizations of remote times. And it was the monuments, the objects made of clay and stone, that were thought to be the embodiments of these magnificent ancient civilizations. The government took steps to place the antiquities under state control because they had become inseparable from the nation's image. This was a task that involved plucking them out of their context, out of the landscape and out the grasp of a variety of people who claimed them as their own and used them day by day. The Porfirian archaeological project was in large part a response to what was happening in the ancient cities, to what can be considered daily life at the ruins, the first topic we will explore.

PART ONE

Ruins and Meaning

CHAPTER ONE

A Day at the Ruins

✦ NATURE HAD CONQUERED THE FALLEN CITIES AND TURNED THEM into landscapes, but that did not mean they were abandoned. The ruins were alive with people. Everyone from Indians to pothunters and scientists believed they had a claim to the pieces of the past. They used them in different ways and found in them a variety of meanings, from the practical (the ruins were a convenient source of stone), to the more symbolic (they were links to traditional rites and rituals). The relics were also a means by which to turn a quick profit; they got channeled into an international market in material culture that took them far from Mexican soil. The Díaz regime would try to put an end to the use and sale of the artifacts, taking control of the monuments and turning them into objects of the nation and science. Let us begin, then, by examining the everyday uses of the sites. The various activities that took place there made associates of unlikely people, linking peasants with the most sophisticated of European dandies. We can begin with the locals, the people who would have been most visible at these sites.

The Locals

Each community had a different relationship to the ruins. Some people actually lived in the well-built, ready-made structures; this was not particularly common, but it was a practice that stretched all the way back to pre-Hispanic times. Teotihuacán, as we know, saw settlers arrive soon after its fall. By the

Porfiriato, dozens of residents still lived at the site, with one lucky fellow inhabiting a particularly dazzling room, where he ate and slept under brilliant frescoes depicting "two priests in their cult of adoring the sun."[1] Some of Mexico's ruins had also been remodeled. Two brothers in Teotihuacán transformed one structure into a ceramics workshop, complete with kiln, where they cooked up fake artifacts for gullible tourists along with small souvenir busts of Porfirio Díaz. Miles away in Oaxaca, a section of Mitla had been converted into a Catholic parish, complete with living quarters for a priest and a stable for his hay and horses.

As might be expected, the ruins had also become farmland. Some sites had been divided into grid-like patterns by the small plots of peasants, creating a checkerboard effect, while others had become completely engulfed by huge haciendas. Many ruins were found on public lands; others were located on private property and amid the fields of indigenous communities. Communities often possessed titles to these lands, sites they had occupied for generations or, as the customary phrase explained, "from time immemorial." Yet whether it took place on a small plot or a hacienda, the act of farming destroyed the ruins. The more desperate planted directly on the monuments, what centuries of exposure to the elements had turned into dirt- and plant-covered mounds or "artificial hills," as they were called. Others dug furrows around the mounds, leaving them standing like islands of wild flora jutting out over neat rows of corn, although in digging the furrows, they ended up chipping away at the base of the monuments. Farming was not the only problem. The grazing of sheep and cattle, along with the fires that were set to prepare the land for sowing, also wore away at the ruins.

Sites were also exploited for resources that grew naturally. Loggers in Chiapas chopped down the mahogany and rubber trees that carpeted the pyramids of Yaxchilán. Back in Teotihuacán, a place that dominates this story, the locals tapped the huge maguey plants growing on the Pyramid of the Sun. They cultivated this type of agave, a versatile plant whose many varieties are especially prized for the making of alcoholic drinks such as the popular fermented beverage pulque and its distilled cousins mescal and tequila that are more favored today. To separate their plots of maguey, the locals built fences of stone. According to one observer, more than 250 people had crisscrossed the site with "stone fences two meters tall and a meter and a half wide."[2] They had pried this stone from the ruins.

What were once sacred places, sites of gods and kings, had become quarries for the making of new structures. This was the most common use for the ruins, a use that, like many others, had roots deep in history. The first experts in the recycling of stone were the pre-Hispanic peoples themselves; they built new pyramids on top of old ones using the materials from earlier cultures. Next came the Spaniards, who shattered the Indians' temples in their search for stone to construct the churches, palaces, and other pillars of the new order. Centuries later, during the Porfiriato, the locals could still be found hammering away at the ruins. They sliced off great chunks of Xochicalco, in the state of Morelos, to make a dam, leaving the site in "a lamentable state." They pried at the walls of Toniná, Chiapas, with "crowbars" to gather stone for a new town hall. A piece of Teotihuacán, it was said, had become a part of everyone's home within "a radius of no less than four leagues."[3]

Often this destruction was purely wanton and aimless. Bored shepherds near Perote, Veracruz, passed away the time throwing rocks at a monument of "two Aztec soldiers."[4] While this sort of target practice was the amusement of choice, the locals never seemed to lack for more clever ways to destroy things. The residents of Orizaba, for example, tried using firecrackers to blow up a statue known as "the giant."[5] Most artifacts, though, met with decidedly less spectacular endings, the most common being in the small hands of children. In the words of one observer, "Idols and figurines . . . were so abundant that generation after generation of children played with no other toys than these dolls."[6] Needless to say, at the mercy of their tiny captors they were quickly turned into dust.

But it would be a mistake to imagine the locals simply as destroyers, since many cherished the ancient objects around them, just as they do today. The ruins were not only embedded in the rituals of ordinary people but played an important role in their identities and histories. Porfirian observers, however, dismissed these types of relationships as idol worship, lamenting the "idolatry persistent . . . in the Indian race."[7] The historical record is full of "idolatry" sightings. A "priestess," for instance, tended a "temple" outside of Mexico City that was made up of a "cave full of idols"; a statue on a mountainside in Morelos inspired the "veneration of the Indians"; and a curious Catholic Virgin could be found in a chapel in the state of Guanajuato.[8] The Virgin seemed to be just a regular Catholic icon until the day a lightning bolt tore through the chapel ceiling, grazed the altar, and charred her clothes. When her garments were removed, her true form was revealed. Underneath all those layers of fabric she had been a pre-Hispanic relic all along, a Virgin carved from an ancient statue of a snake no less! Unfazed by this revelation, if it was one at all, the "Indians . . . placed her on the altar and their worship continue[d] just as fervently as before."⁹

One community with a particularly strong relationship to a site was Tepoztlán, a village in Morelos made up of five thousand Nahuatl speakers of "almost pure aboriginal blood."¹⁰ Its inhabitants had (and continue to have) a connection to the Tepozteco pyramid that sits atop of a hill just outside the village. According to legend, this was the temple of the town chieftain, Tepoztécatl, who, depending on accounts, was either a mythical or historical figure. In stories still told today, the chieftain defended the town from enemy attacks both before and after the Spanish conquest, using the pyramid as a fort on at least one occasion. Every year, the people of Tepoztlán reenacted these events in a celebration held in honor of the chieftain.¹¹ For them, Tepozteco was a source of identity and a link to the spiritual world.

Still, while most communities had a connection with nearby sites, others feared them. When the famous French explorer Désiré Charnay camped out at Uxmal in the 1860s, he was forced to spend many nights alone, as his Maya guides would abandon him at sundown. The very thought of sleeping there, he claimed, filled them with "mortal terror."¹² Often, it was not a site but a single object that provoked this sort of unease, like a tomb in Mitla that awakened "the fear of the Indians" or a monument in Guerrero that they shunned, so great was "the fear and respect it inspired."¹³ No matter how the locals responded to or interacted with Mexico's ruins, it is clear that the ancient places mattered to them. And, apart from their importance in traditional rites and rituals, in local histories and identities, apart from their significance as sources of land and stone, the ruins also happened to be a source of income.

The Antiquities Market

There was money to be made in the pieces of the past, in tunneling through temples and rummaging through tombs, in crushing bones and statues under foot. Mexico's relic hunters left behind huge pits and other obvious signs of their presence at the ruins. But they left little imprint on the historical record. There was the story of the "Indians" in Oaxaca who combed through graves for objects "with the desire of profiting from their sale," of the people who believed the fragments of Mitla would "sooner or later, turn to gold," of those who dug deep into the mounds of Chalchihuites, in the state of Zacatecas, "tempted by the foolish superstition they will find money there."[14] But equating mounds with money was not foolish at all. Antiquities had become coveted commodities. They were status symbols, trophies of empire, and specimens of science. The market for them was booming by the late nineteenth century, creating a demand that was satisfied by a mixed group of suppliers with diverse motives and aims. Local people, archaeologists, antiquarians, and travelers scoured the ruins for relics and went about their business in a variety of ways, from the peasant who came across a figurine every now and then to the tomb raider who made burrowing through temples a full-time job.

Torn from the ruins, Mexico's artifacts entered what scholars know as the "commodity state." Those who study how objects are transformed into commodities, a part of what anthropologist Arjun Appadurai calls the "social life of things," point out that a complex intersection of "temporal, cultural, and social factors" works to shape this process.[15] When it comes to antiquities, they stress, the objects nearly always move from south to north, from poor countries to rich, with little, if any, "countervailing flow."[16] Mexico's relics got funneled into a network of trade that carried them to the museums and collections of the United States and Europe. The fascination the West had for these objects can only be explained by examining the international market in material culture. It was a market embedded in an increasingly globalized world in which transportation and trade were facilitated by technological advances in steam and rail, a market tied to many other developments associated with modernity, such as capitalism, consumerism, and the bourgeoisie, imperialism, the rise of the nation-state, the museum, and archaeology.

In its broadest sense, the quest for antiquities was part of a more general craze in collecting that took off in the nineteenth century. While collecting or human acquisitiveness may be, as some scholars maintain, timeless, an instinct or impulse that drives us to accumulate and display, most agree that the urge to accumulate intensified with the nineteenth century, as "no other age collected with such a vengeance and to such spectacular proportions."[17] It was an era fascinated with things of all kinds, an era of parlor rooms full of knickknacks, a product of the consumer culture that had emerged with the expansion of the middle class in the wake of the growth of capitalism and the industrial economy. It was the era of P. T. Barnum and the freak show, of Madame Tussaud's wax museum and the World's Fair. It was, in the words of Germain Bazin, "the Museum age."[18]

Collecting not only intensified, but also changed in significant ways. What had once been a practice dominated by private exhibits—rooms full of rocks and paintings—gave way to the modern, public museum. While the first of these institutions, London's British Museum, opened in 1753, museum building did not really take off in the world until over a century later. It accelerated after 1850 and especially after 1875. Many scholars see this surge in museums as a product of the Victorian obsession with order; Victorians, incidentally, are often called the "great Museum builders."[19] As Barbara Black explains, the museum was part of the "impulse or spirit that infused the age and many of its projects," "system-building projects [that] involved compilation, organization and display" such as "the triple-decker novel; collected works; encyclopedias and dictionaries; and phenomena as ordinary as keepsakes, dollhouses and rock collections."[20]

But no change drove the museum craze like the rise of the nation-state. Museums are often thought to hold the cultural goods that belong to the citizens of a nation. They are "palaces of the people," testaments to the democratization of culture that accompanied the emergence of the nation-state. By the nineteenth century, developments such as increased literacy, the communications revolution, and the growing public sphere meant that culture was no longer the sole province of the elite but had become the realm of the people. One classic example is the Louvre. The French Revolution transformed this royal palace into a public museum, making the treasures of the monarchy accessible to the citizens of France. To put it more dramatically, the birth of the museum is, as Georges Bataille has claimed, "linked to the development of the guillotine."[21] Like the killing machine that eliminated Louis XVI and the ancien régime, making way for a France of citizens rather than subjects, the museum is a "people's instrument of power . . . a symbol of the new order."[22]

The Louvre may have been a people's palace but it was also a warehouse of imperialism, filled with the spoils of the colonial campaigns of France, such as Napoleon's invasion of Egypt. Many museums housed the loot taken directly during conquest expeditions, like the British Museum, which overflowed with ivories from the Benin Raid. Others held the objects of internal colonial subjects; the museums of the United States, for instance, were packed with the belongings of Native Americans, "who were at that very moment being conquered."[23] Just as colonial powers extracted resources such as lumber and ore, they extracted cultural artifacts. "Economic and cultural plunder," writes Robert Aguirre, "rode on parallel tracks." The Western fascination with the objects of others, then, was no accident but a reflection of the "historical relations of power." Western countries used the artifacts to fashion their national and imperial identities, to communicate their reach and grasp, their "power to possess and dispossess."[24]

Ironically, the same changes associated with colonialism also threatened the West's sense of order. As Glenn Penny explains, the expansion of international trade and the constant steam-powered movement of ever-growing numbers of people—diplomats, soldiers, explorers, and tourists—unleashed a flood of new information about the diversity of humanity. Stories about alien new cultures flowed into the ports of the West, along with exotic material goods. This new information challenged older schemes of knowledge. It "undermined Europeans' confidence in their own belief systems and led many to feel as if 'the world had been turned upside down.'"[25] Collecting the artifacts of others was a way to take charge of this rapidly changing world, full of strange peoples and places. Put in museum cases, the objects, and by extension, the people they were thought to represent, were, in effect, placed under control. As anthropologist Michael Ames points out, "When we 'museumify' other cultures we exercise conceptual control over them."[26]

Placed on museum shelves, the artifacts lent support to the racial hierarchies that justified imperialism. This was, after all, the heyday of social Darwinism, the racialist thinking that divided humanity into superior and inferior races, with whites on the top and darker peoples on the bottom. Herbert Spencer, the chief exponent of this line of thought, had taken Charles Darwin's theory of evolution and applied it to human society, arguing that some races were more fit to survive and thus suited to rule over others. A people's "inferiority" was thought to be a matter of flesh and blood, immutable and inherent. This inferiority was also thought to be capable of being measured by science, a belief reflected in anthropologists' turn to craniology, a now-defunct field that held that human intelligence varied according to the size and shape of the brain. Using bizarre tools, anthropologists measured the lumps and bumps on human heads, which were taken to be evidence of the diminished intellectual capacity of nonwhites. Museums lent credence to these racist ideas. By putting skulls and artifacts on display, they helped create the notion of the primitive, inferior other.

Collecting artifacts not only helped construct the primitive other but also a Western identity in opposition to it. A collection, scholars point out, is ultimately a mode of self-fashioning. It operates at the level of illusion, taking objects out of their original contexts and making them stand for abstract wholes—an Aztec vase, for instance, becomes a metonym for Aztec culture. Through the arrangement of objects, a collection aims to produce a "coherent representational universe," a self-enclosed, hermetic world that is organized according to the principles established by the collector.[27] A collection thus reflects a collector's own identity rather than some sort of exterior reality. For centuries, moreover, the act of collecting has been central to the Western notion of self. Scholars link collecting to the concept of "possessive individualism" developed by the political theorist C. B. Macpherson. According to this idea, since the seventeenth century, a sense of self as owner has operated in the West, the ideal individual being someone who surrounds himself or herself "with accumulated properties and goods." Collecting the objects of primitive peoples is thus a testament to "the knowledge and taste of a possessive Western subjectivity," a sign, in other words, that one is not only Western but sophisticated and refined.[28]

Not surprisingly, the most avid collectors of Mexico's artifacts were British, American, and French. All three powers had dominated the nation in general, Britain and the United States through economic investments that led to informal empires and France by taking it further and trying to create an actual empire. In fact, no country was more captivated by Mexican artifacts than France; the Louvre had an extensive collection in its Musée Mexicain by as early as 1850. This collection swelled the next decade during the French intervention, when Napoleon III invaded Mexico, unleashing a troop of relic-hungry scientists in the country, just as his uncle had done in Egypt. "Our scholars are . . . going to march once more in the tracks of our soldiers" was a motto of the French Scientific Commission of Mexico.[29] While other powers made off with Mexico's artifacts in a piecemeal fashion, the French did it in one fell swoop with this elaborately organized expedition. Working alongside the French army, the commission carried out studies of Mexico's animals, peoples, and plants. It also excavated and documented the ruins. At a time when "science animated and underwrote the extension of European power overseas," the French expedition was at once "a colonial project to render Mexico as scientific object" and a mission designed to "civilize" the nation through the reconstruction of its past.[30] The result was an archaeological conquest: the antiquities that were shipped back to the Louvre delighted observers, drawing crowds so large they supposedly "'fought to get in.'"[31]

By the late nineteenth century, pre-Hispanic antiquities had become a "special source of wonder" for jaded Europeans and Americans, who were accustomed to the stuff of the rest of the globe. As Elizabeth Williams explains, the "oriental" world had lost its feel of strangeness and been "assimilated into European sensibility through periodic vogues of *chinoiserie*; the 'true' *arts primitifs* of Arctic, African and Oceanic peoples could be unambiguously categorized as the work of savages." But the pre-Hispanic world was different. It fascinated because of its "high level of material development," on the one hand, and "its apparent independence from the fonts of Old World creativity," on the other.[32]

This fascination emerged in tandem with the development of the science of archaeology, a discipline derived from the Greek word "arkhaiologia," meaning "the discourse about ancient things." While today's archaeologists study the human past through the recovery and interpretation of its material remains, this was not always the case. For much of its history, archaeology was more of a trophy hunt than formal science, a pursuit or hobby of tomb raiders and antiquarians who coveted ancient objects because they regarded them as treasures. By the latter part of the nineteenth century, this sort of antiquarianism began to give way as archaeology developed into a formal science within the context of the museum, its original institutional setting. The discipline saw the emergence of professional training and organizations, and fieldwork also began to be guided by more systematic methods—or at least the notion that such methods should exist. Still, archaeology was a science in formation. It lacked the consistent, reproducible methods that we associate with any given science today. There were a wide range of practitioners, with varying degrees of training and rigor, from the armchair scholars who rarely left the comfort of the museum to those who braved the elements and set out on digs.

By this time, moreover, a whole intellectual movement had emerged that was dedicated to pre-Hispanic antiquity. Known as Americanism, this broad scholarly field encompassed virtually all disciplines related to the New World as well as all historical periods. Most Americanists, however, specialized in the pre-Hispanic past. France, once again, led the way, establishing the first scholarly society devoted to Americanism, the Société Américaine, in 1857. Britain, Germany, and the United States also produced some of the most active Americanist scholars, as did Mexico and other Latin American nations. In 1875 they began meeting regularly at the International Congress of Americanists, which was held in a different country every two years. As the field grew, so did the desire for Mexican antiquities, many of which wound up in museums, especially the institutions dedicated to anthropology that were established at the time. The first of these was Harvard's Peabody Museum of Archaeology and Ethnology in 1866, and others soon followed: the Ethnological Museum of Berlin (1868), the Trocadéro Museum in Paris (1878), and the Museum of Archaeology and Anthropology at the University of Pennsylvania (1899). These institutions functioned much like huge trading houses, selling and swapping artifacts with one another.

Museums, in general, were considered a gauge of a nation's progress. If scientific knowledge is one of the great metanarratives of modernity, as Jean-François Lyotard has claimed, then museums, as centers of science, were testaments to a country's modern standing. This means that they were also places onto which people projected their anxieties about the nation. Europeans and Americans worried about the place of their museums within the world of science. The Germans, for instance, were constantly comparing their institutions to those abroad. They not only worried about keeping up with the others but wanted to set the "pace in scientific and cultural" achievements. But the anthropology museums were special. As institutions dedicated to the study of the diversity of humans throughout the globe, they offered up an extra dose of cultural capital or prestige. They were evidence of a nation's "connection with the wider world," a sign of being cosmopolitan.[33]

Within this context, artifacts took on new meaning as objects of science. Catalogued, labeled, and put on display, they underwent a transformation, writes Carolyne Larson, a "rite of passage" or initiation process "through which they ceased to be mere things and became museum pieces." These pieces, though, were not just considered visual aids or objects meant to facilitate learning. Instead, they were thought to be the "physical embodiments of knowledge."[34] One simply had to contemplate them, to study and observe them closely, to gain direct access to their meaning. It should come as no surprise, then, that archaeologists displayed a type of hoarding mentality when it came to the objects. They equated the act of possessing them with having more knowledge; more was better, in other words, and by the same token, limited collections were thought to lead to "equally limited conclusions."[35] Put another way, the study and collection of antiquities were considered "practically synonymous." Eduard Seler, the famous German archaeologist who carried out a great deal of research in Mexico during the Porfiriato, made this clear when he said, "We came to this country to study the antiquities, or to collect them, in other words."[36] Yet even though the artifacts were regarded as objects of science, their appeal as a type of treasure would never fully disappear. Archaeologists continued to seek out the most magnificent specimens, especially huge sculptures, instead of more mundane items of daily use such as crusty old pots and tools. And as the pieces of Mexico's past got drawn into this trade, the authority of science made them more valuable. And the more sought after the objects were, the scarcer they became, which only made them that much more coveted and valuable.

Even so, most European experts did not consider Mexico's antiquities "fully 'beautiful.'"[37] Before the primitivist revolution of Picasso and the avant-garde artists of the early twentieth century, Westerners questioned whether pre-Hispanic objects had aesthetic qualities; some found them to be completely ugly. The French explorer Charnay considered Aztec relics "horrific and repugnant." Another authority on the pre-Hispanic past, the French anthropologist Ernest-Théodore Hamy (known as E. T. Hamy), the first director of the Trocadéro Museum (1880–1908), thought many of Mexico's artifacts were "grotesque."[38] Ideas about beauty mimicked the racist thinking of the times, as art was believed to have evolved along a trajectory that culminated in European standards. Europeans considered Mexican antiquities interesting but decidedly inferior to anything produced in the Old World. The objects were no match with those of Greece and Rome. And they were usually not up to par with those of Egypt either, the Old World culture to which Mexico was most frequently compared.

Institutions like the Trocadéro acquired the ancient objects through a variety of means, quite often with the aid of Mexican collectors. Accumulating artifacts had been a pastime of Mexicans for centuries. By the Porfiriato some of the most well-known antiquarians included Guillermo de Heredia and Francisco Plancarte y Navarrete. Many collectors were landowners or had some sort of contact with the soil. Heredia worked as an engineer, while Plancarte, a historian and bishop of Cuernavaca, had dozens of loyal landowning friends, so much so that when he told them about his passion for the ancient past they carried out excavations on their properties just "to please" him.[39] Collections like Plancarte's contained several thousand items and took years, if not lifetimes, to accumulate. When they were put up for sale, they were often quickly snatched up by representatives of museums abroad.

Foreign antiquarians living in Mexico also supplied items to Western museums. Some of them owned shops in the Mexican capital, like the Frenchman Eugène Boban, whose Scientific Museum doubled as a store where one could buy antiquities along with rare books and antiques. A member of the Société Américaine, Boban arrived in Mexico in 1857. After serving as the archaeological consultant to the French Scientific Commission during Napoleon III's invasion, he remained in the country for several years, supplying museums and posh auction houses abroad. In 1886 he tried to sell a life-size skull carved in quartz, what eventually became known as the Boban skull, to the Smithsonian Institution. The Smithsonian rejected it, but Boban went on to find another buyer with the help of George Kunz, the vice president of Tiffany and Company in New York City. The skull eventually became the property of the British Museum, where years later, in the late twentieth century, its crystal powers attracted a steady stream of New Age devotees. Today, most scholars believe the skull is a fake, a creation not of the Aztecs, as it was initially believed, but of a nineteenth-century German jeweler, a forgery quite possibly commissioned by Boban himself.[40]

In addition to suppliers like Boban, there were private individuals living outside of Mexico who sold objects. The vice president of Tiffany's, Mr. Kunz, for example, claimed he bought Mexican artifacts right on the streets of New York City, where, according to him, "bric a brac dealers" peddled obsidian, jadeite, and onyx pieces. In 1888 he purchased one, a votive ax, "the largest and finest object of blue-green Mexican jadeite" he had ever seen. Like the Boban skull, the artifact eventually took the name of its owner, becoming known as the "Kunz Ax." Kunz did not know how the ax had ended up on the New York City streets, nor did he care. His only interest was in acquiring "the finest things."[41] Apart from these sorts of antiquarians, another important source of artifacts were foreign explorers, the many adventurers who traveled through Mexico in the late nineteenth and early twentieth centuries, during what is often known as the "heroic age of archaeology."

The Great Explorers

Pioneers in the field of archaeology were making fabulous discoveries all over the world. The period opened in 1870 when the German merchant Heinrich Schliemann unearthed the city of Troy in modern-day Turkey, confirming his belief that the writings of the ancient bard Homer were based on actual events. It closed with perhaps the greatest find of them all, the tomb of Tutankhamen discovered in Egypt in 1922 by the Englishman Howard Carter. Foreign archaeologists were similarly rummaging through Mexico's ruins. The problem was that the line between scientist and sacker was not only thin but more often than not nonexistent.

A host of adventurers trekked through Mexico with a sense of entitlement, taking possession of the artifacts they came across and portraying it as an act of "heroic preservation."[42] In seizing the objects, they claimed to be rescuing them from decay and thus aiding the cause of science. They also claimed to be rescuing them from the Mexicans, who they considered too inept to care for them, dismissing the sovereignty of the Mexican nation and depicting its people as unworthy of inheriting their own past. But Mexicans did care. The exportation of relics, in fact, had been outlawed since the early years of independence. Decrees like the Maritime and Border Customs Act of 1827 prohibited the removal of "monuments and antiquities," along with valuable resources such as silver and gold.[43] The same decree also gave the Mexican government the power to grant exceptions and issue permits for exportations, as long as the objects were intended for the purpose of science or the "study of sages." Throughout most of the nineteenth century, foreign explorers were either unaware of this legislation or simply ignored it. Mexico was also too weak to effectively enforce it, leaving explorers free to haul off whatever they pleased. And, while the Díaz regime would try to put an end to this practice, the results were inconsistent.

One of the most famous explorers during the age of Díaz was Désiré Charnay, the archaeologist and pioneer photographer. Charnay toured dozens of ruins during his four trips to Mexico, battling malaria, bugs and jungle, heat and rain, all the while lugging about heavy, fragile photographic equipment, along with numerous bottles of French wine—adding up to close to four thousand pounds during his first visit in 1860. Some of the only images we have of Mexico's ruins at the time were photographed by Charnay. But other aspects about Charnay are less admirable. His second trip in 1864 was in the company of Napoleon III's troops. Although his exact role in the French Intervention is unknown, Charnay believed Mexico should have been proud to see the French invade: France had come to "shake Mexico out of its slumber," something the country "should only applaud." Charnay turned his colonial gaze on the antiquities, too: "Does it not correspond to a nation like ours, leader and light of the world," he asked, "to take possession of these precious monuments?"[44] During his third trip in 1880, a visit marred by serious complications, Charnay had his workers excavating at a frantic pace, digging up forty artifacts a minute. He left behind a sexualized account of his deeds: Mexico's soil, he wrote, "was virgin, . . . awaiting the happy explorer."[45] The colonial mentality of explorers like Charnay was highly gendered, as Carmen Ruiz notes. For archaeologists, Mexico was not just a space full of raw materials for science but a feminized space "in need of scientific penetration."[46] Charnay, it seems, took advantage of this space so thoroughly during his last trip in 1886, a visit lacking any sort of federal authorization, that he nearly stripped Jaina, an island off the coast of Campeche, bare of relics.

Like most archaeologists, Charnay relied on the labor of the local Indians, people he considered inferior, a view that was not limited to the foreign explorers. He was constantly frustrated by the workers. "It has been difficult for me," he complained in 1880, "to fight against the bad will of the Indians who, when it comes to serious excavations, take a most hostile attitude, refusing men, opposing work, or claiming as theirs all the objects found on their territory." Charnay, like most archaeologists, failed to record how he recruited the men, but he most likely acquired them through labor contractors. In Yucatán, he found the Indians especially resistant; although he paid them three times more than the Indians in central Mexico, they failed to do even "one-fourth as much work." "There is no help for it," he grumbled, since "the simplest remark pronounced with the air of authority would provoke a mutiny."[47] Charnay's writings are obviously skewed. Like those of other explorers, they silence the voices of the Indians. But a picture does emerge of how the Indians frequently responded to the archaeologists who tried to pay them, coax them, and even force them to work. Sometimes they cooperated and sometimes they did not. But overall, one gets the sense that they often kept their distance. The archaeologists come off as a sort of nuisance, like a pesky fly one simply wishes would go away.

This was especially the case with Augustus Le Plongeon, the eccentric English-born explorer who concocted some of the wildest theories in the history of archaeological thought. A Mayanist, Le Plongeon argued that a "race of dwarves" had built El Rey, the ancient trading post that now sits amid the hotel strip that lines Cancún. He also believed the Maya had founded the civilization of ancient Egypt, an idea that would not be completely discredited until the 1890s, when archaeologists confirmed that the Egyptians had preceded the Maya.[48] But Le Plongeon's claim to fame was his "discovery" of the Chacmool of Chichén Itzá, the famous statue of a reclining human figure, with its head turned to the side. The archaeologist risked life and limb for the statue, working in 1876 during the middle of the Caste War, the armed conflict between Mexican forces and the Maya. As a precaution, he was often accompanied by the military. He also went about armed, as did his wife, Alice Dixon Le Plongeon.

Like Charnay, Le Plongeon had a difficult time getting the Indians to work. He competed for them with a nearby sugar mill at one site, and those he did find "worked badly and unwillingly."[49] They suffered from severe attacks of "laziness," wrote Alice, "pretending to do a great deal, and in fact doing nothing." Both Augustus and Alice, a scholar of the Maya in her own right, ran into other problems. The Indians constantly claimed to misunderstand them, a ruse they devised to avoid having to work, believed Alice. They also feared disturbing the ruins: touching certain relics would make them sick, they said, and excavating at one site would cause them to turn "into statues." Were these really strategies to evade labor? Ascribing special powers to ruins was not uncommon in Mexico, as we have already seen. In any case, Augustus resorted to various tactics to get the Maya locals to work. He played on their fears. When they were afraid to move a huge urn at Uxmal, he claimed to have supernatural powers that would protect them, a claim he backed up by dipping his finger into the urn and ingesting its contents—tiny fragments of mother of pearl. "We did not attempt to take away their fear," explained Alice. "It was convenient that they should have it." "Some will think this very stupid, others very wrong. But we had to manage, one way or another, the men we had with us. They were full of superstition[.] To try and shake it was useless."

Le Plongeon's tactics did not end there. He threatened to withhold the workers' pay. On at least one occasion, he even threatened them at gunpoint. And to the most recalcitrant of men, he gave the most onerous of tasks: pointless chores, like hauling heavy monoliths back and forth for no apparent reason other than to show them he was the boss. But the Indians resisted. They deserted him. They infested his hair with lice, according to Alice. And they sabotaged their own labor, pushing the Chacmool back into the altar in Chichén Itzá's Platform of the Eagles and Jaguars where it had been found and into a position that made its extraction all the more difficult. Le Plongeon, however, finally did get them to remove the statue and haul it to his camp in Pisté, a small town about two miles outside of the ruins. From there, he planned to take the precious monument to the port of Sisal and on to Philadelphia for display at the 1876 World's Fair.

Had foreigners not seized Mexico's artifacts, the claim is often made, the objects would have been destroyed, exposed to the ravages of people and time. This argument, however, merely justifies the appropriation of the objects as an act of "heroic preservation." It also ignores the fact that the explorers were often some of the monuments' main destroyers. "Violence,

dismemberment, and defacement," frequently accompanied the appropriation of antiquities, even by some of the most celebrated archeologists, like
the British diplomat Alfred P. Maudslay.[50] Maudslay did posterity a great
favor, carrying out pioneering research at Maya sites in the 1880s and 1890s.
He worked with great care, meticulously describing artifacts and documenting his excavations. He made maps and drawings and took photographs of the ruins. But he also took parts of them home. One of the
features of Maya sites from the Classic Period (AD 250–900) are lintels
carved with hieroglyphics and depictions of gods and nobles during important events—births and deaths, weddings and wars. The celebrated
Mayanist wanted to ship a lintel from the ruins of Yaxchilán to London.
But the piece was too heavy, so he decided to make it more portable. The
task was no "easy matter," he wrote, since he had not brought along the
right tools. Maudslay's workers ended up using a "broken pickaxe and
some carpenter's chisels" to slice off the lintel's "undecorated" part.[51] They
successfully cut the artifact's weight in half but mutilated it in the process.
At the time, there was some confusion about whether Yaxchilán belonged
to Mexico or Guatemala, as the site straddled the frontier between the two
countries on a boundary that had yet to be formally established. In 1882
both nations signed a preliminary accord that placed Yaxchilán on the
Mexican side of the border, an agreement not finalized until seventeen
years later. Maudslay was aware of the border dispute and worried about
the reaction of the Mexican government, according to his biographer.[52]
Even so, he did not bother to ask the Mexican government for permission
to export the lintels. Today a total of seven of them are in the British
Museum. An eighth graced the Ethnological Museum of Berlin until World
War II, when it mysteriously disappeared.

But of all of the nineteenth-century explorers who set foot in Mexico,
none would devise a more elaborate scheme for gathering artifacts than
Edward Thompson. An amateur archaeologist, Thompson launched his
career in 1879 with an article in *Popular Science Monthly* in which he argued
that the Maya had originated in the legendary land of Atlantis. The article
gained the attention of Stephen Salisbury III, vice president of the American
Antiquarian Society in Massachusetts, who decided to sponsor Thompson to
explore the ruins of the Maya. Through some maneuvering, Salisbury got
Thompson appointed as the American consul to Yucatán, and in 1885
Thompson set off to fill his post. Far from freewheeling, independent explorers, men like Thompson were, as Aguirre has shown, part of the imperial

quest for antiquities; they not only worked, quite often, as agents for museums and collectors but also gathered the objects while serving as state officials.

Thompson visited Maya sites for the next forty years, collecting artifacts at various times for the American Antiquarian Society, Chicago's Field Museum, and the Peabody Museum. He immersed himself in Maya culture, learned to speak Yucatec Maya, and ate what he called "Indian food." In 1894 Thompson paid a small sum for a property near Chichén Itzá made up of thirty square miles and an old hacienda, where he became known to his many Indian servants as Don Eduardo. According to Thompson, much of the site of Chichén Itzá lay on his property. One of his so-called possessions just happened to be one of the site's most striking features: the Sacred Cenote, a natural well more than 100 feet deep and 190 feet in diameter. For geologists cenotes are sinkholes, wells that form with the collapse of the limestone layer. For the Maya they were (and continue to be) sacred places, portals that link the earth to the realm of the rain god Chac, pools into which the ancient people threw ritual offerings. For Thompson, however, the cenotes were places to plunder, and that's exactly what he did. The thought of seizing objects from the depths of the Sacred Cenote obsessed him: "It became a mania which would not let me rest." Thompson toyed with the idea that disturbing the well would be a violation of the sacred: if extracting the Maya's "long-held treasures" made Chac angry, he quipped, by the end of the ordeal the old rain god would surely be in a state of "frenzy."[53]

With the backing of the Peabody, Thompson dredged the Sacred Cenote of Chichén Itzá from 1904 to 1910. The local Indians aided him, operating a huge steel crane, unearthing objects the Maya before them had sacrificed to the gods. "My Indians," Thompson said, referring to the men as possessions, were "about thirty in number" and "each had his appointed task."[54] At first nothing interesting surfaced from the well, just some cow bones and rotten trees. But then, the antiquities began to appear: rubber balls, copal or incense, and human remains—close to one hundred ancient skeletons. Thompson wanted to test his hypothesis that the skeletons were similar to those of the modern Maya in order to prove that the ancient and contemporary people were related. So he ordered a search for human remains in some of the newer cemeteries in the area. He compared the skulls of the modern Maya with the older ones and concluded, somehow, that the people were linked. While today most archaeologists are cautious about disturbing the dead, Thompson worked at a time when archaeology lacked any sort of code of ethics. But what about his Indian assistants? Were they the ones ordered to rummage through the graves? Did the other Indians not try to stop them? Why some locals chose to aid archaeologists and others did not has no simple explanation. Perhaps they were motivated, in this case, by the "high wage" Thompson supposedly paid them. The Indian workers were surely driven by their own needs and aims. But what these were is open to question since Thompson, like most explorers, recorded little information about the men; even their identities remain vague. The Sacred Cenote, however, had been a Maya pilgrimage site for centuries. According to legend, it was also guarded by huge serpents. Even the eccentric Le Plongeon had complained about his workers' fear of the well. Did Thompson's men not share this fear? Were they unaware of the legends? Perhaps they were not from the immediate vicinity.

After much dredging, Thompson realized that his huge crane could not reach the smaller, heavier objects at the bottom of the well, so he decided on a new course of action. With the aid of a Greek diver he had hired, a couple of makeshift scuba outfits, and copper helmets that weighed some thirty pounds, Thompson and "the Greek," as he called him, dove in. They had zero visibility in the "chocolate-colored porridge," water so cold that their lips turned blue. The two men had to feel their way along the bottom of the cenote. Grasping about, they took hold of one of the most fabulous collections of Maya artifacts: gold rings, "tiaras," and figurines; jade tablets, ornaments and beads; copper masks, disks, and bells—"the bells of the ancients," Thompson's assistants exclaimed. At least two of the workers decided to take advantage of the situation. One squirreled away some of the gold and melted it down into a necklace. Another managed to hide a few artifacts that he later sold to an "archaeologist" in the area, who then sold them to an unspecified museum abroad.[55]

But these losses were a tiny fraction of Thompson's vast cache—anywhere from twenty to thirty thousand artifacts!—which were all shipped off to the Peabody. There, to use Thompson's exact words, the objects would be part of "a great institution, safe from the grasp of vandals."[56] In return, Thompson was paid by Charles Bowditch, the Peabody's benefactor, and Frederick Putnam, the museum curator and professor of American archaeology at Harvard. For years, the Peabody had been searching for a subject worthy of study. The institution had "faced a strong predisposition in established Boston circles against the worthiness of 'primitive' peoples and their artifacts."[57] It needed to find a subject prestigious enough to gain the support of the New England elite as well as the respect of the scientific community.

The ancient Maya provided the solution, and Thompson's terrible crane, in turn, supplied the loot that quenched the Peabody's thirst for respectability. Perhaps the water god Chac, however, ultimately did get his revenge. Years later, while Thompson was rearranging a collection of figurines from the well, a statue depicting an "attendant" of the life-giving rain god fell on one of Thompson's feet and crushed it, leaving him "half crippled" for the rest of his life.[58]

Foreigners were absolutely wild about the Maya and visited the ruins of this culture in the Yucatán even in the midst of the Caste War. Why the Maya madness? Some have attributed it to the Maya's aesthetic sensibility, which is often considered more "Western" than that of other Mexican cultures and thus more attractive to foreigners. In the words of one contemporary Mexican archaeologist, the art of the Maya conforms most closely to "the aesthetic ideals of the Western world."[59] Yet while Maya art differs from that of other Mesoamerican peoples (like the Aztecs, for instance, Aztec art being more geometric and static), exactly how Maya aesthetics are somehow more "Western" is not clear. One could just as easily argue that the art of both people is equally "non-Western." The penchant for the Maya, then, was most likely not a function of aesthetics but a result of the culture's long-standing reputation as a peaceful, pyramid-building society. For centuries, Maya culture was considered "the highest culture the New World had produced."[60] In the mind of Westerners, it was a civilization governed by rulers who devoted their time to astronomy and philosophy, activities that elevated the Maya above the sacrifice-addicted Aztecs, the other Mexican culture that inspired a major field of study. This romanticized notion was not shattered until the last decades of the twentieth century, when the decipherment of Maya hieroglyphics and findings like the gory murals at Bonampak revealed that Maya life also revolved around blood and war. The long-standing view of the Maya as exceptionally peaceful and sophisticated and therefore somehow more Western only exposes scholars' own biases about the West. A more basic explanation for the popularity of the Maya lies in geography. Cut off from the rest of Mexico by distance, dense jungle, and, until the early twentieth century, by the Caste War, the isolation of the Yucatán facilitated its exploitation by foreigners.

Outside of the Yucatán, some of the most popular ruins included Tula, Xochicalco, and Teotihuacán. In addition to the famous explorers, common travelers visited these as well as other sites. Touring the ruins of the world had become increasingly common by the late nineteenth century, as the advances of steam and rail had made travel quicker, cheaper, and thus a "regular part of human existence."[61] Europeans and Americans not only trekked through Italy and Greece but Cook's Tours, the famous travel agency, also hauled them to the Holy Land and to an Egypt that they supposedly "did" "in little over three weeks." And everywhere they went, the tourists zealously collected relics, so much so that when the great American writer Mark Twain visited the pyramids of Egypt, he joked about how he thought he saw a wart on the jaw of the sphinx, but, on closer inspection, it turned out to be a dangling tourist "trying to chip off a souvenir."[62]

In Mexico, the common travelers like the ones Twain describes are difficult to track, whether foreign or national. They tread the historical record lightly, leaving behind only an occasional and faint footprint, like the easily overlooked mention of a "group of Germans" spotted climbing the pyramids of Xochicalco in 1900.[63] Who were they? What were they doing there? Some travelers visited the ruins with the sole intent of gathering antiquities, like the Spaniard who was caught leaving Mexico with "various handbags and suitcases" stuffed with relics.[64] Others were sightseers; they trekked through the ruins out of curiosity, inspired, most likely, by what historians of tourism call "travel for education."[65] Yet even this type of tourist seems to have been incapable of leaving without an ancient souvenir. The Mexican journalist known simply as Plutarch, or Plutarco, poked fun at tourists who were convinced they had acquired priceless treasures. In their eyes, an ordinary piece of flint was "nothing less than the weapon that the romantic *Yoloxochitl*, lover of *Moctezuma*, used to kill herself," and a common pot became a "sacred vessel that gathered human blood, still warm."[66]

Mexico's tourists not only seized antiquities but left behind a trail of graffiti. They carved dates and names into the pyramids: a Mr. James R. Hitchcock of New York, for example, let posterity know he had been to Uxmal in 1846, along with his friend Mr. Scripture.[67] The travelers often left behind verses, some foolish, others profound, and some with advice on the right way to experience the ruins: "It is better to contemplate and be silent for the truth is mute," read one message in Uxmal. Even the companions of famous archaeologists could not resist the temptation to leave their mark, like Dr. Samuel Cabot of Boston. A surgeon and amateur naturalist, Cabot etched his name into the temples of Chichén Itzá and recorded that he was traveling in the company of John Lloyd Stephens and Frederick Catherwood, the famous explorers whose journeys brought worldwide attention to the Maya, initiating the field of Maya studies. "A detestable habit exists among all the visitors," wrote one Porfirian observer; they not only believe they have "the authority to write their names on the walls . . . but to seize fragments [of them] as mementos."[68]

What drove them to take possession of these ancient things? Was it the unique allure of the pre-Hispanic past? Or was it simply because the objects were old? That antiquities come from remote times is often thought to give them a "sense of 'depth'," a special quality that makes them particularly appealing.[69] The artifacts seem to have functioned as souvenirs. But what is a souvenir, anyway? According to Susan Stewart, the souvenir has many functions. Much like collecting, the act of possessing a souvenir is a mode of self-fashioning. It is a status marker, a statement of participation not in an event "but in the prestige generated by the event." Possessing an exotic object, Stewart argues, is a form of cultural imperialism. It allows the tourist "to appropriate, consume, and, thereby, 'tame' the cultural other." A souvenir also typically negates the present—it is a sample of an experience outside of present time and space—and speaks to the possessor's survival "outside of his or her own context of familiarity," to the "capacity for otherness."[70] Is this what Mexico's artifacts had come to mean? That the people who acquired them had the leisure time and discretionary income to travel? That they were cosmopolitan, powerful, and refined? Was this the meaning of the chunks of Mitla, for instance, travelers were said to have pried off "as a souvenir of their visit"?[71]

Often, they did not need to pry but were able to buy the objects straight from the locals. The sale of antiquities has long been a source of income for those living near ruins, so much so that archaeologists jokingly refer to it as the second oldest profession in the world. In Mexico, local involvement in the trade ranged from the Indians who peddled an occasional figurine to those who worked in the industry full time. Many locals were "subsistence diggers"; they sold antiquities and used the profits to support a subsistence lifestyle, like the enterprising Indians near Mitla who kept batches of artifacts on hand. When a visitor asked to see what they had, one woman offered up "four broken heads of idols," while another presented "a necklace" of gold beads.[72] The more clever locals didn't just sell their artifacts to the first person who offered to buy them. A visitor to Teotihuacán in 1878, for example, found them "waiting to sell to the highest bidder."[73] Yet savvy or not, the locals were hardly getting rich from their sales; like today, they earned little and usually got cheated. The case of one man from Teotihuacán "who trafficked in idols from burials" was typical. The man sold "an emerald 4 inches long and three inches wide . . . to an Englishman for 100 pesos." The confident local apparently thought he had cashed in on a "piece of green glass," but the Englishman knew better.[74]

Today, there are some archaeologists who support subsistence digging or a people's "right to dig." They defend the practice on moral grounds, on the idea that those who live in poverty are justified in using antiquities as an economic resource. Even though the local from Teotihuacán was cheated, they might say, he gained what for him was a small fortune. He took home the equivalent of about three months of a day laborer's pay. Defenders of the "right to dig" might also add that the local was a victim of the global market, exploited by the demands of collectors and dealers—the true villain in this case was the Englishman. Yet as Julie Hollowell and others explain, there are several problems with the "right to dig" argument. To begin, who is entitled to the right? The argument lacks clarity in this regard. It also inaccurately portrays the locals as victims, when in reality, native peoples, even today, enter the antiquities market on their own initiative and exploit it for their own gain. What is more, the act of digging might not be driven solely by economic motives, as people "dig for a variety of reasons." In her own research on the inhabitants of Alaska's St. Lawrence Island, Hollowell has documented how families go "digging together on weekends for recreation" and how children do it for fun.[75]

Most archaeologists stress the problems with subsistence digging. The artifacts, they believe, should not be treated as commodities since they are a public good, a type of wealth or patrimony that belongs to all of humanity, a quality that places them above the realm of commercialization. Many also point out that subsistence diggers, no matter how noble their cause, not only damage the ruins but the archaeological record. In tearing the artifacts from their context, they destroy information that allows archaeologists to deduce the objects' function and meaning and thus recreate the past. In selling the objects, the people also lose their cultural heritage, and in exchange, they have gained very little. The artifacts are then sold and resold on the market, generating a wealth the subsistence diggers never see. To speak in economic terms, they have exploited a finite or nonrenewable resource in an unsustainable way. But this argument, the "right to dig" camp would counter, privileges the archaeological record over the people. Besides, selling artifacts is not the same as selling one's heritage; "to imagine otherwise amounts to fetishising [the] objects." In fact, some native people, like the islanders studied by Hollowell, consider artifacts a type of gift left to them by their ancestors, a wealth they can use as they please. Digging is thus a birthright, a part of "every Islander's heritage, an activity that actually strengthens one's connections with the past."[76]

On one point, however, the archaeologists do agree: it is the middlemen (and women) more closely connected to the demand side of the market who rake in the true profits. According to one recent estimate, they pocket a whopping 98 percent of an artifact's final price.[77] In Porfirian Mexico they also made off like bandits. They bought cheap and sold high, like the "woman in Jalapa," Veracruz, who did "fabulous business" buying relics from Indians "at despicable prices" and "selling them to a company in Hamburg for the price of gold."[78] And while it wasn't just foreigners but also nationals that assumed the role of middleman, Mexicans often accused foreigners of luring locals into sacking; they "get the Indians involved," claimed one journalist, and "awaken their greed." But others pinned the blame on their fellow countrymen: "the sons of this soil . . . who part with everything related to our history for a fist full of coins."[79] According to this last reporter, it was not the "ignorant people, nor the Indians who live deep in the mountains" who traded away the nation's patrimony for pesos. It was the well-heeled, the more prosperous Mexicans who, due to some "inexplicable perversion, abandon historical objects in the hands of the first person who offers them a profit." That foreigners could so easily make off with the objects, and that Mexicans were often so eager to help, outraged this one observer. Protecting the nation's past, he insisted, needed to become "the first duty of patriotism." Taking charge of the past did, in fact, become a type of duty, a state endeavor, during the age of Porfirio Díaz. The government would try to take control of the ruins, objects that for centuries had had other functions and meanings, and put them to state uses instead. Because this was an effort managed by the country's political and intellectual elites, it is to them and to their motives that we now turn.

CHAPTER TWO

Ruins and the State

❧ THERE IS A FAMOUS PHOTOGRAPH OF PORFIRIO DÍAZ, MEXICO'S supreme leader, posing with the artifact commonly known as the Aztec Calendar. The eighty-year-old dictator looks proudly at the camera, propped up in front of the massive basalt disk with his cane. The photo was taken in Mexico's National Museum in August 1910, just months before the revolution that brought Díaz's thirty-five years of rule to an end. It is an image that marks the climax of an era. It is also an image that marks the height of a government effort to take charge of the remains of the pre-Hispanic past. Antiquity had taken on a variety of meanings for leaders of a country that was generally perceived as backward and inferior. It had become entwined with their nationalist sentiment and their efforts to build the nation. Mexico's intellectuals and statesmen would turn to antiquity and to the science of archaeology to shape and defend the nation's image as they constructed an official history rooted in pre-Hispanic times, one that not only gave Mexicans an ancient and impressive pedigree but a common origin. It was a usable past, indeed. At the same time, the making of this past was a difficult, contentious process, one that saw its share of squabbles as the elites struggled over the meaning of the ancient objects and the proper way to go about controlling them. While ordinary Mexicans would aid the state, the archaeological project that unfolded was ultimately an elite project; it was managed by the elites and reflected their concerns about the nation.

Like other elite endeavors, however, this project was couched in terms of broad national interests. Mexican leaders argued that the government had to take possession of the ruins for the good of the nation and science. But what was the nation? And what was science? Mexico in the age of Don Porfirio was a land of "largely rural, illiterate, dispersed, and heterogeneous societies."[1] Close to 40 percent of the country spoke indigenous languages when Díaz came to power.[2] To claim that a unified, modern nation existed, in other words, was to grasp at straws. Even the elites seemed to sense this, as they consistently expressed their concerns with controlling the past with a degree of apprehension about Mexican nationhood or the state of being a nation. Their statements often lacked the ring of full conviction, as if they themselves found them hard to believe. And if the nation was hardly a nation, archaeology, as the next chapter reveals, was hardly an established science. Yet even so, the appeals to nation and science would form the basis of the government's claims to the past. The archaeological project was rife with other contradictions, not least of which was the fact that the celebration of the ancient peoples occurred alongside the rejection of the contemporary Indians.

By the time of the Porfiriato, the Indian past, or more precisely, an elite construction of that past, had become the foundation of Mexico's official history. This was evident in *Mexico through the Centuries* (1887–1889), the nation's first work of historical synthesis, a five-volume series that took the different periods in the Mexican past and fused them into a single story. Sponsored by the government, *Mexico through the Centuries* was written by several authors and overseen by the celebrated intellectual, statesman, and general Vicente Riva Palacio. Lavishly decorated with maps as well as images of Mexican landscapes, monuments, and historical figures, it began with a volume on antiquity written by the historian and archaeologist Alfredo Chavero and went on to examine the colonial, independence, and modern periods. *Mexico through the Centuries* gave the nation a history that stretched back to remote times. It placed antiquity at the beginning of a sweeping narrative that turned the different phases in Mexico's past into parts of one grand "evolutionary process."[3]

The series argued, in effect, that "beginning with the Spanish Conquest, a mestizo nation had emerged as a natural fusion" between the conqueror and conquered.[4] It portrayed Mexico's disparate inhabitants as a single people, a mestizo people of both Indian and European descent, giving them a common heritage and origin. The mestizo would eventually become the great national unifier, a concept promoted by the revolutionary state to bridge the many divisions found among Mexico's population. Yet even by the

Porfiriato, as Alan Knight and others have shown, an official mestizo definition of the nation had already begun to take hold. As one journalist of the
time explained, the Mexican is "a product of the fusion of two races: the
autochthonous and that of the conqueror. This mix, this biological amalgam
of aborigines and Spaniards, formed the Mexican of today." The Indian past,
in other words, had become essential to the "definition of a self-assured
national identity."[5]

But this past was an exclusive club—it admitted only certain Indians.
The official history the elites created was a selective reconstruction of ancient
times. It celebrated the dominant groups of antiquity like the Toltecs,
Mixtecs, and Maya, societies that were marked by hierarchies with ruling
elites and high priests, and that left behind visible vestiges of "high culture":
works of architecture, temples, and ceremonial centers. It ignored the vast
array of other Indians, such as the nonsedentary peoples of the north. And
it emphasized the Aztecs, the "most powerful empire on the American continent," according to one observer.[6] Mexico was celebrated as an Aztec
nation, a portrayal that took many forms. It can be seen in Chavero's chapter
in *Mexico through the Centuries*, where he compares the Aztecs to the Otomí
and Maya and claims they were "the most perfect and powerful" of the
three.[7] It also showed up in paintings with Aztec subjects and themes; in the
statue of Cuauhtémoc, the last Aztec ruler, erected in 1887 on Reforma
Avenue, the fashionable main street in the capital; and in the Aztec Palace,
the building that housed Mexico's exhibition at the 1889 Paris World's Fair.
It could be seen in the country's archaeological projects as well, as the government focused on excavating and rebuilding the ruins of the central plateau, the heartland of the Aztec empire. (The only other place to receive so
much attention was the state of Oaxaca, the birthplace of Porfirio Díaz.) The
Aztec-centered vision cropped up in the museum, too, in exhibits in which
the Aztecs overshadowed all the other cultures. It was a vision that legitimized the power of the Mexican state by giving it an existence that stretched
back to Aztec times, one that reflected the elites' perception of the nation
and their place within it. As Chavero, an archaeologist with especially close
ties to official circles, succinctly put it, "The Aztecs are the most important
to our history, and they are the closest to us."[8] Still, the dominance of the
Aztecs did not go completely unquestioned. The most famous opposition
newspaper of the time, *The Son of the Scourge* (*El Hijo del Ahuizote*), made
fun of the elite's Aztec fixation in a simple cartoon. The image depicts the
Aztec Calendar, only the god at the center of the monument has been

replaced with a portrait of President Díaz sticking out his tongue, and the glyphs surrounding him have been swapped out with caricatures of well-known elites. Wedged between the different faces of the elites are words like "favoritism" and "gambling," which emphasize the corruption of the regime.[9]

But what about the gory aspects of Aztec culture? How did elites come to terms with things like cannibalism and human sacrifice? Mexican scholars, at least, did not shy away from these topics. In fact, some dedicated whole works to sacrifice, like Manuel Orozco y Berra, who was not only a historian but a geographer and archaeologist as well. Orozco y Berra wrote in gruesome detail about ancient sacrificial stones. Sacrifice was truly barbaric, elites like him agreed. But they also justified it by characterizing it as a practice found in many of the world's cultures. Europeans had no right "to raise a fuss," charged Orozco y Berra, since they too had committed this "crime." Let he who is innocent, he declared, "cast the first stone." Sacrifice was not only universal, a "stain on all humanity," but a practice that was thought to occur at a specific stage in a people's development, a stage out of which they would eventually evolve "both morally and physically." What about cannibalism? This equally or even more delicate subject was handled in much the same way. The Europeans had been cannibals, too, wrote Orozco y Berra, basing his claim on the Roman historian Pliny the Elder's account of cannibalism in the ancient Mediterranean world. Besides, there was a huge difference between the ancient Mexicans, who ate human flesh "*solely* for religious purposes," and true cannibals like the Caribs of the Caribbean, who practiced the "immoral and repugnant" custom "of hunting after humans to devour them." The cannibalism of the Aztecs was an act of reverence, a sign of devotion to something higher than themselves, while the Caribs simply ran around chomping on thighbones like "wild animals."[10]

Outside of these grisly aspects of antiquity, however, the Indian past was generally perceived as a period of sophistication, an era that gave Mexico deep and prestigious roots. The elites often referred to it as the authentic past, or "the genuine national civilization," in the words of archaeologist and historian Antonio Peñafiel.[11] Yet for all their talk about the ancient Indians as "our fathers" and "our ancestors," Mexicans were still somewhat ambivalent about incorporating this past into the official narrative. They did not necessarily consider it the most important era in the nation's history, as Rebecca Earle has revealed; instead, this status was usually reserved for the independence period. The statesman Justo Sierra made this clear when he referred to antiquity as a mere prelude to the nation's "true" history: "We have incorporated" the pre-Hispanic world, he said, "as a preamble that lays the foundations for and explains our true national history."[12]

Elites like Sierra were grappling with a problem faced by other postcolonial countries: that of forging an "authentic" national past in a Western-dominated world, a world whose racial hierarchies and cultural standards Mexican leaders had not only imbibed but would reinforce. Porfirian elites were deeply influenced by the Eurocentric racist thinking of the times. Even though they took pride in Mexico's Indian past and often criticized the Spanish conquest, they had accepted the idea of the superiority of whites and the West to the point of being incapable of making antiquity, a time devoid of Europeans, the most momentous period in the nation's history. Their attempts at constructing an official past were rife with other tensions that were never reconciled. On the one hand, for instance, they were attracted to antiquity because they thought it gave Mexico a prestigious, ancient past like Europe's, a pedigree like that of the Old World. But they were also lured by its potential to highlight features that made Mexico unique, and uniqueness, as many scholars point out, is a quality essential to the making of all modern nations. In the words of Mauricio Tenorio-Trillo, nationalism is an arena in which each nation "tries to develop a synthesis of history, culture, and traditions" that sets it apart from the others.[13] The towering pyramids and majestic rulers of ancient Mexico, features that made the country a one of a kind, gave it a way to enter this arena.

Mexico's ancient past, then, was at once similar to Europe's and different from it. And this difference, too, was a source of pride, a means to challenge the Western values that the elites ironically had absorbed. Not surprisingly, they spoke about the past in ways that simultaneously reinforced and defied these values. They interpreted antiquity in contradictory ways, but always in the shadow of the constructs of the West. Many studies have stressed how the elites portrayed the Indian past within the Europeanized framework of classical antiquity, how paintings of the time depicted pre-Hispanic peoples dressed in togas and with Western features. With a few brushstrokes, like magic, the Indians became Greeks and Romans. Even in the distant, imagined past, writes Stacie Widdifield, the Indian was an "object of conquest, of westernization."[14] When it came to the actual pieces of the past, Mexicans similarly compared their nation's relics to those of Greece and Rome: Teotihuacán's Street of the Dead resembled the "Street of Tombs of Pompey"; a statue from Palenque looked like one of

"Janus"; another was so well crafted that it seemed to have come from the "hands of Phidias," the ancient Greek sculptor.[15]

The classical world set the standards, but the canon of great civilizations was much more elastic in the eyes of Mexicans—it had to be for their nation to be included. And so they stretched their comparisons beyond classical antiquity, arguing for similarities between ancient Mexico and Egypt as well as India and China. These cultures were repeatedly linked together in a mantra-like fashion, with an occasional Persia and Assyria thrown in. In this way, the elites placed Mexico within a more universal order, a canon of civilizations that in including those of the non-West admitted Mexico's ancient peoples and gave the nation an oriental gloss. Mexico was the "American Egypt." The temples of Tlaxcala looked "like those of China." One of the features of the Maya site of Palenque was "the Hindu arch." Another observer saw in Palenque a kaleidoscope of great cultures; the site had elements of Etruscan, "Roman, Greek, Egyptian, Hindu," and even Aztec art—everything, amazingly, but Maya![16] Sometimes Mexican artifacts outdid all the others, like the ceramics of Mitla, which, according to one reporter, were superior to those of "the Greeks and Romans." But every now and then, Mexicans felt forced to admit defeat: the ruins of Teotihuacán, confessed one observer, "are very far from the level of Egypt, Assyria or Chaldea." The journalist Plutarco, once again, could not resist poking fun at this comparison craze: Mexico City lacked a Coliseum like Rome's, he pointed out, but it did have the "coliseum of Vergara."[17] (Was this the public bathhouse on Vergara Street? The nearby National Theater? Or the Hotel Vergara?)

Plutarco's inside joke aside, Mexicans were struggling with pre-Hispanic aesthetics, a form of beauty that did not accord with the standards of the West. One man in 1898, for instance, proposed that the Legislative Palace, whose construction was under deliberation at the time, be designed after a temple in Mitla or Uxmal. Why not build it "according to the architectural taste of our ancestors?" he asked.[18] Why look to foreign models when Mexico could draw inspiration from its own ruins? English buildings lined Hyde Park and French buildings, the Champs-Élysées; Mexico, he argued, also needed to make structures that were "genuinely national." The newspaper dubbed the man the "patriotic carpenter" and ridiculed his proposal, pointing out how uncomfortable the members of Mexico's Congress would be if the Legislative Palace were designed after the squat and narrow structures of Mitla—especially representatives Luis Pérez Verdía and Manuel Peniche, the first of whom would be too fat to enter the building and the second much too tall. Instead, observers tended to support the idea of melding pre-Hispanic and Western aesthetics. One journalist, for example, insisted that the ancient ruins "revealed a grand civilization" that could easily be blended with "modern" tastes.[19] When a building inspired by this melding principle did materialize it took the form of the Aztec Palace at the Paris World's Fair. This structure, which was designed by the archaeologist Antonio Peñafiel, amounted to a "Western reconstruction of the Indian past" down to its façade made up of pre-Hispanic gods and rulers dressed in togas.[20]

But buildings and paintings are different from the actual pieces of the past. Unlike the depictions of antiquity found in works of art, the relics could not be embellished; each had to be taken as it was. This was pre-Hispanic aesthetics without camouflage, and at times Mexicans were just as repelled by the objects as Westerners were. Gumesindo Mendoza, for instance, an archaeologist, chemist, and early director of the National Museum (1876–1883), described the statue of Chalchiuhtlicue, the Goddess of Water from Teotihuacán, as "monstrous."[21] But comments like these were few and far between. Another observer had this to say about the same goddess: "The public better not expect the monument to be a Venus de Milo . . . or the Apollo of Belvedere . . . ; that expectation reveals an absolute ignorance" of Mexico's ancient history.[22] Thus, as Mexicans embraced antiquity in an attempt to equate their country with the great civilizations of the world, they were simultaneously coming to terms with what one reporter called "our national art."[23] They had no choice, since Mexico's artifacts could not be reconciled with Western standards. No piece would benefit more from this appreciation of pre-Hispanic aesthetics than the sculpture of the ominous Coatlicue, an Aztec earth goddess with a serpent's face, which could never be made to conform to Western ideals of beauty. The goddess had been hidden in the museum for close to a century, but during the Porfiriato she was finally put on display and even complimented: Chavero would call her "the most beautiful idol in the National Museum."[24] Objects like Coatlicue and the Goddess of Water were thought to be embodiments of Mexico's glorious past, testaments, wrote Justo Sierra, of the "labor, intelligence, and extraordinary artistic refinement" of its ancient people.[25]

The problem, though, was that these objects were being steadily siphoned away. "When you want to study the history of the Indian civilizations of this land," complained one journalist, "it is necessary to go and search for the documents, codices, hieroglyphics, and most important pieces in the museums of Europe." "This is why we are seen as an ignorant people," he

continued, "incapable of taking an interest . . . in our origins and our ancestors, and incapable of understanding the importance of the treasures that
our soil holds." For a country that had been plagued by invasions, with one
that left it half its original size, the concern with antiquities was intertwined
with anxieties about controlling the national territory. Artifacts, of course,
are typically found embedded in the earth, which closely associates them
with the territory itself, a fact that was not lost on Mexico's elites. They spoke
about the antiquities as treasures, as resources, the "riches of the land,"
equating them with other objects found in the soil.[26] Yet while the elites
encouraged the foreign exploitation of the country's natural resources—the
economic boom of the times was based largely on the exportation of raw
materials—they would try to exert more control over the ancient ruins.

This desire for control extended to the scholarship on antiquity as well,
which up until then had largely been dominated by foreigners—the British,
Americans, Germans, and French. "It seems incredible," declared writer
Manuel Rivera Cambas, that others "have made a more enthusiastic effort at
getting to know our nation's ancient objects . . . than we Mexicans."[27] No one
would express these sentiments more fiercely than Leopoldo Batres, an
archaeologist whom we will come to know quite well. Mexico's lack of control over its antiquity, he maintained, was "a constant source of humiliation."
It made foreigners regard Mexico as "one of the inferior countries" and
forced Mexicans "to be consistently malleable" and "to bow to [Europeans']
desires."[28] Mexico emerges as meek and passive in Batres's statement. It is the
flip side, we might recall, of explorer Désiré Charnay's depiction of himself
as plunging into Mexico's virgin soil. Having power over the past, it seems,
had taken on gendered connotations for Mexicans as well. As Carmen Ruiz
points out, this sort of rhetoric on the part of the elites "positioned Mexico
(the nation) as a feminine entity" that needed to be shielded "by the Mexican
state (its masculine protector)."[29] Perhaps Sierra said it best when he declared
that in protecting the past, the government was defending the "honor" of the
nation.[30]

But Mexico's elites were also drawn to the antiquities for some of the
same reasons foreigners were. Put another way, the motives that led
Westerners to seek out Mexican artifacts drove Mexicans to try to keep
them. Like the foreigners, Mexicans saw the act of collecting the objects as a
sign of being sophisticated, scientific, and modern. All forward-looking
nations, the elites believed, preserved the pieces of their past. In neglecting
them, Mexico risked "the condemnation of the scientific world," explained

Jesús Sánchez, a medical doctor and director of the National Museum (1883–1889). Like others, Sánchez equated the "civilized" countries with those considered modern. "If the cultured nations," he declared, such as "Germany, France, England, Italy, and the United States, spend large sums acquiring and studying the antiquities of Egypt, Greece, China, and Mexico, then it is only right that we give our antiquities the importance they deserve."[31] If the most sophisticated countries collected Mexican artifacts, then Mexicans needed to do the same. Mexico had to take possession of its relics, Sánchez seemed to be saying, not to protect them from foreigners but because the foreign interest in them made them worthy of preservation. Ironically, Sánchez was legitimizing a nationalist impulse—Mexico's drive to control its antiquities—by making reference to imperialist behavior on the part of the West. Controlling the artifacts was thought to be a way to put the nation on par with the most modern powers of the globe; as Inspector Batres would say, Mexico needed to conserve its past as it was "usually done in the civilized nations."[32] How this control would be achieved, however, was a source of intense disagreement. When enacting measures to protect the past, Mexican leaders did not see eye to eye, a situation that was made obvious early in the period by a famous scandal involving the French explorer Charnay.

The Charnay Affair

Funded by the government of France and the American tobacco mogul Pierre Lorillard IV, Charnay arrived in Mexico in 1880, on his third trip to the country, hoping to assemble "the richest and most complete collection" of pre-Hispanic antiquities in "the entire world."[33] Since his last visit, however, Mexico had passed a law that would impact his plans. A decree issued in 1868 under Benito Juárez had prohibited archaeological excavations, forcing those who wished to carry them out to apply for permits from the Secretariat of Education, the ministry in charge of all matters related to archaeology. This ruling, along with the 1827 decree that allowed the government to issue permits to export antiquities, may have set the legal precedent for Mexico to grant contracts to individuals to both excavate and take artifacts out of the country. Initially, there were no consistent, formal guidelines for drafting these contracts. They were instead drawn up on a case-by-case basis and given to foreign archaeologists who worked for museums abroad that wanted to do research in Mexico and acquire antiquities.[34] Their purpose was to promote archaeological investigations, since many Mexicans believed their nation lacked the resources to carry out its own excavations. But these contracts were also a way to put an end to the days when foreign explorers roamed freely, since one of their stipulations was that a representative of the Mexican government supervise the activities of the archaeologists and keep track, for instance, of all sculptures, amulets, and other discoveries. Aware of this legislation, Charnay requested and received one of these contracts in July 1880.

The terms of Charnay's contract were broad. He could excavate anywhere he wished, but he had to send the artifacts he uncovered to the National Museum, where the director would have first pick of two-thirds of them. The remaining third Charnay could keep and take back to France to line the shelves of the Trocadéro Museum. In exchange, Charnay had to give Mexico's National Museum photos and casts of the items he exported, which would be used for study and display. The government appointed a young army engineer named Lorenzo Pérez Castro as Charnay's supervisor; Castro would watch over Charnay's work, keep track of the artifacts, and ensure that he did not damage the ruins. Charnay could begin digging immediately but could not export his share of the antiquities until the Mexican Congress approved of his concession. From the outset, the Frenchman was unhappy with the agreement. He wanted more favorable terms, pressed for modifications, and obstructed the inspection process. But he went on to excavate several ruins nonetheless, including Teotihuacán, Tula, Uxmal, Chichén Itzá, Palenque, and Yaxchilán. At two sites alone he unearthed nearly nine hundred ancient objects. He sent these, along with many others, to Mexico's museum, expecting to return to France with his portion.

But instead, the Mexican Congress voted overwhelmingly against Charnay's contract, 114 votes to 6, a decision that unleashed a fierce debate. Although Charnay's concession was technically legal, most of the delegates in Congress believed it violated Mexico's "dignity" and everything the country held "sacred." It was shameful, noted Gumesindo Enríquez, a representative from the state of Mexico, to see the antiquities, the "inspiration and evidence for the writing of history, become a part of the museums of foreigners and not of our own." It made Mexico appear "semisavage." It was ridiculous, moreover, to suppose that some measly photographs could stand in for the relics. Such an unequal exchange was, another deputy chimed in, like a marriage that takes away the daughter, only to leave her father with her portrait! Rounds of applause broke out, and one of the few dissenters dared to speak. The delegate, Antonio Carbajal, pointed out that Mexico had done a terrible job preserving its past. Charnay's excavations would help enrich the National Museum at no cost to the Mexican government; the contract was no cause for alarm since the museum director would have first pick of the relics. To this argument the representative Enríquez responded that Charnay would surely find a way to make off with the most precious pieces. Mexico might have a terrible record of conservation, but the coming years would surely bring a change. The country, he emphasized, did not need to rely on foreigners to uncover its history. Throughout this whole debate the delegates made no mention of the fact that Mexico was reestablishing formal diplomatic ties with France, relations that had been severed since the French Intervention of the 1860s. But the war with France was far too fresh in their minds for them to allow Charnay to carry out his plan. In vetoing his contract the delegates were essentially carving out a bit of power for their nation. At least in the realm of archaeology, they seemed to be saying, Mexico would not be subservient to France.

The debate intensified when Justo Sierra spoke out in defense of Charnay's contract. The fledgling politician who would soon become one of Mexico's most influential figures belonged to a younger generation less impacted by the brunt of foreign domination. He began by explaining that he was devoted to the cause of science and its "universal mission." Archaeology was the realm of the "community of experts of the globe." Mexico needed to turn to this community and seek the aid of foreigners, Sierra continued, because it lacked the resources to adequately explore its ruins. It was the Europeans, after all, who had brought the history of Egypt to light, just as they had in Mexico, Sierra claimed, referring to the French Scientific Commission that had rummaged through the nation's ruins. At this point, Vicente Riva Palacio, the coordinator of *Mexico through the Centuries* and a general who had made his reputation fighting against France, intervened: just because foreigners studied Mexico's past did not mean the country had to forfeit its treasures to them. "I love science, but I am savage about patriotism. I would perish in flames before foreign domination," Riva Palacio dramatically declared. More applause broke out, and then Sierra dared speak again. It was wrong for Mexicans to be blinded by a patriotism that obstructed the cause of science, he said. Mexico needed to abandon this sort of "savage" patriotism for a more "enlightened" approach, one that put science above the nation. Approving Charnay's contract would further this aim, since it would promote archaeology, a science Mexico had long neglected. The poet and politician Guillermo

Prieto then responded and had the last word. Prieto reminded Sierra of the many Mexicans who had studied the nation's ancient history. How could Sierra overlook Orozco y Berra's decipherment of Mexican hieroglyphics, he asked? How could he support giving foreigners license to tear off pieces of those ancient "alphabets," to destroy the civilizations of the past? How could he allow Mexico's ancient remains to be scattered about "like loose pages out of the book of our history?" And how, above all, could he compare Mexico to Egypt, a country that allowed its antiquities to be dispersed across the globe, a clear sign of its "degradation"? (Egypt, it seems, was a role model for the making of artifacts, but not for defending them.) Mexico's patrimony, Prieto emphasized, needed to remain in the country. With this, the debate ended, and on that day, 28 October 1880, Congress voted to reject Charnay's contract, much to the dismay of the French, of course, and of Charnay.[35]

Instantly, the French began to press their claim to the artifacts Charnay had gathered. The famous anthropologist Armand de Quatrefages, one of the leading figures in the French Scientific Commission, urged his government to take action but with the "greatest prudence," since Mexicans had an "unmeasured sensitivity" about matters concerning their sovereignty. The French government pushed the matter, and so did French nationals living in Mexico, as well as Charnay. Charnay even tried to pressure the museum director, Gumesindo Mendoza, into relinquishing the relics, but Mendoza would not budge. Charnay was insulted. He was a scientist, a benefactor who had come "not to plunder Mexico but to enrich it," yet he found himself being treated like a common "vandal." But the word "vandal," it turns out, was not far from the truth. Charnay had violated the terms of his contract, both before and after the congressional veto, by gathering antiquities that he never revealed to the Mexican government. Utterly brazen, he had once observed that it was hard to smuggle "large pieces" because they were "difficult to hide" but "easy to pass the small ones." The French explorer interpreted the rejection of his contract as an "illegal" "confiscation" of his relics. "Our treasure . . . went to fill up the shelves of the Mexican museum," he would later complain.[36] And there it remained, stored in five sealed crates, a state of affairs we will return to in due time.

The debate over Charnay's contract was about many things—about patrimony, imperialism, and the legacies of Mexico's violent, chaotic past. But underneath it all, it was about two different approaches to nationalism and science, as scholar Clementina Díaz y de Ovando has suggested. The first, the "savage" nationalism of men like General Riva Palacio, as well as the majority of Congress, was a more absolute, uncompromising stance. Its representatives distrusted the presence of foreigners in the study of Mexican archaeology and adopted a more defensive attitude toward the artifacts. The other position was what Sierra labeled "enlightened patriotism." Its advocates, like Sierra himself, were less wary of foreigners. They were influenced by universalist notions of science and believed that since archaeology belonged to the "community of experts of the globe," it should not be hindered by national boundaries. Providing concessions to foreigners connected Mexico to this community and furthered the cause of science. But this "enlightened" approach was not necessarily any less patriotic. Allowing for a limited exportation of antiquities from the country, people like Sierra believed, made it possible for the evidence of Mexico's glorious past to be part of museums abroad, where it would shine for all to see. It also did not imply a loss of control over the objects, since most of the "enlightened" leaders wanted the exportations to be regulated, granted only on a case-by-case basis. Both of these approaches to patrimony would coexist throughout the age of Díaz, with the defensive, "savage" stance dominating early in the Porfiriato, when wounds from foreign invasions were still fresh, and the "enlightened" stance gaining momentum later in the period. In the end, the two views had one thing in common: they were driven by a desire to project a better image of the nation. The first focused more on issues of sovereignty and the second on appearing sophisticated and cosmopolitan.

The Charnay affair not only brought these two views to light but was Mexico's most high-profile case involving the foreign appropriation of antiquities. It raised awareness about the importance of taking measures to control the past, a consciousness Mexican leaders would act on by developing institutions like the National Museum and the Inspectorate of Monuments. This support for archaeology grew as time went by and became especially intense later in the period, when Justo Sierra served as subsecretary (1901–1904) and secretary of education (1905–1911). An ardent promoter of archaeology, Sierra had a profound interest in the pre-Hispanic past, to the point of calling himself the "admirer of Quetzalcoatl," the famous feathered serpent, one of Mexico's greatest of gods.[37] But how could Sierra adopt such a name? How could the Indian past have been admired at all? How could any form of Indian identity have been celebrated by a regime so hostile to Mexico's Indians, one that stripped them of their lands and waged war against them? To understand this question it is useful to turn to the slippery subject of race.

Although the elite's ideas about race were far from uniform, they operated within the general framework of social Darwinism. Mexican leaders
had imbibed the racist thinking that held nonwhites and mixed people to be
inferior. But that does not mean they accepted it completely. What future
would their country have, after all, with a population that was inherently
and therefore permanently inferior? What's more, many elites, including
President Díaz, were mixed people themselves. As Sierra explained, to adhere
to such "dogmatic declarations" about race would cause Mexicans to "lose
all hope in ourselves."[38] Instead of fully reproducing racist thought, elites
tailored it to their nation's context. They adapted it in ways both contradictory and pragmatic, accepting and resisting it at the same time. This tension
surfaced in their ideas about the mestizo, the racial type put forth to unify
the nation. Even when they departed from the belief in the inferiority of
mixed people by glorifying the mestizo, they did so within the "rigid frame
of reference" of social Darwinism.[39] Andrés Molina Enríquez, for example,
the most pro-mestizo thinker of the time, would characterize the mestizo as
the "strongest [racial] element," a product of "advanced selection" and "adap-
tation to the environment."[40] The embrace of the mestizo, moreover, did not
signify a rejection of the European side of Mexico's racial equation. Sierra,
for instance, considered the mestizo the most "dynamic factor in our history." But he also advocated European immigration to the country, since
"only European blood could keep the level of civilization . . . from sinking."[41]
As a matter of fact, the mestizo was exalted even by Mexico's most ardent
Hispanophiles, like the journalist Francisco Cosmes: "Our national spirit is
a consequence of the union of two races," Cosmes declared.[42] But he believed
that the Indian had contributed just the raw material to this "spirit," while
the Spaniard had contributed all the valuable qualities. *Mestizaje*, or misce-
genation, was embraced precisely because it held out the promise that the
Indians could be "whitened." Embedded within the concept is a whitening
ideal, a trajectory that sees Indians eventually becoming mestizos and thus
moving closer to Western ways. Mestizaje promised to "mexicanize" the
Indians, to dilute their many ethnicities by cloaking them under a homog-
enous national identity.[43]

This reworking of racist thought surfaced in the ideas about contemporary Indians as well. Although Mexican elites considered the Indians to be
backward and uncivilized, most did not believe they were biologically and,
therefore, inherently inferior. Instead, they claimed the Indians suffered
from a degraded culture, a condition attributed to a wide array of factors.

While Sierra and others denounced the abuses of Spanish colonialism, Molina Enríquez blamed the fact that the Indians had been deprived of land. In his *Great National Problems* (1909), Molina argued that the Indians' communal landholdings were central to their well-being. That they had been dispossessed of them was "disastrous," wrote this intellectual and local judge whose ideas would go on to influence the policies of the Mexican revolution. Yet even though Molina was one of the more compassionate observers, he too believed the Indians existed in a degraded state, what he called "evolutive backwardness."[44]

Of course, there were some hard-core social Darwinists who attributed the Indians' backwardness to race. The most notorious, again, was Cosmes, who considered Mexico's native peoples completely barbaric. Cosmes even rejected the idea that Mexico had had a sophisticated Indian past. He scoffed at his countrymen who glorified antiquity, at those who got a glimpse of the Aztec Calendar and were "ready to swear that the inhabitants of Tenochtitlán [had] discovered the planetary system before Copernicus."[45] The Porfirian enthusiasm for the ancient past, then, was not universal. It had its share of critics, like the anonymous journalist who believed it was more important to modernize the nation's infrastructure than to dig up relics, more critical "to pave the streets of the capital" than to excavate them in search of "fossils, mummies, and other old things."[46]

But apart from Cosmes and a few others, observers usually attributed the degradation of the Indians to culture rather than biology. They turned to what anthropologists refer to as "culturalist definitions of race." And here, we should not be fooled, since using "culture as a marker of difference," as Marisol de la Cadena explains, is a form of "'racism without race.'"[47] Moreover, when it came to daily life, what mattered were not these abstract notions and debates, but the sheer and simple fact that Mexico's Indians were considered lesser beings, a view that provided justification for taking away their lands and turning them into field hands on haciendas. And yet the embrace of a culturalist definition of race did offer the elites a way out of the stark racist thinking. It gave them a faith in their nation's future potential, since cultural traits, such as language and dress, were thought capable of being changed.

To this end, several solutions were proposed to what the elites perceived as the "Indian problem"—the idea that Indians were an obstacle to Mexico's progress. For some, the answer lay in education. Education had the power to turn an Indian into a "Juárez," wrote one observer, referring to Mexico's famous full-blooded Zapotec president.[48] Sierra, one of the strongest proponents of indigenous education, had this to say: the social problem of the Indian race "is a problem of nutrition and education; . . . let them eat more beef and less *chile*, let them learn the useful and practical lessons of science, and the Indians will transform themselves: that is all there is to it."[49] As Sierra's remark also suggests, another popular solution concerned diet. Some Mexicans believed the indigenous staple of corn had turned the Indians into weaker beings. They advocated that corn be replaced with wheat, the grain of the superior Europeans. The "language of proteins and carbohydrates," a scientific explanation for the Indians' degeneracy, allowed these observers to evade the deterministic racist doctrines of the times.[50] Another solution was to simply encourage more Europeans to immigrate to Mexico, an idea that operated at the level of both culture and biology, as observers hoped that an influx of Europeans would Westernize the nation's population and infuse it, in the words of Sierra, with more civilized "blood." Still, while the elites' solutions to the Indian problem were varied and complex, they shared a common goal: to Westernize or de-Indianize the Indians. Mexican elites, then, may have viewed the Indian past as a type of confirmation or proof that indigenous peoples could be "uplifted"; they had once been civilized, the logic went, and could be made civilized again. Sierra's claim that the Indian "race" had "shown signs of colossal energy" and that "the precise moment has arrived to awaken it" suggests an embrace of such a belief.[51] Some scholars have pointed to this reasoning as evidence that the Porfirian interest in the ancient past was a sign that Mexican elites had finally come to accept the Indians as part of the nation.[52]

But statements like Sierra's were rare. Observers usually made no correlation between antiquity and the contemporary Indians' potential to be uplifted. Instead, most simply stressed that the ancient past was a sophisticated state from which the Indians had fallen. The views of people like Mendoza, the museum director who refused to yield to Charnay, were typical. Unlike most of the other scholars of the museum, Mendoza was neither white nor mestizo. Instead, he was an Indian of Otomí descent, with a story much like that of the legendary Benito Juárez. Mendoza began his life as a peon on a hacienda and then moved up in society through the aid of a local priest. But that did not stop him from declaring that Mexico's Indians were "ignorant," a pale reflection of the "industrious and wise" civilizations who had built the "solemn and majestic ruins."[53] Like Mendoza, observers who compared the contemporary Indians with those of long ago emphasized the gulf rather than the link between the two. They characterized the contemporary Indians as obstacles to Mexico's development, calling them ignorant, backward, and lazy, but celebrated the ancient peoples in ways that fit Western ideals of progress, depicting them as great scientists, mathematicians, astronomers, and artists. In fact, as Rebecca Earle has argued, the glorification of antiquity was predicated on this rift, on the idea that the ancient "cultures had little or nothing to do with contemporary indigenous peoples," on the certainty that the Indian past and present were "utterly disconnected."[54]

Thus, there were dark undertones to the celebration of antiquity by this anti-Indian regime; it represented a retreat from the contemporary Indians, a negation and denial. Much like the embrace of the mestizo and the culturalist notions of race, the glorification of antiquity offered an escape from the bleak racist thinking. It allowed Mexican leaders to construct an indigenous heritage for their nation through the ancient rather than contemporary Indian, the Indian contained in far-off times, shut out from the present, tucked away in scholarly spaces and museum displays and embodied in the ruins and stones—this was the type of indigenous heritage the elites came to incorporate into their idea of the nation. In order to take possession of the old stones and craft this sort of vision of history, the government would promote archaeology, a discipline that not only reflected but helped reinforce the gulf between the Indian past and present through its practices and through the ways in which the nation's ancient peoples were imagined, a task that was placed in the hands of Mexico's archaeologists.

PART TWO

The Archaeologists

CHAPTER THREE

The Museum Men

✦ MEXICO'S ARCHAEOLOGISTS WERE A SERIOUS BUNCH. THEY WERE dedicated to a life of study and devoted to the nation. Many of them were linked to the government through the National Museum. Some were directors of the institution, while others were professors who served as researchers, curators, and docents in the different departments. One, and only one, Leopoldo Batres, the focus of the next chapter, worked in the Inspectorate of Monuments, the agency he headed from its inception in 1885 until the fall of Díaz in 1911. It was through these two institutions—both of which were supervised by the Secretariat of Education—that the Mexican government set out to take control of the relics and ruins. The archaeologists furthered this aim, supported financially and institutionally by the government. A tight link was thus forged between the state and science, as the archaeologists helped construct an ancient past for the nation and legitimize the government's claims to the ruins. At the same time, archaeology was not yet an established science. Mexico's archaeologists had very little training; they were short on technique and carried out their work amid much confusion, as they lacked even the most basic sense of pre-Hispanic chronology. The science often had a certain nebulous or hesitant quality to it, a tentativeness that made the state's claim to the ruins seem all the more strained.

 But it would be a mistake to regard Mexico's early archaeologists as pawns of the federal government. They were dedicated scientists moved by the concerns of their discipline, men like Francisco del Paso y Troncoso, whose commitment to antiquity seems almost superhuman. Del Paso became the director of the National Museum in 1889 and literally lived there—he slept on a cot in one of the rooms and every day had his sister bring him his food—until 1892, when he took up another monk-like existence, this time in the libraries and archives of Europe. The Díaz government sent him there on a special mission to transcribe every document he could find on Mexico's history, especially its pre-Hispanic past. (Like the antiquities, many of the old codices had also ended up in Europe.) Del Paso worked around the clock, barely sleeping and eating. He suffered from poverty, ill health, and inept research assistants, and he ended up sacrificing the last twenty-four years of his life copying a massive body of texts, including works that were vitally important to Mexico's history, such as the sixteenth-century friar Bernardino de Sahagún's *General History of the Things of New Spain* (also known as the *Florentine Codex*). Del Paso never saw home again; he died in Italy in 1916. Years later, his research notes were shipped back to Mexico in crates, along with his lonely, tattered suits.[1]

Mexico's archaeologists hardly lived the lifestyle of the upper crust. Many barely scraped by, and some, like museum professor Jésus Galindo y Villa, died in absolute poverty. Still, as members of the intellectual elite, they had power. What's more, a good number of them served as politicians and public officials; they lived "halfway in between academia and politics."[2] Alfredo Chavero, the author of the chapter on antiquity in *Mexico through the Centuries*, was a museum director (1902–1903) as well as an undersecretary of foreign relations and a member of Congress. As part of the tightly knit intelligentsia of the times, the men had scholarly affiliations that stretched well beyond the museum. Apart from being a medical doctor, museum director, and author of several studies on the Indian past, Jesús Sánchez served as a professor of zoology in the museum, at the national preparatory school, the national teachers' college, and national school of agriculture. Mexico's archaeologists also dedicated themselves to many other activities geared at learning about the nation. Perhaps the best example is Antonio Peñafiel, the designer of the Aztec Palace. A surgeon by training, Peñafiel became the museum taxidermist in 1879 and went on to become a top-ranking statistician, heading the General Directorate of Statistics and carrying out Mexico's first national census in 1895. The scholars of the museum wore many hats, and they were also incredibly prolific. Nicolás León, the first professor of anthropology at the institution, a man more celebrated as the nation's father of physical anthropology than for his writings on the ancient past, left behind over five hundred works of scholarship.

Yet nearly none of the men were archaeologists by training, which was also true of archaeologists in other nations; E. T. Hamy, for instance, the director of the Trocadéro in France, was originally trained as a medical doctor. Mexico's archaeologists similarly came from other, more established fields, especially engineering, medicine, and law. Del Paso had studied medicine, while Chavero specialized in law. And although both of these scholars dedicated much of their time to the study of the ancient past, others were just dabblers in the field, like the zoologist Sánchez, who published some studies on antiquity but focused most of his energies on other subjects. The museum professors lived at a time before the divisions between scholarly disciplines had hardened. They were polymaths, renaissance men, experts in several fields—philology, ethnography, linguistics, poetry, and even music. In fact, the list of those associated with the museum reads much like a "who's who" in the intellectual world of the times. Many of these scholars are not typically remembered as archaeologists but were linked to this science in the museum nonetheless, such as José Juan Tablada, the poet famous for sweet verses like the following:

> ¡Del verano, roja y fría
> carcajada
> rebanada
> de sandía!

> From summer, cold and red
> A laugh
> A slice
> Of watermelon!

Although Tablada is known for his writings rather than his interest in archaeology, he served a brief stint as a professor of the science in 1907. This raises the question of what constituted an expert. An expert was not necessarily someone with a formal education in archaeology, as training in the discipline would not be available in Mexico until 1906, when classes began to be offered on a regular basis at the museum. Instead, an expert was someone who studied the ancient past—using either written sources or the more up-and-coming approach of fieldwork—who published on it, and who frequently had some sort of connection to the state, quite often through the

National Museum, the most important center of archaeological study and conservation in the country, the hub of Mexican archaeology.

As warehouses of patrimony, national museums are central to the process of nation building. In Mexico, as in the rest of Latin America, these institutions emerged in the early nineteenth century, soon after independence, alongside those of Europe and the United States. The timing here suggests, as Benedict Anderson has argued, that Spanish America was at the vanguard of the world's nationalist movements.[3] Mexico's National Museum was founded in 1825 by Lucas Alamán, the minister of the interior and foreign relations. According to its founding charter, the institution was designed to teach the public about the nation, "its primitive population, the Religion and customs of its inhabitants," its art and science, "natural resources, climate and terrain."[4] And it did so by putting Mexico's patrimony on display: antiquities, medals, paintings, sculptures, scientific inventions, natural specimens, and objects that were "curious or strange." Still, while the museum was a product of the nationalist sentiment of Mexico's elites, its origins were essentially colonial: the institution was established in the Royal University with the collection that had been gathered years earlier by the Spanish viceroys. Mexico's museum is thus similar to others found in postcolonial settings.[5] Much like those of Africa and Asia, it developed out of an institution created by a colonial power. Unfortunately for Mexico, though, the museum got off to a rocky start; it was transferred from one room to another in the university and then to the mining school in 1843, before Maximilian granted it a permanent home at 13 Moneda Street near the Zócalo in the center of Mexico City. For most of the century, the institution would fail to garner much government support, a consequence not only of Mexico's incessant chaos and the weakness of the state but also of the "uncertain place of the preconquest era" within the nation's official history.[6]

This situation changed with the rise of Porfirio Díaz, not only because his regime created more stability, a stronger state, and an official history more firmly embedded in the ancient past, but also because of what the museum had come to mean. Mexican elites, like other elites around the world, saw the national museum as inseparable from the national image; it was the "type of institution," wrote an observer, that allowed one to judge "the level of the nation's progress." Thus, it was imperative that Mexico's museum not "fall behind those of other countries."[7] And it did not. Instead, it experienced "extraordinary development," its budget growing tenfold over the course of Díaz's many years of rule, a change that was also driven by the thriving Porfirian economy.[8] The museum went from being a cabinet of curiosities to a full-fledged scientific institution dedicated to research, teaching, collecting, and the spread of knowledge.

And something else changed, too: the museum became more specialized in the different branches of anthropology, especially archaeology. At the onset of the Porfiriato, the institution was dedicated mainly to the natural sciences. Although it contained three sections—a library, a department of natural history, and another department combining both archaeology and history—the natural history section dominated the institution with a stockpile of rocks and minerals that dwarfed all the other collections. In the 1880s, however, the professors began channeling more funding and energy to anthropology. They divided the archaeology and history collections into two separate departments in 1882 and created a department of anthropology and ethnography in 1895. Finally, in 1909, they eliminated the natural history section altogether, transferring it to another location in the capital. From this point on, the museum would be dedicated to the fields of anthropology, archaeology, and history, to the study of Mexico's human past and present, in other words. This change was reflected in the institution's new name: the National Museum of Archaeology, History and Ethnology. But the principal attraction, the "favorite of the public and especially foreigners," the professors often emphasized, was the archaeology collection.[9]

Archaeology was more than just a means of conservation. In the eyes of elites, the discipline gave Mexico both the aura of a scientific, modern nation and a place within the world of science—and not just any place. It allowed the country to carve out a special niche; as Sierra put it, "Archaeology is the only discipline that gives Mexico personality in the scientific world."[10] The science provided Mexicans with an international language with which to define themselves and their nation. Mexican archaeologists operated within a global community of scientists. They contributed to international discussions and publications and were active players in the Americanist movement, traveling abroad to present papers at the Congress of Americanists and hosting the event in their own country two times, in 1895 and 1910. They corresponded with foreign scientists, engaged with their works, and received them as researchers in the museum. And they presented their own findings in the *Annals of the National Museum*, the museum journal initiated in 1877 with the purpose of reaching a national and foreign audience. Historians often depict Europe and the United States as "the producers of scientific ideas" and poorer countries like Mexico as places that merely adopt foreign advances, but in this case, as Ruiz has shown, the center-periphery model does not hold.[11] Mexicans dialogued with foreign scientists; they refuted old theories, presented new ones, and developed their own scholarly traditions and sense of the field. And they were held in high esteem by their counterparts abroad: the French authority on the pre-Hispanic past, E. T. Hamy, for instance, considered Chavero a "savant."[12]

The benefits of archaeology did not end there. As we have seen, archaeology is a discipline that is especially useful for nation building. The artifacts it collects are tangible, even portable, making it easy for governments to surround citizens with them on a daily basis. The ruins can be turned into official monuments and museum pieces and into symbols that can be used on national currencies and flags; they can be memorialized in national anthems and songs. More importantly, the data gathered by archaeology is "hardly ever straightforward"; it rarely leads to "unambiguous reconstructions of the past," making the science particularly "susceptible to political manipulation," writes Philip Kohl. While archaeological data is not open to endless interpretation, it has a degree of malleability that lends itself to nationalist reconstructions of the past, to interpretations that prop up certain cultures as the ancestors of a nation. Archaeology can thus provide the stuff on which nations are built, a common history and culture, "a respectable pedigree extending back into the remote past" and firmly rooted in the national territory. Put another way, archaeology is a science that can ground a nation in both time and space.[13]

But what *was* archaeology back then? How did its practitioners go about their work? What were their preconceptions and beliefs? What were their paradigms, to use philosopher of science Thomas Kuhn's term? According to Kuhn, all scientists, whatever their discipline, adhere to certain paradigms, a mix of practices and ways of thinking. Their research is shaped by an existing framework of techniques and conceptual schemes. This makes the nature of scientific activity susceptible to tradition and to the styles of thought of its practitioners, as scientists carry out their work within a behavioral world that is generated by their own profession.[14] But what exactly was this world for the archaeologists of Mexico's museum?

To the present-day observer, most of these scientists would have hardly seemed like archaeologists at all. They worked more like historians, studying antiquity through dusty, old texts such as codices, the writings of scholars like the German naturalist Alexander von Humboldt, and, when possible, the works of fellow archaeologists. They based their research on a close reading of the texts, using the artifacts to supplement their findings. Scholars have characterized Mexico's archaeologists as positivists, as scientists who emphasized direct observation—research carried out through the human senses—as the true source of knowledge. Yet these were positivists who relied quite heavily on written texts to analyze the very objects they had right in front of them. Sometimes, they examined an artifact to verify the information found in the texts. More often, they did the opposite: they sifted through page after page and text after text in order to decipher an object's meaning. Dozens of studies in the museum's journal focus on what Sahagún or Humboldt or some other scholar had to say about a specific piece, a style of research, again, that was not limited to Mexicans. The Frenchman Hamy carried out his work in much the same way, analyzing artifacts with the heavy aid of written sources. Archaeology was born in Mexico's museum "attached to history," a phrase that captures more than how the scientists went about their work.[15] Not only were the archaeology and history collections initially held together in the institution, but a single scholar, a professor of archaeology and history, ran both departments until 1903, well after they had been separated. Archaeology was an "important aid to history," as the multitasking Peñafiel explained.[16] Even the metaphors used to describe the artifacts lay bare this connection to history; the objects were the nation's "archives," "the purest sources," "the delicate pages" of our history books.[17]

Compared to other countries, moreover, archaeology in Mexico seems to have been more detached from the branches of anthropology that concern live people. Ethnology and physical anthropology did not take off in the National Museum until late in the Porfiriato, much later than they did in France, for instance, where the disciplines played an active role in the country's colonial expeditions. Mexican archaeologists tended to avoid these fields and were less likely to shift back and forth between the study of the Indian past and present. Foreigners like Hamy, in contrast, were more apt to make these sorts of leaps, carrying out research on both ancient and contemporary people. Hamy was not only an expert in antiquity but in anthropometry, the study and measurement of human skulls and body parts that was so fashionable among French scientists of his day. In Mexico, the boundary between the study of the ancient and contemporary Indians was simply more fixed, a reflection, perhaps, of the rift that separated the Indian past and present in the minds of elites.[18] Scholars such as Chavero and del Paso focused their attention on the Indians of long ago, research they carried out, nearly always, ensconced in the museum.

In fact, most of the museum archaeologists, especially the older ones like Chavero and del Paso, hardly ventured out into the ruins. This was also not unique to Mexicans. Hamy never set foot in the Americas and did not carry out many formal excavations. Archaeology had yet to become completely associated with fieldwork. While Mexico had its share of armchair scholars as well as diggers (and some who did a bit of both), it was the armchair types who dominated the museum. Those who did go out into the field, like the energetic Peñafiel, usually did so of their own accord and at their own expense, as the museum would not begin to fund expeditions on a regular basis until 1904. It was only then, toward the end of the Porfiriato, that fieldwork began to gain ground, a trend in other disciplines around the world as well. Even so, it was the ethnographers of the National Museum, rather than the archaeologists, who went out into the field, scholars like anthropology professor Nicolás León. León not only carried out fieldwork in his discipline but also seems to have done more research at the ruins than the archaeologists. For León, the study of the ancient past was a way to corroborate his findings in ethnology, a means of verifying the origins and linguistic and ethnic makeup of the contemporary Indians. The archaeology professors, in contrast, had much less experience with fieldwork.

Of course, even some of the most die-hard armchair scholars occasionally set foot in the ruins, like museum director del Paso, who in 1891 was commissioned to carry out what is often considered Mexico's first state-sponsored excavation since the time of the Bourbon rulers. For two months, del Paso explored the monuments of his native land of Veracruz. The Mexican military aided him, along with the local Indians, who cleared the structures of vegetation, allowing him to sketch, map, and photograph much of the ruins. Del Paso uncovered Cempoala, the Totonac city so crucial to the Spanish conquest, as well as Villa Rica de la Vera Cruz, the first settlement established by the conqueror Hernán Cortés. He went on to explore several more sites, including El Tajín. The artifacts he gathered, along with thousands of other pieces from the National Museum, were shipped off to Spain for the Columbian Historical Exposition of 1892, the celebration that marked the four-hundred-year anniversary of the "discovery" of the New World. Del Paso attended the event and remained in Europe to carry out his special mission of gathering ancient Mexican texts. He took an indefinite leave of absence as museum director but retained his title, since it was not clear when he would return, making those who occupied his position throughout the rest of the Porfiriato just interim directors. But

apart from his work at Cempoala, the man often touted as the most important Mexican archaeologist of his time carried out next to no excavations.
What is more, those he did perform were "woefully deficient in theory and
technique."[19]

And he was not alone. Mexican archaeologists worked with little technique. They did not use stratigraphic excavation, for instance, a procedure in
which archaeologists treat a relic much like a geologist treats a fossil, recording its location in the strata or layers found in the earth in order to establish
its relative age. To the modern-day "dirt" archaeologist, context is everything. The place of an artifact in the soil is an invaluable source of information—without it, the object does not offer much insight into the past.
Stratigraphic excavation allows an archaeologist to read the ground, much
like a text, and to deduce the chronological order in which the artifacts were
created, since those found in the bottom layers are most likely older than
those found closer to the surface. It allows scientists to measure the passage
of time and to date cultural changes, as well as related developments such as
invasions, migrations, and the diffusion of cultures.

Although stratigraphic techniques had been used in the Old World for
some time, in the Americas they were uncommon. There is much contro-
versy on the matter, but recent research has revealed that some Americanist
scholars did use these methods: William Henry Holmes, the first curator of
anthropology at Chicago's Field Museum, made stratigraphic observations
in the Valley of Mexico as early as 1884. The professors in Mexico's museum
were also familiar with the techniques. When railroad construction in the
state of Guanajuato unearthed some "prehistoric" remains in 1902, the
museum sent out two professors, one in anthropology and another in geol-
ogy, to investigate, ordering them to "meticulously" record the position and
depth of the objects found in the soil.[20] But Mexicans and Americanist scholars as a whole did not use stratigraphic excavation frequently or systemati-
cally. They also did not use it to record the passage of time or cultural change.
This does not mean their science was backward or lagging. In fact, archaeology is thought to have become professionalized in Mexico between the 1880s
and early 1940s, about the same time as it did in the Old World. Instead, the
neglect of stratigraphic excavation was a result of several factors specific to
the field of Americanism, not least of which was the common belief that
human occupation in the New World had been so short lived that little cultural change could have occurred in the first place.[21] The technique would
not become popular in Mexico until the so-called stratigraphic revolution in

the second decade of the twentieth century, which is thought to have been led by the anthropologist Manuel Gamio.

Until then, Mexican archaeologists had a limited understanding of things like chronology and the succession of cultures. They had almost no sense of historical or absolute dates and were at a loss when it came to relative dating, the placement of objects and cultures into a chronological sequence. Their studies never made reference to time; antiquity was left dangling, treated as some faraway, nebulous past. "When was this pyramid constructed?" asked archaeology professor Galindo y Villa when pondering a ruin in Veracruz. "The monument is thought to be from very remote times. To guess its age is to lose oneself in useless speculation."[22] To complicate matters, the archaeologists were also unsure about which cultures had built certain ruins. When in doubt, the mystery sites were usually attributed to the Toltecs—the Toltecs were a sort of default culture, not only for Mexican but foreign scholars as well. (Some archaeologists in the United States even credited the Toltecs with building the famous earthen mounds of Ohio.) As Peñafiel explained, "Everything that is unknown, everything that is uncertain, everything that is marvelous" is unfortunately considered Toltec.[23] Yet, ironically, while Mexico's archaeologists glorified Toltec culture, they paid little scholarly attention to the Toltec capital of Tula.

The men of Mexico's museum spent much of their time scrutinizing artifacts rather than the context in which they were found. They focused on amassing, organizing, and displaying the pieces, on determining what they represented, and on labeling them. Like their counterparts abroad, they equated having more artifacts with having more knowledge. More was definitely better. And as the professors concentrated on trying to decipher the different pieces, labels became a near obsession; they were the "soul" of the museum, according to Genaro García, the institution's director in 1909.[24] Labels, as scholars point out, serve to simplify a collection. They transform artifacts into writing, reducing the "ungainly, three-dimensional objects to flat, combinable 'inscriptions.'"[25] They make collections more manageable. For the museum professors, who often harbored doubts about their findings, the labels must also have served the important function of helping to fix the meaning of the artifacts.

How to organize these objects, moreover, posed endless problems for the museum men. The archaeology collection was in a constant state of chaos. It had pieces "mixed up from different peoples," lamented one professor; it was nothing more than a "depot of curiosities," wrote another. This sort of chaos, though, was typical of museums around the world. The guiding principle behind the organization of the Trocadéro, for instance, was the availability of storage and floor space. Organizational principles were in flux, as museums were beginning to shift from a system that arranged antiquities by type (the typological collection) to one that organized them by culture (the so-called tribal arrangement). For most of the Porfiriato, the professors grouped the artifacts by type, breaking them down into "weapons, musical instruments, instruments for sacrifice, domestic utensils, [and] adornments."[26] Scattered among these, until the creation of the anthropology department in 1895, were ethnographic objects not only from Mexico but also from abroad. While we often imagine state projects as monolithic, structured, and methodical, when it came to the organization of Mexico's archaeology collection there was no consensus to be found. The professors did not agree on how to arrange the antiquities in part because they lacked knowledge about the origin or provenance of many of them. Instead, they spent the entire period organizing and reorganizing the pieces, a process that came to absorb the labors of several key scholars, including Del Paso, Chavero, and Peñafiel.

The professors compared the antiquities to one another and to those found in the written sources, recording their attributes—measurements, material composition, and features—in painstaking detail. Yet outside of their own judgments and a relatively small number of texts, they had little to go on. So they turned, quite often, to examples from abroad, which they used as additional points of comparison. Mendoza, the indigenous museum director, carried out some of these studies, comparing Mexico to Asia, an association also made by foreign archaeologists. In "Aztec Idol of a Japanese Type," he examines a tiny Aztec figurine in the National Museum, only to conclude that it has "all the characteristics of a Japanese woman," down to the "oblique eyes" and hair wrapped in a bun, the style "still worn by the women of that empire today."[27] In some of his other writings, Mendoza seems driven by an almost-unrelenting quest to prove that Nahuatl, the language of central Mexico, derived from Sanskrit, an idea that might seem odd but that elevated Nahuatl to a superior status by linking it to what was considered one of the world's more sophisticated languages, an "Indo-European" language, as one observer made sure to note.[28] But overall, Mendoza's Sanskrit theory reflected the rudimentary state of Mexican archeology at the time. Like most of his colleagues, Mendoza was painfully aware of the limits of his field; he was not only aware of them but quite humble. "Surely we have committed grave errors" that will later be rectified, he wrote. "Our work is imperfect and our

National Archaeology is still not well known."[29] To remedy these errors and gaps in knowledge the professors decided to turn to the very people they were supposed to be instructing: the museum patrons. As late as 1915, a sign posted at the entrance of the archaeology department asked visitors to inform the management of any mistakes in "classification and origin of the pieces on display."[30]

And while the professors considered archaeology an empirical science, they spoke about it and about the ancient past in almost-mystical ways. Chavero wrote poetically about archaeology, about how it "satisfies man's desire to know the truth about his past, so that he does not feel as if born without any ancestors, like a lone tree sprouting on a plain, or a solitary rock that tumbles after breaking from a high mountain."[31] Chavero's statement depicts archaeology as a sort of portal into a genuine past, a past as natural as the trees and mountains, rather than a past that is constructed and contrived. Not knowing the "truth" about this past is precarious; it can lead to solitude (the lone tree) and to fragmentation and separation from a larger entity (the falling rock). It can lead to conditions that are antithetical to the sense of unity and belonging that the national project is meant to instill. And if archaeology was a type of portal, the language used to describe its methods usually implied motion, a gaining of access or entry. Archaeology "penetrate[d] the shadows of the past." It also exposed: it lifted "the veil" from antiquity, it stripped it of "myth," it "uncovered the truth."[32] "I have read these stones," pronounced Inspector Batres at one site, "like an open book."[33] The idea that archaeology provided a direct connection to the ancient past was simply taken on faith. David Lowenthal has likened this devotion to patrimony and objects of heritage to a "cult, almost a religious faith." Like a "spiritual calling," he writes, "the creed of heritage . . . relies on revealed faith rather than rational proof."[34]

Even the subjects Mexico's scientists studied had an ethereal quality. The archaeologists tended to avoid mundane topics—the lives of ordinary people, what they died of, what they ate. They were also not concerned much with the lives of the nobility. Instead, they focused on what was considered higher knowledge: pre-Hispanic hieroglyphics, language, religion, cosmology, and the measurement of time—evidence of the ancient Indians' intellectual achievements. Not surprisingly, the artifacts they chose to study were a reflection of these topics, pieces like the Aztec Calendar, codices, and statues of gods and goddesses. These, too, were spoken about in ethereal ways. The artifacts were "the mute witnesses of the past," objects thought to hold essences or truths about the national being.[35] Néstor García Canclini characterizes this approach to patrimony as "fundamentalist traditionalism." Its main feature, he writes, is a "metaphysical vision" of a "national being," whose "expressions of grandeur were exhibited in a hazy past and which today survive only in the objects that recall them." Mexico's ancient Indians took on the form of abstract "essences." Their majesty and splendor were thought to be captured somehow in the old stones. Archaeology was thought to have the power to make these stones, the "mute witnesses," speak, to make the nation's glorious past apparent, a mistaken belief, since "all scientific and pedagogical procedures dealing with patrimony are a metalanguage; they do not make things speak but rather speak about them."[36]

Like all other sciences, then, archaeology is not neutral. While it hides behind a "façade of empirical objectivity," its depiction of the past is embedded in the contemporary context; its practitioners are shaped by the values and concerns of their time.[37] Mexico's archaeologists during the age of Díaz envisioned the ancient Indians in ways that never veered too far from a nationalist agenda bent on glorifying the past. Thus we find Inspector Batres declaring that the only scholars capable of carrying out Mexico's "arqueología patria," or national archaeology, were the "sincere lovers of science," full of "enlightenment and selfless patriotism."[38] The government wholeheartedly supported this sort of patriotic archaeology, and to implement it, it would rely less on the armchair bookworm types of the museum and instead put its faith in one man. Let us now meet Inspector Batres, the leading actor in Mexico's archaeological project and the protagonist of this story.

CHAPTER FOUR

El Inspector

✢ IN 1885, LEOPOLDO BATRES HUERTA BECAME THE HEAD OF THE Inspectorate of Monuments, the first agency created in Mexico with the exclusive purpose of protecting the remains of the Indian past. The position gave Batres a great deal of power—this was the agency, after all, that eventually became the INAH, the National Institute of Anthropology and History, Mexico's present-day guardian of the past.[1] Batres was in charge of nothing less than caring for all of the nation's ruins. Although his position also required him to look after "historic" structures such as colonial churches, he focused nearly all his time, funding, and energy on the monuments of antiquity. His job was to ensure they were not disturbed in any way. To this end, he created and supervised a network of guards at ruins throughout the country. Batres also monitored the work of individuals who had been granted government contracts to excavate, making him the ultimate authority in matters of archaeology. He himself, however, could carry out excavations and reconstructions at will. Batres wielded the "official pickaxe" ("zapapico oficial"), as he once claimed.[2] His agency was central to the government's goal of taking charge of the relics and ruins, the objects through which Mexico would construct a sophisticated antiquity. It was also proof that Mexico took care of its past, a sign, in other words, of its status as a scientific, civilized, modern nation. And while in theory Batres was accountable to the Secretariat of Education, in practice he enjoyed a considerable amount of autonomy, ruling the Inspectorate, an institution with dozens of employees, as his own tiny fiefdom. But who was Batres, and how did he land such a prestigious job?

According to his autobiography, Batres had developed a passion for the ancient past early on, during his childhood visits to the home of his grandfather, an avid collector who kept a small museum that contained coins, paintings, and minerals but that was mostly made up of pre-Hispanic antiquities. If we are to believe his story, Batres came from a long line of notables, a family with over seventy counts and marquises as well as two of Mexico's original conquerors: Bernal Díaz del Castillo, the foot soldier of Hernán Cortés, and the notorious Pedro de Alvarado, Cortés's second in command, as cruel a man to the Indians as Mexico has ever seen. Both of Batres's parents were prominent individuals. His father, Salvador Batres, served as consul general to Germany during one of the many regimes of Antonio López de Santa Anna. Salvador was also a businessman who traded in everything from tobacco to artillery until the early 1870s when, for some reason, he went bankrupt. Batres's mother, Francisca Huerta, was an astute woman of "extraordinary talent," according to her son. She had originally planned on becoming a nun but decided against it after falling in love with Salvador. As a liberal, part of the nineteenth-century political faction that aimed to modernize Mexico, Francisca's opinions were supposedly so sought after by the leading figures of the day that little Leopoldo, who was born in Mexico City in 1852, grew up in a home surrounded by famous politicians and thinkers such as Melchor Ocampo and Miguel Lerdo de Tejada. In fact, it was his mother whom Batres credited with filling his heart with "patriotism."[3]

Around the age of twenty, Batres joined the military. He became a cavalry captain, traveling widely in this capacity and most likely exploring Mexico's ruins. In the early 1880s he took his interest in the ancient past a step further, setting off to study archaeology and anthropology in Paris at the Museum of Natural History, the most prestigious scientific institution in France. While Batres is often considered to have been a self-taught archaeologist, he did in fact receive some formal training, an experience that set him apart from Mexico's other archaeologists. An admirer of French culture, he spent about a year studying under Armand de Quatrefages, the chair in anthropology at the museum. An even more important influence on Batres was Hamy, a protégé of Quatrefages's who was in charge of organizing the anthropology collections in both the Natural History Museum and the brand-new Trocadéro, which Hamy helped to establish.

Next to nothing is known about Batres's time in France. What did his training consist of? While both of his mentors were experts in the pre-Hispanic past, they were also dedicated to the practice of anthropometry.

Quatrefages spent much of his time amassing and analyzing human skulls, putting together a cranial series "for the racial identification of different human types."[4] He and Hamy coauthored *Crania ethnica* (1882), a celebrated work that categorizes more than a hundred skulls by race and country of origin. The two men also taught classes in anthropometry in the museum focusing on the "how-tos" of measuring heads and body parts, courses that were wildly popular with the students. Batres most likely attended these, but they do not seem to have impacted him much, as craniometry did not become a significant part of his career. As inspector, he practiced anthropometric techniques only rarely; he would take out his tools at an archaeological site to measure the skull of an Indian or two in order to document "the types of races that inhabit the ruins."[5] This research was actually designed to gain insight into the past, as Batres believed the contemporary and ancient inhabitants of sites must have been similar in appearance. He used the local Indians as examples of what the pre-Hispanic peoples must have looked like. He compared the Indians' features to those found on the ancient statues and skulls at the sites. These studies, though, appear in less than a handful of his many writings on the ruins and are tacked on at the end, much like an afterthought. Compared to his French mentors, Batres paid little attention to anthropometry.

What about his training in archaeology? How did Batres feel about studying under Hamy, a mentor whose understanding of the pre-Hispanic past was tainted by his Eurocentric views? While Hamy had a "profound love" of all things Mexican, he also found the country's relics to be plagued by a "perverse aesthetic."[6] Like most Europeans, he considered them inferior to anything produced in the Old World. One wonders how Hamy's opinions impacted his young Mexican student. Batres would later claim that his experience in France had only served to strengthen his feelings of nationalism, and it appears not to have left him too bitter, since he would continue to correspond with Hamy later in life. But what did Batres's training actually consist of? While this is also unclear, his activities must not have strayed too far from those of Hamy, an archaeologist who focused mainly on deciphering the origin and use of relics found in the museum, knowledge he gleaned from written sources. Yet unlike Hamy, who was mostly an armchair scholar, Batres went on to have a career involving almost-constant fieldwork, which he carried out with the gusto of an Indiana Jones.

Upon returning to Mexico, Batres's dabbling in the ancient past soon became an official career when he was made inspector of monuments, a position he held for more than a quarter of a century. Much about his job remains a mystery. We do not know where his office was located, whether it was in his home or in the museum. We are also not sure how he got his job. Batres first appears in museum records in May 1881, before his trip to France, bearing twenty-one Zapotec artifacts for sale. He continued to sell antiquities to the museum, becoming one of its best suppliers, until June 1885, when he was hired as the "curator and assistant in the Archaeology Section." Batres complained that the archaeology collection was in a state of disarray, and he proposed a plan to organize it. He began by sorting through what was then a chaotic jumble of objects, separating the ethnographic pieces that were mixed up with the antiquities, but he quit within a month. While it is not clear why he quit, his relationship with the professors of the museum was always tense and strained: he would come to consider two of its directors, Chavero and del Paso, his "mortal enemies."[7] Batres was a man who did not take orders easily, especially when they came from others considered experts in the field. Three months later, in October 1885, he was catapulted to the new and much more prestigious position of inspector.

According to Batres, the Inspectorate was established due to his "initiative."[8] He most likely contacted President Díaz to propose the agency's creation, with himself as its head. Similar agencies had been founded all over the world. France had created the position of inspector general of historical monuments and national antiquities as early as 1830. Ireland established an inspector of monuments in 1875 and, that same year, Italy stationed several inspectors in various regions throughout the country. England followed suit, passing the Ancient Monuments Protection Act in 1882, which eventually led to the formation of an inspector of monuments. Mexicans were well aware of these developments. Within the museum, the professors studied texts on the conservation of monuments from the "civilized countries." They pored over a German tract, for instance, with the dry but fitting title "Steps Taken in Several Countries for the Conservation of Monuments of Historical and Artistic Interest."[9] While one scholar claims that Mexico's Inspectorate was based on the French model, Batres and Díaz may have been inspired by other examples when (and if) they ever met to discuss the creation of the agency.[10]

The two men had known each other for some time, having met, quite possibly, while Batres was still in the army. Batres, however, claimed they first met much earlier, during the war against the French, when he supposedly came to the aid of an injured Díaz, an improbable story, as Batres could not have been more than fourteen years old at that time.[11] While some

scholars claim he was a "protégé of don Porfirio," who shielded him throughout his career, others have characterized their relationship more as a friend-
ship; Batres himself would declare that he was a "very close friend" of Díaz.[12]
Although the exact nature of their relationship is difficult to glean, Batres
most likely did become the inspector as a result of his personal connection
to Díaz. Political and personal connections, writes Mechthild Rutsch, thus
shaped the beginning of "the institutionalization of Mexican archaeology."[13]
President Díaz often picked his military buddies to serve in government
positions. In fact, his regime was packed with warriors, as a good number of
officials, over 80 percent according to one historian, had fought in at least one
of Mexico's many wars, a shared experience that made this the most "homo-
geneous generation" of politicians in the nation's history.[14]

That Batres convinced Díaz to hire him as the director of the Inspectorate
seems likely for another reason: there were other more established archaeologists that the president could have chosen, like Chavero or del Paso. Both
men had government connections and were accomplished scholars, while
Batres was virtually unknown. At the same time, the job of inspector was a
dynamic one, requiring almost-constant activity in the field. Batres was
capable of this sort of work, while Chavero and del Paso were older and
mainly armchair archaeologists. Batres's background in the military also
made him a good candidate for the job; not only had it taken him all over the
country, giving him knowledge of the terrain, but it left him relatively
unfazed by the inconveniences—the bugs, dirt, and travel—of work in the
field. His career in the military had also accustomed him to a world of hierarchies and orders, something that would serve him well as an inspector who
commanded a small army of workers. It is also possible that Batres's style of
archaeology, his vision for the ruins, was simply more attractive to President
Díaz. Batres was not the type of archaeologist to meticulously sift through
soil for bits of pottery, carrying out painstaking, tedious research. He was a
mover of monoliths, a builder of pyramids, a rough-and-tumble archaeologist more suited to the government's project of constructing a monumental
vision of the past. His specialty, in other words, was "monumental archaeology," a way of practicing the science that matched the interests of a Mexican
government that sought to appropriate the cultural achievements of earlier
civilizations and endow the nation with a prestigious past.

That Batres initiated the Inspectorate seems likely for one final reason:
he stood to gain from its creation. The agency not only gave him a great deal
of power but autonomy from the museum, the den of his "mortal enemies."

While in theory both institutions were supposed to work together, with Batres serving the museum by helping to build the archaeology collection, in practice his job put him in a "superior position," giving him the authority to promote or hinder the museum's activities "both in the field and behind office doors."[15] In a new division of labor, Batres assumed some of the duties formerly carried out by the museum. For example, in the past one of the professors or an assistant would investigate reports of vandalism at sites. Now, Batres was in charge of this. The museum had also been responsible for retrieving artifacts discovered throughout Mexico as well as those confiscated at customs houses. (Officials often intercepted boxes full of relics that were being smuggled out of the country.) Batres either traveled to collect these objects or received shipments of them in the capital and hauled them to the museum. As inspector, he essentially took over the tasks involving fieldwork, which had the effect of relegating the museum to an academic role, to research and the spread of knowledge. But the museum would continue to carry out many of its former duties, such as the retrieval of artifacts, duties it had always had and that were not annulled by the creation of the Inspectorate. As a result, Mexico had two agencies with partially duplicate functions that at times set out on the same task; this became a source of friction and even sparks between the two.

Some scholars believe this duplication of functions was an example of President Díaz's practice of creating competing institutions in order to play them against each other: through the Inspectorate, they argue, the president was able to intervene in the museum "without having to do so directly."[16] In truth, there is no paper trail to prove that Díaz was interested in using Batres to interfere with museum affairs; there is little correspondence from Díaz in Batres's archive. What is more, the inspector did not need to be prodded into meddling with the museum, as he was more than willing to do so on his own. And he had plenty of opportunities. In addition to being responsible for transporting artifacts to the museum, Batres was also in charge of taking inventory of the new acquisitions. Though he was a constant fixture in the museum, especially in the archaeology department, he does not seem to have left behind any of these records. (The museum often did its own inventories, though not on a regular basis.) Toward the end of the Porfiriato, in 1908, the government issued a decree updating the inspector's duties. Batres was now in charge of examining each acquisition in order to determine its authenticity, its culture of origin, and whether it had been severed from the ruins. He was also supposed to put together a photo album of the newly acquired pieces and submit it to the Secretariat of Education, but again, these albums do not seem to exist.

Outside of the museum, Batres was a fieldworker for the state. His job took him far and wide, from the southern border with Guatemala to Mexico's northern frontier and beyond to the cliff dwellings of Mesa Verde, Colorado—ruins he was certain were Toltec. Batres tallied his major excavations at over forty. One of the most significant took place on the street of Escalerillas in downtown Mexico City (1900), where he uncovered part of the Templo Mayor, the main temple of the Aztecs, without realizing exactly what it was. Amazingly, the temple's whereabouts had been a mystery since the Spanish conquest and would remain so for decades to come, until the late 1970s, when workers stumbled across it while installing electrical cables underground. Some of Batres's other important excavations included Mitla (1901), Monte Albán (1902), and Xochicalco and Isla de Sacrificios (1910). But his master-piece, his *obra maestra*, was the reconstruction of Teotihuacán's Pyramid of the Sun, a labor of "pharaohs," wrote a later archaeologist, carried out from 1905 to 1910.[17]

Yet even though Batres's fieldwork set him apart from the professors in the museum, like them he operated with little technique. He employed the same procedures, he once vaguely explained, as those used in Herculaneum, Egypt, Troy, and Babylonia.[18] The methods of some of his excavations can be summed up in two words: dig and haul. Others were characterized by a bit more attention to detail. In fact, Batres seems to have understood the principles of stratigraphic excavation and the importance of the technique for recording data. In 1889, he carried out what he called "stratigraphic work" at Teotihuacán, where he discovered two "completely distinct geographic layers" with ceramics of two different styles, evidence of a succession of cultures. Batres attributed the deeper layer to the Toltecs and the top layer, the "ground we now walk on," to the Aztecs.[19] This led him to conclude that Teotihuacán was Toltec, a common belief at the time, although the site is now thought to have been built by the much older, mysterious people known as the Teotihuacanos. Still, while Batres employed some sort of stratigraphic method in this case, he did so in a cursory manner. Rigor was never his strong suit. Yet what he lacked in this regard, as one later archaeologist remarked, he would surely make up for in "enthusiasm."[20]

Of course, Batres had to follow certain protocols. He had to notify the Secretariat of Education about his activities and, if necessary, request funds and the aid of other government agencies. If a project required an extensive period of time, as in the case of rebuilding a pyramid, or complicated procedures, like moving a huge statue, the Secretariat of Education informed the governor of the state where Batres would be working, and the governor then informed the local authorities and requested they cooperate with the inspector. In the case of less complicated tasks, there was no protocol. If Batres came across an easily transportable artifact while riding horseback through the countryside, he simply picked it up and took it to the museum. And to the locals who looked on in curiosity he routinely explained that he was the inspector of monuments, a state official, a pronouncement that usually allowed him free rein. As one local put it, "He presented himself to me in the name of the Supreme Government and I did not choose to oppose him."[21] To ensure this sort of compliance, Batres often went about armed or accompanied by soldiers or the rurales, as their presence, he believed, served "to promote respect."[22] The decree that updated his duties in 1908, moreover, enlarged the scope of his powers in this sense. It allowed him to bypass the Secretariat of Education and deal directly with the local authorities and "solicit their help when needed," but only in the case of emergencies—like when a pyramid was on the verge of collapsing.[23]

With the creation of the Inspectorate, Mexican archaeology thus took on a dual form, an arrangement that persists to this very day. According to Luis Vázquez, the discipline is currently divided between the archaeology of the INAH and that of the Institute of Anthropological Investigations at the National Autonomous University of Mexico, or UNAM. Much like the National Museum during the Porfiriato, the UNAM tends to focus on research. And much like the Inspectorate, the INAH tends to specialize in large-scale projects, such as the reconstruction of ruins, activities aimed at showcasing the ancient past. Of the two, the INAH exercises more power; it dominates Mexico's approach to archaeology and secures the most government funding, just as the Inspectorate would ultimately do during the Porfiriato. As the official in charge of bringing pre-Hispanic remains into the fold of the state, Batres dictated the terms of archaeology in key ways. As time went by, his agency's budget increased by leaps and bounds, growing twice as quickly as the museum's. A rivalry developed between the two institutions that was rooted in conflicts not only over funding, interpretation, and practice but even over who had the right to practice, battles that Batres usually won. The INAH's overbearing influence on archaeology in Mexico today, a problem that is political and institutional but that ultimately concerns "the purpose and objective of knowledge," thus had its origins in the Porfiriato.[24]

Batres became Mexico's turn-of-the-century dictator of archaeology, a reflection not only of the trend toward the centralization of power at the time but also of the way that power has tended to operate in the country in general. And he would prove to be an even hardier dictator than Díaz. Whereas Díaz stepped down in 1880 to allow his friend Manuel González to rule for one term, Batres's reign was continuous.

And his "archaeological dictatorship" was also reinforced by law. The Díaz regime passed two major laws regarding Mexico's ruins, both of which gave Batres more power. The first, which we examine in chapter 6, was the Law of Archaeological Explorations. Enacted in 1896, this ruling placed stricter limits on the contracts the government granted to archaeologists. An even more important decree, however, surfaced the following year, the Law of Monuments, the strongest piece of archaeological legislation that Mexico had ever seen.

The Law of Monuments

By the late nineteenth century, leaders all over the world had enacted laws to protect their ancient ruins. Pope Pius VII passed legislation to conserve the monuments of Italy as early as 1802. Rulers in Germany issued similar decrees around the same time, and Egypt took comparable measures in 1835. Peru outlawed the removal of artifacts from ruins in 1822 and Japan created the Law for the Preservation of Ancient Temples and Shrines in 1897.[25] Mexico was no different. Throughout the century, it had enacted a series of laws regarding the monuments. These rulings, however, not only went unenforced but were often contradictory. While most gave the federal government authority over ancient sites, others placed the care of the ruins in the hands of local officials. A nebulous edict in 1840, for instance, asked "all Mexicans" to undertake excavations and "search for monuments from antiquity." Another decree issued by Maximilian in 1864 called on local authorities to safeguard the monuments and make sure no one extracted pieces of them, "no matter how small." Even Benito Juárez, the leader who banned unauthorized excavations—the measure that forced Charnay to obtain his concession—ordered local political officers, the *jefes políticos*, to "carefully" collect and send antiquities to the National Museum.[26] In relying on the locals, the Mexican government was essentially acknowledging that it lacked the ability to control the many ruins scattered throughout the country.

The Díaz regime overrode this patchwork of decrees with the Law of Monuments, the first law to explicitly grant the Mexican government ownership of the ruins. The law nationalized the "archaeological monuments," declaring them "property of the nation" and prohibiting anyone from "exploring, touching, and restoring" them without permission from the government. It allowed federal authorities to arrest and punish anyone caught destroying the structures with "a class-two fine," criminalizing the act for the first time. But the most novel aspect of the law was article 5. This article gave the government the right to expropriate monuments found on private property for the purpose of "conservation and study."[27] Although the law did not specify how the expropriations would be carried out and was vague in other ways, it gave the Díaz regime the authority to carve out archaeological sites, a power it would act on a few years later in Teotihuacán, the only site it would ever expropriate. In declaring the ruins national property, the Law of Monuments challenged the privatization of land that was occurring at the time, as public lands and the communal holdings of Indians were steadily falling into private hands. In fact, as one scholar has pointed out, much of the legislation enacted under Díaz was designed to safeguard private property—the Law of Monuments, then, bucked that trend.[28] Mexican leaders, in effect, had realized that the government's claim to the ruins needed a stronger legal foundation. At the same time, they enacted the law only after much debate, as the delegates in Congress squabbled over several issues. These discussions echoed the Charnay debate of years before and highlighted the complications that ensued from the government takeover of the ancient remains.

Was the Law of Monuments legal? Some congressmen raised this question, since Mexico's constitution did not give the federal government control over the ruins. The constitution actually made no mention of them. Why should the monuments belong to the federal government and not to the states? The law, some believed, infringed on the states' rights to the ruins. If the constitution did not grant the federal government ownership of the sites, then what was the legal basis for the decree? According to the famous writer and politician Manuel Sánchez Mármol, the head of the committee in the Secretariat of Education in charge of drafting the law, Mexico's states lacked the power to conserve the ancient monuments for two reasons. First, they could not enact legislation over public lands, where the ruins were often located. Second, they could not rule on customs matters, a legal circumstance that limited their ability to stop the smuggling of artifacts. Besides, placing the ruins in the care of the federal government simply made more sense, some delegates added, because it allowed for a more uniform and thus more effective approach to the conservation of monuments than if each state were to take matters into its own hands. Later in the debate, Joaquín Baranda, the intellectual who served as secretary of education for nearly two decades (1882–1901), offered his opinion. Baranda argued that the Law of Monuments was constitutional, since article 125 of the Mexican constitution gave the federal government the right to conserve a "building" if it was deemed "necessary" to the nation, and, according to the many dictionaries and encyclopedias he had consulted, the ruins were technically buildings. The secretary of education ended his speech to Congress with the flimsiest of arguments: if President Díaz, the "illustrious caudillo" who had shed blood fighting in defense of the constitution, approved of the law, Baranda declared, then it surely must be constitutional.[29]

More importantly, pointed out Mr. Sánchez, the head of the lawmaking committee, the ancient monuments had *always* been considered property of the nation; they had belonged to the nation since "time immemorial . . . from the pre-Columbian era through the period of colonial domination" and "up until today."[30] With this, Sánchez placed the roots of the Mexican nation way back in time, in that nebulous, eternal past known as "time immemorial." And he even extended the government's *ownership* of the ruins to the pre-Hispanic period. Sánchez based the idea that the monuments were national property on legal precedent, especially on colonial law. But Mexico's legislation regarding the ruins had been neither consistent nor clear-cut. Although decrees from the colonial period had declared the sites property of the Spanish Crown, later laws enacted throughout the nineteenth century did not grant the federal government definitive ownership of Mexico's monuments. Sánchez, however, dismissed this last fact by claiming that once Mexico gained its independence, the crown's ownership of the ruins had passed to the federal government. This ownership, he added, had recently been codified in a law on public lands, the Occupation and Transfer of Vacant Lots of 1894, which gave the federal government authority over the monuments, or, as the law explained, at least over the land on which they were found: "The lands in which monumental ruins are encountered" "will always remain under control of the Federation."[31] In nationalizing the ruins, the Law of Monuments marked a victory for the federal government over Mexico's many states, some of which were taking their own measures to conserve the pre-Hispanic remains. The law reflected the Porfirian regime's desire to centralize power, its effort to gain greater control over the nation by suppressing the interests of the states.

Curiously, while the Law of Monuments nationalized the ruins, it did not do the same with the antiquities. The decree applied only to fixed or immovable objects: "the ruins of cities, . . . fortifications, palaces, temples, pyramids." It did not give the nation ownership over movable objects such as statues. It simply mandated that the objects remain in the country, or that, as article 6 declared, the "codices, idols, amulets, and other objects . . . cannot be exported without legal authorization."[32] While the law stipulated that the antiquities found by the government were to be housed in the National Museum, it allowed for artifacts to be privately owned and even exported, as long as "legal authorization" was obtained from the government. Why the distinction between movable and immovable objects? Why nationalize one and not the other? Here, once again, the writers of the law cited legal precedent. Sánchez argued that Mexico's previous legislation had not explicitly made the ancient objects property of the nation. But this was not really the case. Colonial law had granted the crown ownership over all of Mexico's subsoil wealth, including antiquities. A more recent decree passed under Juárez in 1868, moreover, had declared that "the antiquities found throughout the entire nation belong to the government."[33] Why did Mexican leaders overlook these rulings?

Concerns about private property seem to have nagged at them. The right to private property was a sacred tenet of classical liberal thought. Mexican elites, like others around the world, considered it the basis of economic development and modern, civilized society. If the elites wanted to take control of the nation's archeological sites, they had no choice but to expropriate the lands where the ruins existed. But they were far more wary of infringing on the right to private property when it came to the movable objects. Even article 5, the article dealing with the expropriation of sites, seemed designed to safeguard this right, as it allowed the state to claim only the "surface area deemed necessary for the care and conservation" of the monuments, letting property owners keep the subsoil wealth, including the artifacts, found on their lands.[34] How the owners would access these artifacts without touching the surface of their lands—an impossible feat of archaeological acrobatics— was not explained. The law also did not clarify if the owners needed government permission to excavate their own properties, as excavating without such permits was illegal. More importantly, the law made no real attempt to distinguish between movable and immovable objects. Naturally, this was a tricky matter, since there was often no clear-cut distinction between the two, as portable artifacts such as carvings and statues are frequently found affixed to temples and other immovable monuments. Subsequent legislation in Mexico would address this problem, but under Díaz it remained unsolved. If an earthquake struck and dislodged a bust from a pyramid wall, for example, did a pothunter have the right to keep it?[35]

Rather than harking back to precedents from much earlier times, the Law of Monuments' position on movable objects was based on more recent decrees, like the Mining Act of 1884, a ruling issued during the Porfiriato that broke with centuries of tradition. Since the colonial period, Mexico's subsoil wealth, even wealth found on private lands, had belonged to the state. The new mining law changed that. It gave property owners the right to both the surface and subsoil wealth found on their lands, a measure the Díaz government enacted to court British and American mining interests by establishing a property regime in Mexico that was similar to the ones in England and the United States. Like the Mining Act of 1884, the Law of Monuments gave property owners the right to the subsoil wealth, the antiquities, found on their lands. The antiquities, in other words, became subject to the civil codes regarding private property. Taken as a whole, then, the Law of Monuments offered Mexico's leaders the best of both worlds. It allowed them to take possession of the ancient cities, pyramids, and temples without completely violating the principle of private property they held so dear. Like the proverbial cake, they could have their ruins and their private property, too. What is more, many of Mexico's leaders, including the congressmen, were antiquities collectors themselves and would have hardly wanted to outlaw their own hobby. That the Law of Monuments did not make the government owner of all the artifacts in the country, however, would pose major problems for Mexico in later years. It became a loophole in court cases when Mexico tried to reclaim objects that had been illegally exported.[36]

Interestingly, one of the hot-button issues during the debate over the law was the ban on exporting antiquities. Some of the delegates opposed the ban, and surprisingly, no one was a bigger opponent than Alfredo Chavero. The congressman and celebrated archaeologist believed the ban was impossible to enforce. Similar decrees had been on the books for the last century and had not been effective. More importantly, stressed Chavero, the ban hindered the flow of artifacts to museums abroad and thus obstructed the cause of science. Here, Chavero launched into a speech that encapsulated the enlightened nationalist approach to the artifacts, the stance that put science above the nation. He couched his argument in terms of free trade, another sacred tenet, much like private property, of Mexican elites. According to him, the ban limited the "free trade of study and history." "Science does not belong to one nation but is the patrimony of all humanity," he declared. What would have become of Egypt's monuments had Napoleon not transported them back to France? The relics would have remained abandoned, in "the sands of the desert," where even "the Arab who passed by on his camel would have ignored them, overwhelmed by his laziness and the heat of Africa." Like Egypt, Mexico could not carry out adequate research on its antiquity by itself and thus needed the help of foreigners, claimed Chavero. Why hoard the relics, he asked, the "raw materials" of science? Chavero made this last point with a bizarre analogy. He compared the antiquities to cotton: it is as if Mexicans have "cotton without knowing how to make cloth," yet prohibit the cotton's exportation that would allow garments to be made, "preferring instead to remain naked." ("Mexicans prefer to go about naked!" echoed a journalist in the press.)[37] By advocating for the free flow of artifacts to the point of opposing any limits on their exportation, Chavero was taking the position of the enlightened patriot to its logical extreme. But his speech failed to win over the delegates and the Law of Monuments passed by a landslide, moving on to the Senate, where it was also approved.

Amazingly, one of the first people to benefit from the new law was none other than Charnay. Nearly twenty years had passed since the Frenchman's contract had been rejected by the Mexican government, and his crates of artifacts continued to wait patiently in the National Museum. French officials had never stopped fighting for them, and soon after the Law of Monuments was enacted, the ambassador of France raised the issue again. Realizing that the law had reaffirmed Mexico's right to authorize archaeological exportations, the ambassador contacted Baranda. As a result, in 1899 Baranda brought a declaration before Congress calling for the release of the crates. He began by explaining that while the initial rejection of Charnay's contract had been inspired by a "noble and patriotic" sentiment, "by the laudable desire to conserve unharmed our invaluable archaeological patrimony," Mexico now benefited from its relationship with France, the "civilizing nation to which we are linked by cordial sentiments of admiration and sympathy." Charnay's artifacts would dazzle observers in the Trocadéro in Paris, "where, in the most frequently visited capital in the world, collections of American antiquities stand out, placed thus for the pursuit of men of knowledge." Science was an international arena, and the pieces of Mexico's past were a part of what Baranda called "universal dominion."[38] Baranda was promoting a patriotism of the enlightened type, and he won. He finished his speech, and Congress moved to approve the exportation of Charnay's crates.

Twenty years had passed, and Mexico had changed. Gone was the intense bitterness the elites had felt toward France. Mexicans were now more strongly Francophile, more spellbound by the cultural hegemony of France. At the same time, they feared the growing influence of the United States and used the Charnay case, according to historian Paul Edison, as a strategy to counteract American power.[39] Both the initial rejection of Charnay's contract and the vote years later in favor of permitting his crates of relics to be exported, then, were a form of political leverage, a way to relay the message, however muted, that Mexico would not completely subordinate itself to the countries that dominated it. And so in 1900, Charnay's crates sailed off to the Trocadéro, which later became the Musée de l'Homme, where today the roughly 1,600 Mexican artifacts he collected can still be found. In the words of museum director Hamy, Charnay had "brought the greatest honor to French science abroad" and made the Trocadéro much richer.[40] But to Mexico, ironically or not, he failed to leave behind the casts and photographs of the relics he had originally promised in his contract.

Mexico had changed in other ways. By 1900, its institutions and mechanisms for controlling the remains of the pre-Hispanic past had developed to the point where the exportation of a few crates of artifacts was not as threatening as it once had seemed. In the words of Baranda, the country lost nothing by exporting the crates, since it had already "amassed and will continue to amass the most valuable examples of Mexican antiquities."[41] As the head of the institution in charge of taking control of these objects, Inspector Batres was the linchpin of the government's archaeological project. Though it is not clear if he had anything to do with the Charnay case—at one point his old mentor Hamy asked him to intervene on Charnay's behalf—Batres most likely did play some role in the creation of the Law of Monuments, which, as the official on the front lines of enforcing it, endowed him with more power.

In 1888, almost a decade before the passing of the law, Batres commissioned the famous jurist and former Supreme Court president Ignacio Vallarta to draft a proposal for a ruling on "the conservation and inspection of national archaeological monuments," a step, he believed, the Inspectorate had to take to carry out its duties. As the Law of Monuments would do, Batres's proposal gave the federal government "dominion" over the ruins and allowed for their expropriation. It placed even stiffer penalties on those caught destroying the monuments, including hefty fines and a prison sentence of up to one year. It also gave Batres more power over the museum, stipulating, for instance, that the archaeology collection be placed "under the surveillance of the Inspectorate." Like the Law of Monuments, Batres's proposal is vague in many respects—how would the expropriations be carried out? How much land was needed to conserve the ruins? But it is more comprehensive in one key way: it included the antiquities, the movable objects, in the definition of what constituted a monument: "pottery, sculptures, . . . adornments, amulets, weapons, and tools," "all objects related to the ancient history of the country," would be placed under the control of the federal government.[42] It allowed the artifacts that existed in private collections and on private lands to remain in the hands of the owners but made all the other antiquities property of the nation. While Batres's proposal most likely served as a template for the Law of Monuments—the two documents are strikingly similar—we do not know why the law materialized as late as it did. In any case, Batres was steadfast in implementing the ruling, a measure he hoped would curtail the "insatiable foreign and national greed" that threatened the monuments.[43] When he caught wind of someone violating it, he either set out to stop them, had the Secretariat of Education order local officials to intervene, or called on his guards at the ruins. Batres had been carrying out procedures like these ever since becoming inspector. In fact, the decree that initially established his position in 1885 was based on the premise that the ruins were federal property; it had placed Batres in charge of "the conservation of all the monuments and archaeological ruins," allowing him to impede excavations and the removal of objects.[44] The Law of Monuments, then, simply formalized the inspector's de facto powers. It strengthened the legitimacy of his position by giving him a more solid legal footing on which to operate.

Of course, it would be impossible for Batres to watch over all of Mexico's ruins, enforcing the law from one border to another. Like the typical bureaucrat, he found out about the destruction of monuments—and often, their very existence—from the daily paper work that crossed his desk. Mexicans were constantly sending letters with these types of reports to him and to the secretary of education. Batres was an avid reader of newspapers, and his other source of information was the press. The implementation of the law, then, was a matter of happenstance, erratic and uneven. It depended on the information that came to the attention of the federal government and on the discretion of the inspector—that is, whether or not Batres believed a case warranted action. It also depended on the level of cooperation he got from both the federal and local authorities, as well as on the many guards stationed at the ruins. Batres did not act alone. His agency was not a one-man show. Instead, he developed the Inspectorate into a full-fledged government institution with an army of workers made up mainly of the guards or caretakers at the sites. These were the *conserjes*, Mexico's first official presence at the ruins, the men entrusted with the awesome task of turning the government's lofty rhetoric about controlling the ancient monuments into actual policy.

PART THREE

Making Patrimony

CHAPTER FIVE

Guarding

† SOON AFTER BECOMING INSPECTOR, BATRES SAT DOWN AT HIS DESK
to record all of Mexico's major archaeological sites. Using a map made by one
Luis Becerril, he plotted the ruins he knew to exist, as well as the railroad and
shipping routes providing access to them. Some of the main sites we know
today are there, from the sprinkling of ancient cities scattered about the
north and the many dotting the nation's center to the Maya ruins of Palenque
and Yaxchilán in the south and Izamal, Chichén Itzá, and Acanech (today
called Acanceh) in the Yucatán Peninsula. Although he probably did not
realize it at the time, Batres was crafting one of the most basic tools of modern state building. Maps, scholars point out, make a nation legible and manageable. With their synoptic "God's-eye view," they simplify an immensely
complicated world. But maps do more than merely summarize the facts; they
have the power to transform, an ability that lies not in the map itself but in
the "power possessed by those who deploy the perspective of that particular
map."[1] As Batres charted out each of the sites across Mexico's vast terrain
made up of over 760,000 square miles, he was carrying out one of the first
steps involved in turning the ruins into patrimony. Taking control of the
sites required gaining knowledge about them.

But maps are more than instruments of state control. As Raymond Craib
has shown, they have the effect of making a nation seem like a timeless, objective reality, a place that simply exists rather than one that has been, and continues to be, forged. They portray a nation as a finished product, its outlines
just waiting to be traced by a cartographer's pen. The presence of ruins from

bygone times give a map, which is essentially a scientific document, a historical depth, infusing "a modern methodology with foundational mythology."
Batres's map, then, is a scientific portrayal of a mythical past. Not surprisingly, it emphasizes the sedentary civilizations of long ago, the Indians who
left behind monuments and cities. Mexico's nomadic peoples have no place on
such a map. Not only did Porfirian elites consider them barbaric, but their
lack of ruins meant they left no "remnants to take one back in time and no
rootedness to satisfy" the need for origins.[2] The sedentary Indians, by contrast, anchored Mexico in the distant past and in the national territory, giving
the country a continuity and fixity, a permanence in time and space.

Perhaps now is the time to recall why the government was so interested in
this past in the first place. Porfirian leaders were constructing an official history for Mexico, an essential part of the process of nation building. This history
was thought to endow the country's diverse population with a common origin.
It also gave Mexico, a nation marked by centuries of colonialism, an "authentic" and prestigious past, one that challenged its inferior place within the global
order. In order to take possession of the ancient sites, the embodiments of
Mexico's glorious antiquity, the government needed to record and survey the
ruins. Batres's map is an attempt at taking this sort of inventory.

At the same time, Batres's *Archaeological Map of the Republic* is curious.
Next to each site is a symbol representing a different culture. The Aztecs, for
instance, are depicted with an asterisk, the Maya with an equal sign or two
horizontal lines, and the Chichimecs with an oval. These symbols do not
stand for the ancient people who built the sites. Instead, they represent the
contemporary Indians or "races that live where there are ruins." The map,
then, is both an archaeological and ethnographic account of the nation. But
why list the contemporary peoples in the first place? Why not label the ruins
with their ancient builders, the more logical choice for such a map? Just like
in his anthropometric studies, Batres must have been trying to convey some
sort of connection between Mexico's contemporary and ancient Indians. But
to what end, and why?

Batres's map is also a confusion of cultures, a testament to his mistaken
beliefs. It labels some of the contemporary indigenous groups with the names
of ancient peoples, conflating the past and present. The modern-day Nahuatl-
speaking Indians, for instance, are identified as Aztecs. According to the
map, Mexico is saturated with Aztecs, from the Isthmus of Tehuantepec to
the northern frontier, giving the Aztecs a reach they never actually possessed. The map is also out of touch with the scholarship of the time, as most

ethnographers in Batres's day did not refer to the Nahuatl-speaking peoples as Aztecs but as Mexicanos. Other cultures on the map are wildly out of place, like the Toltecs and Zapotecs, whom Batres situates in Yucatán alongside the Maya. Did Batres really think the Toltecs and Zapotecs lived in the Yucatán Peninsula? Did he believe the Toltecs, a civilization long since vanished, continued to exist? Perhaps he was pointing to the Toltec influences found in the area. Archaeologists have long noted the similarities between the architecture of the Toltec city of Tula in Mexico's central highlands and Yucatán's Chichén Itzá, although the nature of this connection is still unclear. Was Batres calling attention to this relationship? Batres's map is not only curious but it contains relatively few ruins, giving it an unfinished quality. While today Mexico is thought to possess over ten thousand archaeological sites, the map lists a paltry three dozen. It is especially skimpy in the Yucatán Peninsula, where the inspector records only three ancient cities. Still, with ruins spread from one end of the country to another, the map gives the impression that the pre-Hispanic peoples had taken hold of almost the entire terrain, making Mexico seem like a unified space.

Stretched out on a table or in one's hands, the map is also striking for the sheer vastness of the territory. Seven hundred and sixty thousand square miles full of ruins is a lot of ground to cover, and if Batres ever had any doubts about the feasibility of controlling so much space, he never expressed them in writing. Instead of uncertainties there are lamentations about the sorry state of the monuments, about how their condition shocked foreign visitors, about how this situation reflected poorly on the nation. There is also a sense of urgency, as the archaeological terrain, Batres believed, was in dire need of protection. To bring this about, Batres developed the Inspectorate into a troop of fifty to sixty workers, made up of guards and the manual laborers, or *peones*, who helped them. Nearly all of these employees were local men who lived near the ruins. Every now and then, this troop would swell to include many more—the masons, diggers, and builders who were hired on a temporary basis to perform excavations and special assignments such as the reconstruction of Teotihuacán. Although Batres never mentioned how he gathered these temporary workers, he most likely recruited them with the aid of labor contractors as well as the governors and local officials in the areas where he carried out his projects. Some of the more specialized workers came from the nation's capital.

As time went by, this workforce expanded. In 1898, the government added two employees known as subinspectors, one in the state of Chiapas

and another in Yucatán, authorities that exercised some of the same functions as Batres only on a more regional scale. Later, in 1905, the government
also allowed Batres to hire an assistant inspector of monuments. By that
point, one of the busiest periods in his career, Batres had embarked on the
reconstruction of Teotihuacán, and he desperately needed an aide. To fill this
post, he did not look very far but hired his twenty-two-year-old son, Salvador.
A former secretary in the Inspectorate's small clerical staff, Salvador acted as
his father's right-hand man: he transported artifacts to the museum, helped
with excavations, and oversaw his father's work when duty called him
elsewhere.

But the vast majority of Batres's employees were guards, the conserjes or
caretakers, whose lives were intertwined with the Porfirian archaeological
project in crucial but forgotten ways. While these men have been lost to history, as the government's first permanent presence at the ruins they played a
key role in the making and display of the ancient patrimony: they enforced
the archaeological legislation, aided visitors, and cleaned and maintained the
monuments. Much like other aspects of the archaeological project, the creation of the network of guards grew out of a desire to represent Mexico as a
sovereign nation, one that took care of its past. It was through these men that
the state came into being at the sites. And it was through them that the state
acquired knowledge of the archaeological terrain. Like Batres's map, the
guards made up part of the effort to quantify, describe, and record the pre-
Hispanic remains. And it was through them, too, that the government
extended its reach into the farthest corners of the nation, into the ruins of
Mexico's deserts and jungles. The guards, then, were agents of the larger process of political centralization that was occurring under Porfirio Díaz, as the
state sought to extend its control over the national territory.

Tucked away in places often far removed from any federal oversight,
however, the guards enjoyed a great deal of autonomy. As the sole representatives of the government found at the ruins, the fate of the monuments rested
largely in their hands. The condition of a site and the government's authority
over it often depended on the actions of the guards. If a guard remained at
his post, carrying out his many duties, the state not only had an obedient
worker but a presence at the site. If the guard decided to leave, say, to go on
a drinking spree, the state's authority disappeared along with him. The government's claim of ownership over a site was often only as effective as the
caretaker who watched over it, making this facet of the archaeological
project—and of Mexico's political centralization—tenuous and inconsistent.

Scattered across Mexico's immense terrain, the guards were not the satellites of state power that Batres and the federal government wished them to be. Most of these men were motivated by their own interests, which, as might be expected, did not always coincide with those of the state.

Batres began hiring the guards soon after becoming inspector, a power granted to him by the decree that established the Inspectorate as well as by the subsequent Law of Monuments. He started off by appointing a conserje at Teotihuacán in October 1885 and went on to create at least thirty-three positions if not more, the last as late as January 1911 at Tlalixcoyan, Veracruz, in the midst of the Mexican revolution. By then, caretakers could be found at sites throughout the country: in the north at Casas Grandes, Chalchihuites, and La Quemada; in central Mexico at Teotihuacán, Xochicalco, Tepozteco, Tescutzingo/Texcoco, and Huexotla/Tepetitlán; in Oaxaca at Mitla, Valle de Mitla, Quiotepec, Monte Albán, and Xoxocotlán; in Veracruz at Papantla, Cempoala, Maltrata, Isla de Sacrificios, and Tlalixcoyan; and in Michoacán at Pátzcuaro (to watch over the ruins of Tzintzuntzan, among others). Some positions were ephemeral; Tula, for instance, had a guard early in the Porfiriato, but the post was eliminated soon after. The lion's share of care-takers (fourteen of thirty-three) were posted at Maya sites: Palenque, Uxmal, Labná, Chichén Itzá, Chacmultún, Kabah, Kiuic, Dzulá, Sayil, Chacbolay, Xkichmook, Cobá, Izamal, and a place that Batres and others referred to as Tzitzi (today known as Tzitzilá).[3] The most heavily guarded territory, then, was the land of the Maya, an area that was full of ruins and relic hunters and that was also difficult for Batres to reach.

If we compare the list of guards to the map Batres made earlier in the 1880s, it becomes clear that the inspector gained knowledge of the existence of more ruins over time, especially in the Yucatán Peninsula. This region, which he originally depicted with just three sites, ended up with thirteen guards. It also becomes clear that Batres chose to protect certain ruins but not others; many of the places on the map, like Querétaro's Ruinas del Doctor, would never see a guard. How Batres determined where to post a guard is not known, but he probably took into account the size and fame of the site as well as its popularity with pothunters and travelers. Scientific dis-coveries also seem to have played a role. For example, Batres hired a care-taker at Tepozteco, the hilltop pyramid near the village of Tepoztlán, shortly after it was introduced to the world of archaeology. In 1895, a young architect and engineer from Tepoztlán named Francisco Rodríguez excavated the pyr-amid and presented his findings at the Eleventh Congress of Americanists, which was held in Mexico that same year. In the words of one observer, Rodríguez's study "attracted much attention and led several archaeologists to visit the temple, and later to the appointment of a custodian of the ruin."[4]

Batres's method for hiring the guards was usually straightforward. After visiting a site and deeming it worthy of a federal presence, he began his "research." He asked local authorities and prominent people in the area to suggest a candidate with a "good record" or reputation.[5] Once he appointed the guard, he occasionally took inventory of the site; he made maps, took photos, and sometimes even counted the slabs of stone that made up the monuments. In this way, the government recorded its property and also made it known that it was familiar with the condition of the site, a warning for the conserje not to get lazy and allow it to be destroyed. The guards were not only liable for the ruins but could be fined if parts of them were torn off or went missing.

Although Batres frequently handpicked the initial caretaker at a site, the local authorities, especially governors, often sent him recommendations for subsequent candidates. On rare occasions, it was these officials who prompted the creation of the conserje position, like the town council of San Carlos in the state of Veracruz, which in 1899 asked Governor Teodoro Dehesa for a guard to be stationed at Cempoala. The council explained it had tried to keep watch over the site but lacked the funds to hire a permanent overseer and the legal authority to stop the destruction of the monuments. Governor Dehesa, an antiquarian and frequent donor of artifacts to the National Museum, forwarded the message to the Secretariat of Education, recommending the mayor of San Carlos as the "perfect" man for the job, a request the federal government quickly approved.[6] Still, while governors like Dehesa often played an active role in selecting the guards, many others could not have cared less about the monuments.

Officials like Dehesa used the caretaker job to reward allies for their support. Cronyism was rampant, so much so that authorities frequently proposed candidates without any qualifications for the job, appointments with often-disastrous results. Apart from this sort of patronage, there was also nepotism; the conserje position often remained in the hands of certain families, passed down from one relative to another, especially from father to son. It was also common for members of a family to serve at different sites in a region. At least three men from the Verazaluce clan in Morelos worked consecutively at Xochicalco, while two others guarded Tepozteco. Hiring practices like these may have benefited the federal government. Recruiting from within the same family made it more likely that the guards would be familiar with a site and the responsibilities of the job. Relying on families as well as patronage networks also allowed the government to extend its reach into an area without disrupting the local dynamics of power, an important consideration, as many of the ruins existed on private property and on the lands of indigenous communities. In this way, the government could have a presence at a site without actually having to own it, and amazingly, the landowners do not seem to have opposed the idea, as no protests are recorded in the official documents. (Complaints about specific guards and their actions, however, were an entirely different matter.) Every now and then, someone tried to bypass these sorts of hiring practices and propose himself for the job, a tactic that usually failed. Gregorio Bautista, a teacher at a rural school near El Tajín, got nowhere, for instance, despite his promise in 1891 to keep "faithful watch" over the monuments.[7]

"Faithful" was an understatement, as the guards (the obedient ones, at least) were virtually slaves to the sites. They were sentinels who were required to remain at their posts night and day, making sure no one destroyed the monuments. If they caught someone tampering with them, they sent a telegram to Batres, who would instruct the governor or a local authority to intervene. Sometimes, the guards contacted these regional officials directly, like the caretaker at Mitla, who in 1907 informed a jefe político that some Americans were "really sacking the ruins," "taking countless precious objects."[8]

And that was not all. The guards served as middlemen between the visitors and federal government. They kept track of the tourists, recording the number of nationals and foreigners that came to each site. Some even kept guest books for them to sign, a practice, according to one of the guards, that was also meant to discourage the travelers from the age-old custom of decorating the monuments with their "names and thoughts" and other graffiti.[9] Several of the men provided visitors with transportation, food, and lodging as well as tours of the sites—making the caretakers, quite possibly, Mexico's first official tour guides. Some also aided visiting scientists. When the archaeologist Antonio Peñafiel traveled to Xochicalco in 1887 in the company of the German scholar Eduard Seler and his wife, Caecilie Seler-Sachs, the original guard at the site, Jesús Moreno Flores, supposedly offered them "interesting services in their explorations." Moreno, it seems, went out of his way to welcome scientists and other prominent guests by putting on live "Indian shows." The guard got the local Indians to dance, sing, and play instruments in different places around the pyramids of Xochicalco. These performances were similar to those found in tourist attractions throughout the world today that are designed to bring a native people's culture to life and add an air of authenticity to the experience. When the Mexican archaeologist and lawyer Cecilio Robelo caught a glimpse of one of these spectacles at Xochicalco in the 1880s, the Indians' melodies nearly put him in a trance; he had visions of thousands of "slaves" being forced to build the pyramids "by the whips of fanaticism," along with a high priest ripping out the hearts of sacrificial victims.[10] As representatives of the federal government, guards like Moreno often took pride in their job and were concerned with making a good impression. Such was the case of the caretaker of Mitla, who in 1911 hoped his efforts had left travelers "very pleased, and satisfied with their visit."[11]

And the conserjes did more. They cared for the ruins, or, as Batres explained, they had to "clean the constructions and prohibit the growth of vegetation, which is the principal destructive agent of the monuments."[12] The guards carried out hard manual labor. The work was exhausting, even though some of the men had a temporary helper or two, and others were aided by a more permanent personal assistant (ayudante particular). They pulled weeds, cleared roads, and chopped down trees, a never-ending chore. For those in the jungle who were faced with relentless tropical creepers and vines, it must have seemed like a task made for Sisyphus, as trees grew tenaciously from the tops of temples and vines penetrated through walls. Cleaning the ruins was thought to make them more accessible. Having clear views, unhindered by vegetation, also rendered them more "attractive" to tourists, explained one of the caretakers. It made it easier to photograph, map, and draw the structures, enabling their "contemplation and study."[13] And it facilitated the surveillance of the sites, allowing the guards and Batres to assess any damages to the monuments. The tidying up of the ruins also reflected the Porfirian emphasis not only on order and progress but on cleanliness, too, as hygiene, many scholars have shown, had become a significant "concern of the state."[14] In acting on the old stones, the government was controlling the cities of the ancient Indians, remaking them in ways that were consistent with Porfirian values. Ironically, though, much of this cleaning most likely did more harm than good. In some cases, the thick roots of trees were the only thing holding the buildings together, and the vines worked to support crumbling walls. A guard who chopped down a tree could easily send it crashing into a temple, and a peón who set himself to polishing the mossy stones might erode an age-old relief, causing it to vanish forever.

The work of the guards did not end there. Some made maps of the sites and copied murals, displaying an intellectual interest in the ruins under their care, like Moreno of Xochicalco, who in 1895 asked the federal government to provide him with books and maps so he could study the "interesting science of Archaeology."[15] Many of the guards helped transport antiquities to the National Museum, and some, not surprisingly, also discovered them. This is how the museum acquired several of its finest pieces, like the famous *guacamaya*, or macaw, of Xochicalco, an object the ancient inhabitants of the site had used to keep score during the ritual ballgame. This relic continues to dazzle visitors in the National Museum of Anthropology today. In 1903, the guard at the site, Herculano Verazaluce, came across a tiny piece of the object, a "partecita," sticking out of the ground. He reported his finding to Batres: "I tried to yank it out, but the ground was too hard," so I waited until "the waters fell [and] the earth softened and [then] took advantage of the occasion to remove it."[16]

Verazaluce also drew an exact replica of the artifact, displaying a talent that seems to have run in his family. One of his relatives, Bernardino Verazaluce, was a very skilled draftsman who accompanied Batres on an expedition to copy the murals of Mitla in 1901. The drawings he made were so precise that Batres recommended they be installed in the National Museum. Verazaluce eventually became a guard at Tepozteco, where he made some sketches of the reliefs found on the temples, images that were thought to be more accurate than the photographs taken by the American archaeologist Marshall Saville around the same time. The drawings were the "most prized" data collected on the site, wrote another scientist.[17] A Nahuatl speaker of humble origins from Tepoztlán, a village where people took "great pride in their ancestry," Verazaluce seems to have been a keeper of local lore.[18] He possessed some sort of manuscript recording legends from the area around his village. Both he and his son shared this information with scientists, including Franz Boas, the German American often touted as the "father" of modern anthropology. Sometime after the revolution broke out, Verazaluce quit his job at Tepozteco, leaving the position to his son and migrating to Mexico City, where he became an "enthusiastic but forgotten collaborator" of Robelo, the archaeologist mesmerized by the show of dancing Indians at Xochicalco who, by then, had become the director of the National Museum (1911–1913).[19] For this one guard, then, the conserje position seems to have paved the way to a more formal role in the world of science. While Verazaluce was exceptional, even an ordinary caretaker's job might involve tasks that were crucial to the preservation of data, making the guards the unsung heroes in Mexico's history of archaeology. In order to perform these as well as other chores, the most basic requirement for the job was that the men remain at their sites without fail.

It was a difficult requirement to fulfill, especially since the position initially went unpaid. The job was "purely honorific" until 1895 when at least some of the guards began to receive a wage, but even then, the pay was relatively meager.[20] Batres's records are spotty, but the salaries seem to have varied depending on the importance of the site, a judgment, again, most likely based on the popularity and size of the ruins. In 1900, for instance, the conserjes of Mitla and Teotihuacán took home 492 pesos a year, about the same as a skilled laborer, while the guard at the smaller and less visited site of Cempoala earned 365 pesos, a little over minimum wage—if, that is, he ever actually got paid.[21] Wages were often slow in coming or failed to arrive due to bureaucratic glitches: one desperate guard at Quiotepec complained to the federal government that he had not received "even a centavo" and that he was suffering from "a shortage of food."[22] To make ends meet, the guards most likely relied on their families or took on other jobs. At least one of the men, Ángel Vázquez of Mitla, came up with a novel approach— he solicited tips from the tourists, letting them know that the government was not paying him enough "for his subsistence."[23] Wages were not only unpredictable, but the guards could always be fired or have their pay withheld if they failed to complete a task or if a piece of the ruins disappeared. Yet even so, Mexicans often seem to have sought out the job precisely for its pay. In 1911, Juan Antonio Mendieta, for example, took advantage of the fact that the guard at Mitla had been sent to jail, asking the government on several occasions if he could replace the incarcerated guard. And while he did his best to sweet talk Justo Sierra, who was secretary of education at that point, praising Sierra as a person both "beautiful" and kind, he did not get the job.[24]

Because the guards were expected to sustain themselves and their families on modest wages yet remain in places that were often removed from other sources of income, Batres sought out candidates with two qualities: he looked for individuals who were from "humble origins" and from the area. Put another way, he recruited poor men from villages near the ruins, even specifying, at times, that they should be Indians or "indígenas."[25] In light of this request and the fact that the guards were nearly always local men, it is probably safe to say that many of them were indigenous. Every now and then,

Batres was forced to break from his "poor and humble" policy and hire a more affluent local. This is how at least one military captain, doctor, clergyman, and innkeeper got the job. But these men were the exception to the rule, as the typical conserje was a man of lower-class origins who was literally going nowhere.

While Batres believed these qualities would ensure the caretakers lived "with satisfaction in the place," his logic was flawed. When Moreno, the Xochicalco guard who requested the archaeology books, could no longer scrape by, for example, he moved his family of eight to Amecameca some sixty miles away, where, as he explained, "life is cheaper." From there, he traveled to care for Xochicalco every few weeks and every time his relatives near the site informed him that it had visitors. Unfortunately for Moreno, Batres learned about this long-distance relationship from a group of Germans who visited Xochicalco and found it abandoned. (Moreno's relatives must have been lax.) Poor Moreno had been caught breaking the conserje's cardinal rule: to remain at the ruins at all times. And so it was that Xochicalco's original caretaker found himself begging to keep his job. But Batres would have none of it. "Would it be possible," he asked, "for a doorman to live" so far "from the building under his care without the building getting destroyed?" Batres continued, "One should not forget the constant clamor in the national and foreign press denouncing . . . the state of abandon in which Xochicalco finds and has always found itself." Moreno pleaded with Batres, pointing out that he had been the guard for fourteen years, had "a love" of the site, and would happily return to live there in exchange for a raise, "even if it meant living in one of the caves beneath" the ruins.[26] But Batres refused. He fired Moreno and hired another local in his place. A deserted site gave the impression the government lacked control over the ruins, hardly the message it wished to convey.

Getting the guards to remain at their sites was a constant problem for Batres. The men left because they got sick, got new jobs, or got thrown in jail. Batres even made them promise they would stick around. "He assures me he'll always stay," he said of one new hire.[27] Drawing on the locals as a source of labor most likely did increase the odds that they would stay, as the few outsiders that Batres appointed were less willing to tolerate the hardships of the job, like Aurelio Montes de Oca, a resident of Mexico City who became the caretaker at Pátzcuaro in 1909 only to quit within a few months. Locals were not only likely to be familiar with the sites but could also summon the aid of their communities to care for the ruins if needed. The reliance on locals also made the extension of the government's authority over the ruins more palatable to the people of the area. There was one more quality that Batres sought in a guard: the ideal conserje had to be "energetic" or "enthusiastic," an essential trait not only because there was so much to do but so much to endure.[28]

Life at the ruins was tough. The penniless caretaker of Quiotepec was not only going hungry but was sleeping outside, "exposed to the elements." The rainy season was fast approaching, and he begged the government for a shelter.[29] In the words of Vázquez, Mitla's tip-hungry guard, the job required one to live at the ruins much like "an owl."[30] Batres petitioned the government to construct housing at a few sites, suggesting it erect a small dwelling at Mitla since without it, the guard had to live in town, some "500 meters away," making his surveillance of the ruins completely "fictitious."[31] Some guards also built thatched huts for themselves. But overall, material comforts were scarce, as were tools and supplies. To hack away the brush, the men most likely made use of their own machetes since the government does not seem to have provided them with much equipment other than the guest books for gathering signatures and some axes, presumably for chopping down trees. Mexico's two subinspectors, whom we meet shortly, received a few more items: "tools, books, archives, and the rubber stamp of office."[32] The subinspector of Yucatán also got a stack of copies of the Law of Monuments to distribute among the visitors and locals. The government sent him five hundred of the leaflets to hand out to ensure that "the necessary respect" would be shown to "the notable ruins."[33] The leaflets, along with the publication of the law in the press, were just one of the ways the government made people aware of the ruling and injected the idea of federal ownership of the sites into the national consciousness. The word seems to have gotten out as hoped, as the individuals who notified Batres about the destruction of ruins often referred to the law, down to its specific articles. Yet while the law was frequently used to stop offenders in the act, no ordinary Mexican ever seems to have been fined for violating it. Ironically, the people who did end up getting fined were the guards. The inspector often used the articles of the Law of Monuments as justification to fire them or take away their pay if they abandoned their posts or neglected the ruins.

If the caretakers' supplies were minimal, their job training was even more so. Apart from a few instructions Batres might have uttered when appointing a guard or visiting a site, the men seemed to have learned about their duties through their correspondence with the inspector. They were required to send him a monthly report documenting the state of the ruins and their work at the site, to which Batres often replied with suggestions. Judging from the paucity of these reports and the fact that only certain conserjes seemed to write Batres time and again, it is probably safe to say that many, if not most, of the men were illiterate. ("It takes him much effort to write his name," remarked one observer about a guard.)[34] Communication between the guards and the federal government was a constant problem; messages were slow to arrive or simply never showed up, prompting one caretaker to note, "I'm always shocked by the delay in our correspondence."[35] The wheels of bureaucracy turned slowly, making it difficult to address emergency situations in a timely fashion. When a worker at Palenque requested 250 pesos to build a pillar to support a collapsing façade, the funds were so late that by the time they arrived, an earthquake had already sent the wall crashing to the ground.

Except in the case of emergencies, the caretakers were strictly prohibited from making "repairs to the monuments and from excavating." They were "incompetent" in such technical matters, explained Batres, and would only end up destroying the monuments "in the name of the government."[36] Yet even though the guards lacked any sort of specialized training or expertise, in the eyes of Batres, the very fact that they had obtained the position through the requisite channels—through Batres, patronage, or family connections—raised them above the level of the common citizen. When a man near Cempoala asked to become the custodian of the monuments on his lands, Batres responded that he would never leave the ruins at the "mercy of a common citizen no matter how honorable."[37]

Most of the guards took their duties quite seriously; some even carried them out with "excessive zeal."[38] But every now and then, Batres would come to regret his caretaker appointments, and Mitla, for some reason, was plagued by a series of such hires. The guard in 1893 kept the "ruins in ruins," a traveler complained; the place was so unkempt it was not even worth taking the trip up the "dreadful" road to see it. The only task this one guard performed was to approach visitors with the guest book that "has the airs of being an album in which they can write their thoughts, which are usually nothing more than downright idiotic remarks."[39] Two years later, the guard was replaced with the tip-hungry Vázquez, a patronage appointment it seems, as Batres himself questioned the wisdom of the choice. Vázquez was in his eighties, much too slow and old to adequately carry out his duties, claimed Batres. Among his many failings, he repeatedly insulted the local villagers, including the priest, and left Mitla unattended for months at a time. Batres protested that Mitla, a frequently visited site, was a "caricature" of what it should be, overseen by a guard whom visitors consistently "treat as less than a household servant due to the fact that he does not command respect."[40] Vázquez's downfall came in 1900, when an observer caught him giving away pieces of the pyramids to a tourist, an infraction that quickly got him fired. An exasperated Batres was constantly confronted by the fact that there was a huge gulf between how he envisioned the system of guards and how it actually worked on the ground. The actions and self-interest of the men often served to undermine the state's power.

But the conserje that bedeviled Mitla the most was not Vázquez but his successor, Ángel Navalon, whose first name turned out to be a misnomer. Navalon was also a patronage appointment, hired at the behest of Martín González, the governor of Oaxaca who had come to power as a result of his personal connections to President Díaz. The governor had vouched for Navalon's character, but the new guard turned out to be a drunk who made a habit out of abusing the locals. He stole their horses and food and lived in their homes only to skip town when rent was due. Navalon spent much of his time combing through the countryside in search of mines (and probably artifacts, too), leaving Mitla in the care of his teenage son, who played on the monuments instead of going to school, since he had been expelled due to "bad behavior." When the people of Villa de Mitla confronted Navalon about his abuses, he insulted them and made it known that they were powerless against him since, as he put it, he "was part of the Federal Government." But Navalon's insolence soon caught up with him. In late 1901, a wall at Mitla was torn down over the course of two weeks, the stone from which was used to repair a nearby church. When Batres went to investigate, he found all the prominent locals—the municipal president, ex-president, town trustee, and priest—blaming each other for what had happened. The clever townsfolk decided to use the occasion to get rid of Navalon. In his presence, they let Batres know the guard was never at his post. They presented a petition to have him fired, complete with a page full of signatures. Unable to uncover the truth about the wall, Batres put the blame squarely on Navalon, as it was his "duty to have stopped the destruction," especially since it occurred over a span of two weeks, plenty of time for the guard to have taken action. The town was victorious; Batres fired Navalon and put a new and improved conserje in his place. According to Batres, the new guard kept the ruins in a "perfect state of conservation and cleanliness," an accomplishment about which Mitla's tourists "sang praises."[41] A negligent caretaker like Navalon not only gave Mexico a bad name but also tarnished Batres's reputation, making him vulnerable to criticism. Writing about the neglect of Mitla and other sites in the newspaper *El Tiempo* in 1900, one commentator called into question the very purpose of the inspector: "What function does Mr. Batres serve, famous curator of the monuments of the Republic? Simply to earn a salary, put on airs, and let the ruins fall to ruin?"[42]

As the story of Navalon suggests, one of the perks of the caretaker job was that it transformed individuals into employees of the state, giving them a bit of power and prestige. Some men abused it, like those of Mitla and a certain guard in Texcoco who went around banging on the doors of all the "respectable people," threatening to "kick them out" of town if he found any monuments on their properties.[43] But others took pride in the job and displayed an intellectual curiosity about the ruins, like Moreno, Xochicalco's long-distance guard who wanted to further his studies in archaeology. Some, too, seem to have developed emotional attachments to the sites, like Moreno, once again, who professed a "love" for Xochicalco. Did the conserjes consider themselves guardians of national patrimony? Moreno, at least, seems to have interpreted his job in this way; when he asked the government for the archaeology books he characterized his work as a service "to my patria."[44] But there is also the possibility that some of the men were drawn to the job because it allowed them to defend places important to their community's sense of identity and history, like the draftsman Verazaluce and his son, two keepers of local lore who made contributions to science. These sorts of emotional attachments to a particular site, however, are difficult to discern, as the guards tended to surface in the historical record mainly when they misbehaved, abused their authority, or failed to carry out their duties. Some of the worst offenders, it turns out, were those higher up in the chain of command, the subinspectors of Chiapas and Yucatán.

The Subinspectors

Hired in 1898, Mexico's two subinspectors took over Batres's duties in the land of the Maya. They monitored sites, enforced the archaeological legislation, and appointed and supervised the guards in their states, choosing "poor laborers of good conduct," the same criteria, in other words, used by Batres.[45] While both men often communicated with Batres, and Batres made decisions about them, the subinspectors were not accountable to him but to the secretary of education, an arrangement designed, perhaps, to curtail some of the inspector's power. Batres also disliked the heat and humidity in Chiapas and Yucatán (according to Marshall Saville, an archaeologist who would have many confrontations with Batres), and though his work would continue to take him there, the subinspectors may have been hired to allow him to spend less time in the area.[46]

The subinspector of Chiapas, Benito Lacroix, most likely acquired his position due to family and political connections. His father had served as the guard of Palenque, and one of his relatives had been president of the nearby town of Santo Domingo de Palenque. Lacroix had also previously worked at the site. In 1891 he took part in archaeologist Alfred Maudslay's expedition to Palenque, where he was placed in charge of clearing away vegetation. Once he became subinspector of Chiapas, Lacroix found several ways to profit from the job. He opened a hotel near Palenque. And he also took to selling the ancient objects, an egregious violation of his position that did not come to light until the 1920s. According to the Danish anthropologist Frans Blom, both Lacroix and his father were "the principal sackers of the area." They kept a stockpile of antiquities for sale in their homes, a convenient souvenir shop for the tourists.[47]

The subinspector of Yucatán, Santiago Bolio, also profited from the very objects he was hired to guard. As the official in charge of the ruins in the state of Yucatán, Bolio tangled with the notorious Edward Thompson, the American consul who dredged the Sacred Cenote of Chichén Itzá for the Peabody Museum. Bolio, an engineer, took on the task of establishing the boundary between Chichén Itzá and Thompson's land in 1902. The subinspector concluded that although Thompson's hacienda lay "at a close distance" to the site, none of the monuments, including the cenote, were part of his property. The ruins were thus public domain and belonged to the Mexican nation. Thompson protested the finding, especially the part about the cenote, but he did not have the proper documents at the time to contest it. That did not stop him, however, from entering the site and "invading" the well, according to Bolio. For the next few years, Bolio worked tenaciously to put an end to Thompson's dredging—or at least his official reports portray him in this light. He sent several notices to the Secretariat of Education about Thompson, along with some of the artifacts from the cenote and photographs of the crane used for dredging. The government ordered Bolio to put an end to the dredging and have Thompson send the artifacts to the National

Museum. Each time Bolio approached Thompson and demanded he stop, the American would supposedly comply, pull back his crane, and allow the sub-inspector to search for antiquities in the heaps of mud taken out of the well. But as soon as Bolio left, Thompson would start operating the crane once again. In his letters to the government, Bolio characterizes himself as a model employee, an "honest," "faithful" man with a "clear conscience."[48]

Witnesses told a different story. They said that Bolio was actually in cahoots with Thompson. According to Teobert Maler, a German archaeologist who hated Thompson and denounced his dredging and other activities to the federal government on several occasions, Bolio helped Thompson search for antiquities, breaking into tomb after tomb and gathering stones at one site to use in the remodeling of Thompson's hacienda. At Chichén Itzá, the subinspector destroyed some murals Thompson had studied in order to prevent anyone from carrying out any further research, making Thompson the sole expert on the images. Even Thompson recorded Bolio's complicity. The American had to buy Bolio's silence with small bribes, giving him "money from time to time as occasion seems to demand." Smuggling the cenote artifacts to the Peabody cost Thompson "quite a sum of money," so much, he complained, that he suffered "many sleepless nights and unhappy days," but he knew it was the only way to make Bolio "hold fast" to his interests.[49] If Bolio was ever the diligent official he made himself out to be, he had been quickly corrupted.

In early 1906, Inspector Batres paid a visit to Chichén Itzá. Batres was in Yucatán with Secretary Sierra and other officials for a huge celebration to mark the completion of several public works projects designed to modernize the capital of Mérida. President Díaz also attended the event, the first Mexican president to visit the Yucatán peninsula. The officials toured the new hospital, penitentiary, and mental asylum, along with many schools and haciendas—at one hacienda hundreds of workers waving tiny Mexican flags greeted the dictator Díaz.[50] In the midst of all the banquets and excitement, Batres and Sierra set out to inspect Chichén Itzá, a trip Thompson's enemy Maler arranged in the hope that they would see fit to put a stop to Thompson's activities. Before the officials arrived, Thompson and his trusty confidant Bolio worked hard to cover their tracks, hiding the pits they had dug into the temples. But they did not hide the crane. While Thompson had enough sense to stop his dredging during the visit, Batres and Sierra fully understood what was going on; at one point Maler even ordered Bolio to hand the two men some of the artifacts that Thompson had removed from the well. And, while

Batres may have been disturbed by what he saw, he also had a certain admiration for Thompson's methods: he found the idea of exploring the cenote with a diving suit particularly ingenious. Maler's plan seems to have backfired, as Thompson wined and dined Batres and the officials, and days later, President Díaz himself paid a visit and was similarly received.

Soon after, Bolio died of an unidentified illness. A new subinspector took his place, and the dredging of Chichén Itzá's famous Sacred Cenote continued off and on until 1910. Why the federal government failed to stop Thompson is not well understood. Perhaps it simply believed he owned the land around the cenote and that he thus had the right to exploit it. Most scholars assume the government never questioned Thompson's ownership of the land. But this does not seem to have been the case, since Bolio himself declared the cenote national property in his initial survey of the site. That the government instructed Thompson to send the artifacts he discovered to the National Museum is also curious. Federal officials most likely would not have taken this step if they believed Thompson owned the cenote, since the Law of Monuments allowed people to keep the artifacts found on their lands. To complicate matters, months after Batres's visit, officials ordered Thompson to apply for a contract to excavate, but such contracts were usually only for professional archaeologists. Thompson applied for a contract in April 1907, but whether he received it is open to question. Why the government made this request is another mystery. While Mexican law did not clarify if individuals could excavate their own lands, it seems unlikely that the government would have made Thompson apply for a concession to excavate a piece of property that it believed was his. In demanding he obtain a contract, it may merely have been treating Thompson as a researcher rather than a property owner. Or perhaps it was just trying to obstruct him, since contract recipients were required to have their work supervised by a federal agent. In any case, the official responses to Thompson seem scattershot and inconsistent. It is possible that the government was simply vexed (and with good reason!) by the ambiguity of its own laws and did not know how to proceed. Perhaps the whole problem lay in the fact that Thompson was excavating a body of water rather than soil, an issue not addressed by the Law of Monuments.

Batres seems to have kept a certain distance from the whole affair, as the responsibility for the day-to-day surveillance of Yucatán lay in the hands of the subinspector and, by extension, the secretary of education. Curiously, Batres said next to nothing about the matter, an unusual reticence, since he was never hesitant about attacking other archaeologists. In his personal papers, he mentions Thompson only once, listing him among the many "Yanquis" who trafficked in relics, lamenting the loss of a "multitude of objects to the Peabody."[51] What about Sierra? Why did he not put a stop to Thompson? Although the secretary of education took measures to protect Chichén Itzá, placing a fence around the site and investigating the legitimacy of Thompson's deed to the hacienda, Sierra seems to have worried that denouncing Thompson, an American consul, would have triggered an international scandal. Even subinspector Bolio shared this concern. In 1904, when the dredging first began, Bolio asked the government for instructions on how to proceed, as he feared that hindering the consul would cause "an international complication."[52] This concern, along with the vagueness of the archaeological legislation, most likely explains Mexico's haphazard attempts at dealing with Thompson and his smuggling of one of the country's most dazzling pre-Hispanic findings.

The full extent of Thompson's activities did not surface until years later. It was only after the publication in 1926 of T. A. Willard's *City of the Sacred Well*, a biography of Thompson, that the Mexican government realized just how many relics it had lost. The government seized Thompson's hacienda and sued him for the illicit exportation of artifacts to the tune of 1.3 million pesos, the estimated value of the objects extracted from the cenote. Thompson returned to the United States, where he died in 1935. Mexico's Supreme Court eventually found him not guilty, a decision based on the Law of Monuments, the legislation in effect when Thompson carried out the dredging. The court argued that under the law, Thompson was entitled to the artifacts since the cenote was on his property—a claim, as we have seen, however, that does seem to have been called into question at least once during the Porfiriato. Only Thompson's unauthorized exportation of the artifacts was a crime under the law, with a fine capped at 500 pesos, a small sum that the Mexican government did not try to extract from his heirs. In 1944, the government returned Thompson's hacienda to his relatives, who sold it to the Barbachano family, who today operate it as an upscale resort, a "Mayan eco-spa" that has several rooms, including a master suite, named after Thompson. After years of insisting, Mexico was finally able to persuade the Peabody to return some of the artifacts from the cenote. Today more than two hundred can be found in Mérida's Regional Anthropology Museum of Palacio Cantón, along with a few in the National Museum of Anthropology. But the vast majority of Thompson's artifacts remain in the Peabody, stored in the basement.

Thompson had extracted the objects from the depths of the cenote, writes scholar Spencer Burke, "only to have them returned back to the bowels of the earth, beneath the green pastures of Harvard."[53] Today, the battle between Mexico and the Peabody over these artifacts remains deadlocked.

Just as trafficking today in illicit drugs lures officials, Mexico's market in antiquities was just too profitable for authorities like Bolio and Lacroix to resist. And it may also have been too tempting for Batres. According to Carelton Beals, an American journalist writing in the 1930s, Batres was a "wholesale and retail merchant in antiquities," a man who "rifled the nation of its archaeological treasures."[54] Although it is not clear where Beals got his information, it might have come from the American archaeologist Zelia Nuttall. An independent scholar who began her career as a special assistant in the Peabody under Frederic Putnam (the same Putnam who sponsored Thompson), Nuttall arrived in Mexico in 1903. She carried out research in her home in the capital and in the National Museum, where she became an honorary professor. One of the few female archaeologists at the time, she had several run-ins with Batres.

Her most famous confrontation with the inspector was over the Isle of Sacrifices off the coast of Veracruz, a place she believed was Aztlán, the mythical home of the Aztecs. In late 1909, Nuttall discovered some ruins with red frescoes on the island. She asked the Mexican government for permission to explore the site, promising to protect the frescoes with panes of glass and to send any artifacts she uncovered to the National Museum. The Secretariat of Education authorized her expedition, but before Nuttall could return to the site, Batres beat her to it: he "went quietly down to Vera Cruz and explored the island himself," taking credit for the discovery of the frescoes and also leaving them exposed and vulnerable to ruin. In an article, Nuttall not only charged Batres with obstructing her work but with trafficking in antiquities. She claimed Batres took bribes from smugglers. "As many tourists and scientists are willing to testify," she explained, Batres "openly dealt in antiquities . . . and received payments for 'affording facilities' for taking said purchases out of the country."[55] Batres fought back against Nuttall in his short, combative pamphlet *The Island of Sacrifices: Mrs. Zelia Nuttall de Pinard and Leopoldo Batres.* He denied hindering Nuttall's work and attributed her accusations to "feminine hysteria."[56] But his pamphlet is completely silent about the charge of trafficking. His personal papers, on the other hand, are not. In his draft for the pamphlet, Batres fiercely denied the charge. What proof did Nuttall have? he asked. What artifacts had been smuggled? Who were the "many tourists and scientists" willing to testify against him?

Was the man entrusted with guarding Mexico's patrimony one of its biggest exploiters? Was he a "wholesale and retail merchant" of the past? While these charges have never been proven, some of his actions were questionable. In 1896 Batres tried to sell a collection of antiquities to Mexico's National Museum through the aid of a third party. Somehow, the museum director found out that Batres was the collection's true owner and contacted the Secretariat of Education to inquire if the inspector "was authorized to sell Mexican archaeological objects." Batres defended himself on the grounds that the collection was his private property.[57] He eventually sold it to the German linguist Walter Lehman, a disciple of Eduard Seler. That he sold it, though, does not make him a trafficker, since Mexican law did not prohibit individuals from amassing collections or even selling them. Rumors of trafficking would swirl about Batres, never to be put to rest, and some of his habits only served to fuel them. For example, Batres often stored antiquities he found on the job in his home in Mexico City before taking them to the museum. He also kept a few private pieces in what was known at the time as an Oriental or Arabic room—a type of exotic smoking room, full of "oriental" furnishings, that was popular among elites. Only Batres—who earned a comfortable yet modest salary—decorated his space with rugs from Oaxaca and other Mexican goods, a cheaper, "knock-off" version of the room that put an orientalist spin on Mexico's indigenous heritage.

Still, while Batres's position gave him plenty of opportunities to engage in illicit activities, there is no solid evidence against him. Of course, anyone who benefited from these activities would have most likely kept quiet. But what about all those "tourists and scientists"? What did they have to lose? Batres was a man who would come to make scores of enemies—or at least people *he* perceived as enemies—and it seems logical that if anyone had any concrete evidence against him they would have gladly stepped forward. What is more, trafficking seems a bit out of character. While Batres was a difficult man, he was also an official who made protecting his nation's past his life's cause. That he trafficked in antiquities seems inconsistent with the mission he carried out for twenty-six long years. At the same time, like many of his peers, Batres viewed the artifacts through a hierarchical lens, believing a common ceramic pot, say, was inferior to a finely carved statue; as he explained, certain monuments in Mexico "were of little interest; thousands of these types could be found all over the place and were not important enough to warrant any serious study."[58] Given this view, the inspector may well have considered some objects expendable, less important to retain within Mexico's borders. While it is entirely possible he allowed these and others to slip out of the country, or even trafficked in the goods, the truth is that unless some new evidence surfaces we will never really know. Still, that accusations were lodged against him does cast serious doubt on his honesty.

As inspector, Batres stood at the head of an agency riddled with problems, an institution made up of employees whose actions often ran counter to its very reason for being. The scattering of handfuls of these workers across an immense terrain full of ruins proved to be a fragile mechanism for taking charge of the past—especially when some of the men only facilitated the loss and destruction of the objects they were supposed to be guarding. The Mexican government's control over the archaeological landscape would remain spotty and inconsistent. Foreigners like Thompson and Mexicans like those who tore down the wall at Mitla would continue to use the pieces of the past in their own ways. The Inspectorate of Monuments was simply too weak to rein them in—but it tried. For all its flaws, the agency represented a more concerted effort at controlling the ruins than anything that had come before. It helped establish the idea of state ownership over the ruins, a notion that has become largely embedded in Mexico's national consciousness. The Inspectorate was Mexico's first attempt at creating an archaeological bureaucracy, and while it was tinkered with a bit over time, it is essentially the same entity today. It is also not farfetched to assume that in some instances, with a vigilant guard at the helm, the agency did deter some people from destroying the monuments. As head of the Inspectorate, Batres was the highest ranking of these guards. And he was a gatekeeper in another key way. Batres was in charge of inspecting the activities of other archaeologists, a duty that gave him an extraordinary amount of power over the research carried out in the country and that led him into head-on collisions with more than a few archaeologists.

CHAPTER SIX

Inspecting

✢ IN LATE 1897 BATRES FOUND HIMSELF AT THE RUINS OF PALENQUE watching over the excavations of American archaeologist Marshall Saville. Every shovelful of dirt, every mound, led to "bitter arguments" between the two, wrote Batres.[1] Saville, who was on a research expedition for the American Museum of Natural History in New York City, one of the leading anthropological institutions of the United States, had his own complaints. According to him, Batres had "placed every obstacle" in his way, causing his expedition to be delayed for over a month and preventing him from hiring workers. Labor was scarce to begin with, as most of the Indians in the area worked on the coffee plantations nearby, leaving Saville "practically alone . . . with only a handful of men to clear the forest and to carry on excavations." On top of it all, it never seemed to stop raining. After only a few days of digging, Saville decided to give up: "All hope of working there was abandoned." Batres, on the other hand, claimed Saville had quit because he had come to believe the antiquities he was after had been "completely destroyed by moisture."[2] The inspector lodged other accusations against Saville. He supposedly caught him prying a panel out of a temple and trying to stuff a statue into his suitcase. The American, Batres later declared, was a "gold digger," a mere treasure hunter, with an utter "ignorance of science" and a "tendency to destroy the monuments in search of objects to transport to the Museum of Natural History."[3] That Saville could not tolerate the rigors of fieldwork and was effeminate in Batres's opinion did not help matters. Nor did the fact that he traveled with a friend who Batres considered even more effete—"fifí," or sissy, was Batres's exact word. In one incident, the compan-ion, a wealthy, young American engineer named H. C. Humphries, tried to climb astride a horse but somehow ended up facing backward, much to the delight of the inspector.

In accompanying Saville, Batres was carrying out his official duty of monitoring the work of researchers who had secured government contracts to excavate, which Saville had recently been granted. Saville's concession was the first of its kind since the adoption of the Law of Archaeological Explorations in 1896, a ruling that regulated the archaeological concessions in greater detail.[4] The law established consistent, formal guidelines for the contracts, which up until then had been negotiated on a case-by-case basis. Much like the other steps taken to create Mexico's archaeological patrimony, the ruling was aimed at defending the nation's image. It came out of concerns with demonstrating that Mexico was the master of its past, that foreign sci-entists could not simply rifle through the ancient ruins, appropriating what-ever they pleased.

Batres, however, approached his supervising function much like a duel, a battle to determine who was the "real" archaeologist and who had the right to practice the science. He used this task, as he used so many aspects of his job, as a way to crowd out other researchers and enlarge his scope of power. As the official watchdog of the ancient past, Batres would come to confuse himself with the Mexican nation and to view the field of archaeology as his personal domain. Much of the authoritarian streak of the government's archaeological project can be attributed to him and to the way he went about his job. The inspector was quick to claim any violation of the concession law as he watched over the excavations of Saville.

While individuals often petitioned the Mexican government for con-tracts to excavate, it was Saville's request that spurred the new concession law. Saville got the idea to apply for a contract after visiting Mexico in 1895. He was in the country that year representing the American Museum of Natural History at the Eleventh Congress of Americanists. This was the first time the conference had been held outside of Europe, and it was a momen-tous occasion for Mexico and its archaeological establishment. The congress ended with a trip to the state of Oaxaca, where thirty-two foreign and Mexican delegates toured the ruins of Mitla and the Oaxacan Museum, all the while being celebrated by the locals, who decorated their villages and came out en masse to greet them. Saville's interest in Mexico was piqued, and before returning home to New York, he met with President Díaz to discuss the possibility of obtaining a contract to carry out excavations, an agreement that would involve the Mexican government and the American Museum of Natural History. Saville let Díaz know he wanted the right to half of all the artifacts he discovered. Eager for Mexico to acquire artifacts, Díaz agreed. "One half of the loaf," he remarked, "is better than none."[5] Díaz told Saville to draw up a formal request in order to present it to the Mexican Congress, "as it was necessary for it [the concession] to take the form of a law." Within months, Saville submitted his proposal, asking for a ten-year contract. Pressed by his urgent appeal, the government soon passed the Law of Archaeological Explorations, and Saville was granted a concession under the terms of the new ruling.

Throughout the Porfiriato, the government would dole out only a handful of these contracts, which were aimed exclusively at professional researchers working on behalf of museums abroad even though the law did not make this stipulation. Requests from people who wished to carry out excavations for their own benefit were usually denied, like the plea from one Mexican who wanted to dig up a mound to "extract what is useful from it."[6] If a petition did not involve tampering with the monuments, it was often approved and dealt with in a less formal manner. When the archaeology club of Nuevo León asked for permission to visit several ruins in northern Mexico, for instance, the federal government simply authorized the expedition without drawing up a contract.[7]

The new law placed stricter limits on archaeological concessions. It stipulated that they could last no longer than ten years, made the researchers responsible for their own expenses, and required them to work only at the sites where they had been granted permission to excavate. If the archaeologists wanted to excavate ruins located on private property, they had to obtain permission from the owner. (If permission were denied, one assumes, there would be no excavation.) More importantly, the law required all of the work to be supervised by a "special agent appointed by the government," an official who would not only look out for Mexico's interests but provide assistance to the archaeologist. While in the past, as we have seen in the case of Charnay, there was no agent permanently assigned to this task, and while the law did not specify who this agent would be, the unstated assumption was that it would be Batres. Last of all, the law regulated what the concession holders could do with the artifacts they found. They could take photos and make casts of them, but they could not keep them. All discoveries were "property of the national government," a clause, ironically, that placed the antiquities

more firmly under the control of the federal government than the Law of
Monuments that was enacted the following year.

The sole exception to this rule involved what were considered "duplicates," a strange concept, really, since no two objects made in antiquity, long
before the age of mass production, could ever be exactly the same. The law
referred to these objects as originales iguales (identical originals). A duplicate
was any relic without intrinsic value—an artifact, in other words, that did
not contain precious metals or stones. It was also an artifact not considered
to be unique—a ceramic pot, say, found among several similar pots in a
burial. Concession holders could keep and export one of each duplicate they
found, the selection of which would be overseen by the government's "special
agent." Why make this exception? Rather than enforcing a total ban on
exports, a prohibition the archaeologists could circumvent through smuggling, the duplicate clause gave the government a degree of control over
which pieces left the country. It was also in keeping with the museum practices of the time. The trade in so-called duplicates was thriving around the
world; museums commonly sold and bartered the pieces with one another,
and the archaeological legislation of other countries similarly allowed for the
exportation of such objects. Taken as a whole, then, the law reflected Mexico's
"enlightened" approach to antiquities and to the practice of archaeology. It
shored up Mexico's image as a scientific, modern nation, allowing it to con-
tribute to the greater cause of science by facilitating excavations and scientific exchange. But it also tried to ensure that the objects that did get exported
did not represent a huge loss to Mexico and its national archaeology. It tried
to strike a balance, in other words, between allowing certain artifacts to be
flaunted abroad while making sure the most magnificent ones remained in
the country.

But there is another way to interpret the law. While it can be seen as a
step toward taking greater control over the antiquities, like the contracts in
general, the law made foreigners the active agents in archaeology and made
Mexico a supplier of artifacts, the raw materials of this burgeoning science.
As Carmen Ruiz points out, the archaeological concessions did not imply a
scientific collaboration between Mexicans and foreigners. Foreigners provided the effort, science, and technology—which was often little more than
photographic equipment and paper for making molds —while Mexico provided "its natural wealth: the ruins."[8] Whether one takes this view or sees
the law as an attempt to assume greater control over the monuments, in
either case, Mexico comes across as a colonized space, a nation that at once

accepted and challenged its weaker, peripheral status or at least tried to shape the terms of its subordinate position. It is as if Mexico just couldn't win. Like so many other aspects of the country's archaeological project, the concession law was rife with contradictions. Nevertheless, the ruling did signify a move toward greater regulation. What is more, it may also have given rise to the Law of Monuments the following year, as it made Mexicans aware of the fact that the country needed a more comprehensive piece of legislation, one that did more than simply regulate the activities of foreign explorers. Saville's visit, then, might have been the catalyst for both the Law of Archaeological Explorations as well as the Law of Monuments.

Without mentioning Inspector Batres, the concession law formalized many of his de facto powers. It further solidified his role as the gatekeeper of antiquity, as Batres was not only in charge of supervising the concession holders but also of deciding which artifacts were duplicates and could be exported out of the country. But this would prove to be an odd arrangement because Batres was not an archaeologist of the enlightened type; he was a "savage" nationalist if there ever was one. Batres displayed a fiercely possessive attitude toward the antiquities and a deep distrust of most foreign archaeologists, whom he regarded as little more than thieves. According to him, the Englishman Maudslay, for instance, was a "bandit-like character," whose actions had far-reaching and negative effects on Mexico's "historical and archaeological interests." Batres even compared Maudslay to Hernán Cortés. Like the Spanish conqueror who left Mexico to search for treasures in Central America, Maudslay, too, had traveled south with the sole intent of plundering the lintels of Yaxchilán. This act alone, not to mention the "200 boxes of antiquities" from Palenque that Batres claimed Maudslay had illegally exported to the British Museum, was reason enough for Mexico to "close its doors" to foreigners.[9]

In addition to the archaeological concessions, Batres was also in charge of reviewing the more general requests for permits to export antiquities. Like the concessions, the government granted these permits to representatives of museums abroad; it did not issue them to private individuals or for commercial purposes. Unlike the concessions, though, the assessment of these requests was much less formal. The government simply forwarded them to Batres, whose decisions were based on a sense of justice, a type of archaeological moral code. Batres claimed he approved only the petitions from institutions that had aided Mexican archaeology through research, publications, or service to the National Museum. When the English ambassador to Mexico asked to export some Zapotec statues to the British Museum, objects (unbeknownst to Batres) most likely gathered by Maudslay, Batres ruled against it. Not only were the artifacts "very important" to Mexico, the inspector pointed out to the Secretariat of Education, but the British Museum had never "provided even the smallest service to our nation in any sense of the word." To emphasize the selfish, grasping nature of the British, Batres brought up an incident involving Sir Weetman Pearson, the contractor who oversaw the drainage of the Valley of Mexico and built the railroad across the Isthmus of Tehuantepec, and who also owned the largest oil company in the country. According to Batres, Pearson had tried to make off with some antiquities and fossils discovered during the construction of the drainage canal, a violation of his agreement with Mexico, which prohibited the extraction of any bones or relics. This anecdote, however, failed to persuade the Secretariat of Education, which overruled Batres and allowed the British ambassador to export the Zapotec statues, an unusual move as Batres typically had the last word. (Perhaps the ambassador was simply too important to rebuff.) Although the inspector usually carried out his duties with the support of the Secretariat of Education, occasionally he was challenged and even forced to back down. Batres's mistrust of foreigners ran deep, and it eventually led to an ugly scandal, one that arose from his struggles with Marshall Saville.

Saville's contract with Mexico placed him at the head of the Loubat Archaeological Expedition, a mission to gather antiquities for the American Museum of Natural History that was financed by Joseph Florimond Loubat. Loubat, an American millionaire raised in France, was a patron of archaeology and philanthropist whose gifts to the Catholic Church were so generous that Pope Leo XIII dubbed him the "Duke of Loubat." Like other explorers, Saville believed he was doing Mexico a huge favor; his expedition would bring the country's "history to light," "open new horizons" of study, and earn the National Museum "great fame." Saville compared Mexico to other places (Persia, Turkey, and Egypt) that had opened their doors to foreigners, and his own country (the United States) to England and France, nations famous for sending explorers all over the world. Yet even though Saville was an emissary of a dominant power, he worried about his contract, especially the provisions regarding artifacts. While he had originally wanted to keep half of all the objects he found, he would have to adhere to the new ruling and settle for the duplicates, a clause, he maintained, that Batres had introduced into the law, although there is no proof for this claim. Saville feared his museum back home would be left with "nothing," but he took comfort in the fact that Batres, according to him, had promised to be lenient when determining which objects were duplicates. Nevertheless, even before setting foot in the ruins Saville worried about the inspector, "the only person" who could cause him "problems."[10]

And cause problems he did. Saville had intended to begin his expedition in the far southern site of Yaxchilán rather than Palenque. Batres, however, insisted that Yaxchilán was in Guatemala, a claim most likely made to deter Saville, as the inspector had included the site in Mexican territory in the archaeological map he had made more than a decade earlier. Saville agreed and went to Palenque only to find that Batres refused to take up lodging at the site. Batres often seemed more concerned with using his authority to obstruct Saville than to supervise him, and tellingly, he stayed in the nearby village and made only one or two trips to Palenque over the course of Saville's six weeks at the ruins. The two men also clashed over antiquities. Saville was on a mission to fill the brand-new Mexico Hall in the American Museum of Natural History, but Batres was determined to stop him. The American carried out what he called "sounding tests," probes to determine if the structures at Palenque were hollow; if they were, then that would suggest they contained underground chambers that might be full of relics.[11] But Batres consistently prevented Saville from going any further and excavating. (Saville, it turns out, had the right idea but the wrong pyramid. Years later, in 1952, the Mexican archaeologist Alberto Ruz Lhuillier would follow one of these chambers in the Temple of the Inscriptions to the tomb of Pakal the Great, the seventh-century Maya ruler decked out in an extraordinary death mask made of jade.) Defeated in Palenque, Saville moved on to the Valley of Oaxaca, his main battleground with Batres and the focus of his explorations during what amounted to five years of the Loubat Expedition.

That Saville hunted after antiquities did not make him an incompetent archaeologist, even though Batres characterized him as such. The American was actually a better scientist than Batres. A former student of anthropology under Frederick Putnam at Harvard and a future professor of archaeology at Columbia University, Saville used more rigorous methods for recording data. Both he and Batres carried out reconnaissance studies and surveys of sites. They walked through the ruins, examining, measuring, and taking note of the structures and their features. They documented their findings with diagrams, photos, and drawings, using written sources to engage with the work of earlier explorers.

Saville, however, was more methodical. He carried out the same procedures from one site to the next, leaving behind step-by-step accounts of his
explorations. Batres was much more idiosyncratic and inconsistent. His
studies of Mexico's ruins are organized by the topics that struck him as
important—hieroglyphics, mythology, and so on, and they are full of the
usual suspects, including Greeks, Egyptians, and even Buddhas, along with
Mount Olympus, Memphis, and Thebes. They also feature flowery, extrava-
gant prose ("Perhaps in the times during which these gigantic people flourished with such grandeur, they ascended to Mount Alban by broad stairs"),
along with mystical and existential passages ("The ideal of man is to go after
something more than what is found in this valley of tears" and to seek protection "in the struggle he sustains, from birth till death, against [the] natural enemies sorrounding [*sic*] him").[12]

But the biggest difference between the two men was their treatment of
context. Saville paid much more attention to detail, recording more information about the in situ location of objects. Unlike Batres, he catalogued and
gathered all the artifacts he discovered, not just the best ones or finest examples. And unlike Batres, Saville employed standardized field techniques,
dividing the ruins into grids to ensure a more thorough investigation. His
studies provide a much better sense of the layout of the ruins, to the point,
though, of exhausting even the most determined of readers, as this passage
about a temple in Mitla suggests:

> The upper part of the first doorway at the entrance is about 3.2 feet
> below the cement floor of the court. It is about 3.5 feet high, 2 feet
> long, and 2.75 feet broad. It leads into a small chamber of irregular
> shape (see ground-plan), about 5.4 feet in height, 3.3 feet in length,
> and 5.4 feet in width at the outer entrance and 7.5 feet at the inner
> end. In the center of this wall is a second doorway.[13]

One hardly wants to learn more about the next door! Yet even though
Saville was a more exacting archaeologist, both he and Batres shared one
thing in common: they focused on describing the ruins rather than trying to
reconstruct the past, doing relatively little to piece together how Mexico's
ancient people had actually lived.

That Saville carried out most of his work in Oaxaca with Batres in tow is
one of the reasons the Mexican government ended up paying so much attention to the ruins in that state. Saville claimed he went to Oaxaca on the

suggestion of Batres, advice most likely driven by the inspector's own desire to study the region. Mitla, the focus of Saville's explorations, was one of Batres's favorite sites: "To speak of Mitla," he would say, "is to speak of past grandeur."[14] Archaeologists at the time were unsure who had built the ruins; some, including Batres, proposed the Toltecs and others the Zapotecs. Saville, who at one point suggested it had been the Aztecs because the murals at the site were "Nahuan in character," went to Mitla in 1899 to find out.[15] He traveled in the company of his brother, Foster Saville, the only other member of his expedition apart from the fifty Indian workers he had hired. (His friend Mr. Humphries had fallen ill in Palenque and returned home.) Batres brought along his son Salvador, who was not yet assistant inspector. He took advantage of the occasion to engage in research of his own, something he was not supposed to do. Saville's contract prohibited other archaeologists from working in the area at the same time, but Batres, as inspector, must not have believed this clause applied to him. Batres also carried out several projects in Oaxaca during Saville's off-seasons, as the American worked in the state only during the winters. The inspector spent most of his time trying to reconstruct Mitla.

Mitla had become something of a national embarrassment, especially after the visit by the Congress of Americanists delegates a few years earlier, the trip that had originally sparked Saville's interest in the area. Although the aim of the congress had been to highlight Mexico's scientific credentials and magnificent ruins, the delegates arrived to find Mitla "abandoned and without surveillance." Not only was the conserje nowhere to be found, but the site was teetering on the brink of collapse. In response, the delegates wrote to President Díaz, informing him, "respectfully," of the importance of caring for Mexico's "archaeological riches," monuments famous throughout the world. Mitla, they claimed, attested to the "vigorous civilization of the Zapotec race," a "wise and enlightened" people.[16] Signed by the many delegates, including Saville, the letter spelled out the steps Díaz needed to take to protect the ruins: post a guard, protect the structures from decay, and build a fence around the site to prohibit access. Batres must have been mortified upon reading the letter, which was also published in the press. He quickly reacted by firing the guard, which led to the hiring of an even worse caretaker, the eighty-year-old, tip-hungry Vásquez. He also decided to gather the materials he needed to reconstruct the site, which he would not put into use until 1901, while on assignment with Saville.

Over the centuries, Mitla had suffered a series of remodelings. During the colonial period, officials had torn down several structures and replaced them with a Catholic church. The buildings left standing consisted mainly of palaces, rooms with murals and large windows overlooking square court-yards and covered in friezes or fretwork of elaborate geometric designs. These, too, had been altered. The windows had been filled in with bricks and the murals concealed under heavy coats of whitewash so as "to prevent the Indians from continuing their worship, etc., etc.," explained Batres about the remodeling.[17] One of Mitla's palaces was also transformed into the presby-tery, or house of the priest, along with a stable for his horses.

Batres worked to undo the remodeling. He extracted the bricks from the windows and somehow removed the whitewash. That was the easy part, com-pared to the task of trying to stop the monuments from falling to pieces. Not taking action would be "a terrible shame for the spirit of the civilized world," he declared.[18] Batres focused on propping up the structures; he installed heavy steel beams in the doorways and made retaining walls out of wooden planks, which he covered with a mixture of sand and cement, a type of waterproof sealant. While the use of these sorts of materials was standard practice, Batres's methods were questionable. To protect some of the murals, he covered them with thick panes of glass, a common technique at the time. To fasten the glass, though, he drove large metal bolts into the temple walls, leaving behind huge, gaping holes. Batres, however, claimed he worked with the goal of being as "faithful to the monuments" as possible, a statement he would repeat time and again. He rebuilt the steps near Mitla's Palace of the Columns, for instance, modeling them after the "primitive ones" still intact. Like most Mexican archaeologists of his day, he did not resort to any theo-retical models as he reassembled Mitla's dismembered parts. He simply went about his work as he saw fit.

There was more piecing together to be done as Batres turned to the friezes. The elaborate stonework had been "ravaged by the elements and human hands," yanked out by everyone, as he put it, "from the priest down to the last Indian of Mitla."[19] Batres carefully glued on the fallen pieces using calcium oxide or quicklime, a key ingredient in the making of cement. Over the years, "thieves" had also "stolen" chunks of stone from Mitla, leaving it pockmarked as if it had been pummeled by cannon fire. So Batres set off on a hunt for the missing stones, finding a total of 450, some large, others small. According to one present-day archaeologist, the search was more of a "military incursion," as the inspector entered the homes of the locals to seize the pieces of Mitla that had become part of their patios and kitchen walls. Batres downplayed the event. He failed to mention the use of force, explaining tersely that he retrieved the materials, "not without much effort, from the church, private homes, and corrals."[20] He then measured each hole on the palaces of Mitla and, as if he were doing a puzzle, found the exact piece of stone to insert. In order to show off Mitla's elaborate stonework, he also made several casts of the palaces, which were sent to Mexico City and set up in the patio of the National Museum.

Next, Batres focused on securing the site. In his zeal to keep out the "idle" folk who laid waste to the monuments, the inspector nearly turned Mitla into a fort. He asked the federal government for funds to build a wall around the ruins, following the suggestion made by the Congress of Americanists delegates years earlier. Batres also planned on installing iron bars on the doors of the palaces. Luckily, Ezequiel Chávez, an official in the Secretariat of Education, vetoed the idea, claiming it would "destroy the purity of the architectural style."[21] So instead, Batres put up an iron gate with a lock around the section of Mitla that he thought had the best stonework. To prevent anyone else from entertaining the idea of tampering with the monuments, he also embedded a plaque in one of the temples with a warning, which ironically did not teach by example:

> Warning: It is prohibited to write on the walls of these buildings, and also to scratch or soil the constructions or remove their stone. All violators of this regulation will be brought before the federal authorities and be penalized accordingly. The General Inspector and Curator of Archaeological Monuments: Leopoldo Batres.[22]

Batres also took on the difficult task of ousting the priest who lived at the site with his horses. Visitors often complained about the animals, troughs, and hay. But here, the inspector proceeded with caution. In order to avoid depriving the locals of their presbytery and causing them "harm," he asked the federal government for funds to build a new home for the clergyman near the ruins. For some reason, though, the construction project dragged on, allowing the priest to remain at Mitla for the rest of the Porfiriato. But Batres did manage to get rid of the stable, an act the priest seems to have fiercely protested. While the process took several more visits over the years, in 1907 the inspector was finally able to send the government this short but victorious telegram: "Destroyed the mangers, cleaned the patio, and secured door with a lock."[23] The key to this lock and to the one on the iron gate were placed in the custody of the conserje, who was responsible for allowing visitors into the sealed structures.

That Batres completed at least some of this work while watching over Saville means he did not give his supervising duties his full attention. In fact, the inspector often seemed more interested in promoting himself than in monitoring the American. At Mitla, he prevented Saville from excavating the Temple of the Columns and let his son Salvador, who had no archaeological experience, carry out the procedure. The elder Batres grew bored. Watching over Saville as he carefully sifted through the soil with his trowel was tedious. So he asked to borrow some of Saville's workers. Saville agreed, and Batres set off with five of the men on his own explorations, leaving his son in charge of Saville, something else he should not have done as inspector. Free to roam, Batres moved about constantly. He never "spent more than one day working in any site," he allegedly told Saville.[24] Soon, a group of structures in Mitla came to light. Batres initially credited Saville with the discoveries but then changed his story and claimed them as his own. "Fearful of becoming fatigued," he explained, "the American limited his work to the perimeter of the known buildings and, although it was not my exploration to carry out, I took advantage of some of Mr. Saville's resources [the workers] and . . . discovered the monuments that the American should have found and which I am sure he will present as his own in the next Congress of Americanists."[25] Eager to head off the publication of Saville's research, Batres prepared a book taking credit for most of the explorations. He promised Saville he would install a plaque at Mitla acknowledging the work of the Loubat Expedition but instead "had his own name carved on the lintel of the Temple of the Columns" calling attention, Saville complained, to his own restorations, "several of which are open to serious criticism."[26]

Saville went on to explore other ruins, including Monte Albán, where he carried out some minor excavations. Batres, in contrast, worked more extensively at the site, using Saville's "resources" at first and then hiring workers paid for by the Mexican government once funds had been released. Determined to tear off the "vale [sic] which for centuries had enveloped that mysterious city," Batres surveyed the ruins and unearthed several objects: temple walls, earthen heads, ceramic vases, findings of "greatest importance," he noted in his English-language text *Explorations of Mount Alban.*[27] The antiquities both he and Saville collected throughout their explorations in Oaxaca were shipped off to Mexico's National Museum, and although it is not clear how Saville's relics were divided up, the "duplicates," one assumes, eventually made their way to the American Museum of Natural History in New York City.

Throughout this entire period, Saville had been busy buying ethno-graphic objects from the local Indians, straight out of their homes. These too found their way back to the museum in New York, even though their collec-tion was not a part of Saville's contract. Unfazed, Batres did not mention the pieces to the federal government. Neither the Law of Archaeological Explorations nor the Law of Monuments protected these sorts of objects—it was only the stuff of the ancient Indians that mattered. Mexican law, then, reflected the elites' contrasting perceptions of the Indian past and present; it placed value on the ancient artifacts but ignored the objects made by the contemporary Indians. And the law also ignored human remains. Farther north in the country, around this same time, the government allowed Alës Hrdlicka, the famous Czech anthropologist and future curator of physical anthropology at the Smithsonian, to collect and export several skeletons. Hrdlicka's shipment was the result of a particularly gruesome find near Hermosillo, Sonora. In 1902, the Díaz regime, in order to expel the Yaqui Indians from their land, slaughtered 150 men, women, and children in a mas-sacre. Hrdlicka arrived fresh on the scene; he decapitated some of the decom-posing bodies (a practitioner of craniometry, he was after the skulls) and threw away the corpse of an infant attached to a headboard (he simply wanted the headboard). The skulls and other items, including blood-splattered blankets, were shipped to New York, to the same museum that commissioned Saville. There, they remained in storage for over a hundred years, until the Pascua Yaquis of Arizona successfully had them returned for burial.[28]

The tensions between Saville and Inspector Batres would finally come to a head at the Thirteenth Congress of Americanists that was held in New York City in 1902. Some of the biggest names in Mexican anthropology were there: Saville, Hrdlicka, Maudslay, Seler, Boas, and the Duke of Loubat. The Mexican government did not send Batres to head up its delegation, but his "mortal enemy" Chavero, the director of the National Museum at the time. Both Chavero and the Duke of Loubat were aware of the fact that Batres had used a few of Saville's men to undertake work at Monte Albán, and during one of the opening events, Chavero took the stage to give some of the credit for the excavations at the site to the Loubat expedition. Batres was stunned. The discoveries at Monte Albán were his, financed by the Mexican govern-ment and not the Loubat Expedition. Batres interrupted Chavero with an outburst only few in the audience understood. He demanded Chavero retract his statement, but Chavero refused. In crediting foreigners for

research carried out by Mexicans, Batres claimed, Chavero had stripped
Mexico of its scientific laurels, made the Mexican "government look completely ridiculous at an international conference," and made him, the
inspector of monuments, seem incompetent.[29] In truth, Batres had used
workers funded by both the Loubat Expedition *and* the Mexican government, and so it is possible that the most "important discoveries" were made
under the Mexican-paid employees. Later, several of the congress delegates
supposedly approached Batres in a show of support. A reporter from the
New York Herald even doubted Chavero's nationality, questioning whether
he was Mexican (was he actually Cuban?) since no citizen would have
insulted his own country in that way. When Chavero did not return to the
conference the next day, Batres could be heard boasting that the museum
director was hiding out of shame. More than just a clash of personalities,
the conflict between the two men was rooted in their differing approaches
to science. As an "enlightened nationalist" Chavero welcomed cooperation
with foreigners; as a "savage nationalist" Batres did not. Batres was wary of
anyone stealing the limelight from Mexico or, more accurately, stealing the
limelight from him. His actions were not simply those of a savage nationalist. While he couched his arguments as a defense of the Mexican nation and
its patrimony, as on so many other occasions, he seemed less driven by
patriotism than self-interest and an obsession with safeguarding his scientific credentials.

Soon, another incident took center stage when Batres brought up the
Monte Albán discoveries again, this time with the Duke of Loubat, the honorary president of the congress. A witness saw Batres "speaking firmly and
gesticulating with great excitement, becoming more intense by the minute,
even alarming all the bystanders."[30] Unruffled at first, the duke reproached
Batres for taking credit "for the work done by Saville and my Indians."[31]
Tensions escalated, and finally, when the duke could no longer take Batres's
ranting, he pounded his fist on the table—in a manner more American than
French, noted the *New York Sun*. Not one to retreat, Batres reacted with violence. "I punished that offense to Mexico," he said, "by lashing out at that
neurotic old man with my hand."[32] Batres was told to leave the conference,
"and his corpulent figure was not seen again," wrote one reporter. The
Mexican government immediately ordered him home. For the Mexican
press, it was not Chavero's statement but the "loud and ugly" "Batres incident" that had brought shame to the nation, in front of more than two hundred delegates from dozens of countries.[33] Years later, Batres would claim he

had heard Chavero gossiping about him during the conference, telling everyone he was "an ignorant nobody," a man who became inspector only because
President Díaz, in a moment of weakness, "had taken a liking to him."[34] The
incident also seems to have sparked a coup against Batres. Saville, most likely
joined by two of Batres's other rivals, Maudslay and Nuttall, led an effort to
have him fired and replaced with "someone less hostile" to foreign researchers, a plot that obviously failed.[35] When it came to hindering the work of
others, though, Batres was an equal opportunity obstructer. He did not discriminate on the basis of race or gender. Nor did he discriminate on the basis
of nationality. Batres was just as territorial with his fellow Mexicans, a problem that had surfaced years earlier as Mexico prepared to host the Congress
of Americanists in 1895.

Inspecting the Countrymen

Preparations for the event unleashed a flurry of activity. The National
Museum, the seat of the congress, underwent a complete renovation, as the
professors worked furiously to make improvements and enlarge the collections. They opened boxes of artifacts held in storage, set out pieces recently
returned from the Columbian Historical Exposition in Spain, and asked
politicians and antiquarians from all over Mexico to send the most "curious
objects" they could find.[36] They lined the museum walls with maps and
images of the ruins, set the monoliths on brand-new pedestals, and replaced
the institution's wooden shelving with modern cabinets made of iron and
glass, paying attention to every detail, down to the last label and thumb tack.

It was then, in preparation for the event, that they established the
Department of Anthropology and Ethnography, working quickly to fill it
with human remains. These included bones that Batres had fetched from the
Mexico City drainage project, along with eight full skeletons, several jaws,
forty "Indian teeth," and a mysterious "monstrous head."[37] The professors
installed the anthropology department upstairs, on the second floor, leaving
the archaeology collection on the lower level. They thus reinforced the gulf
they perceived between the Indian past and present in the layout of the
museum, a separation still found in the National Museum of Anthropology
today.[38] The professors also hung charts and paintings on the walls that documented the country's racial mixtures as well as a diagram comparing the
eye maladies of "Mexico with those of Europe."[39] They organized these and

all the other materials according to the latest "craniometric and craneoscopic studies," based on the methods of Hamy and Paul Broca, France's leading authority in anthropometrics—the methods, the professors emphasized, advocated by the Society of Anthropology of Paris.[40] They placed more ethnographic objects on display, along with tools of the Comanches and Tarahumara, photos of Indians, linguistic maps of the nation, more pictures and charts, and at least three mannequins that were most likely dressed up to represent certain groups of Indians. They gathered so many objects, and the museum got so full, that the government had to relocate the city's fire department to another building in order to grant the professors more space in the National Palace. Once finished, the professors were completely "fatigued." They had tried to give the institution a "certain dignity."[41] If it could not have "the luxury and décor of the museums of Europe," explained one of the men, then at least it would have "the cleanliness and decency that corresponds to our civilization and culture."[42]

In preparation for the congress, President Díaz also sponsored the exploration of Teotihuacán. He personally commissioned Antonio García Cubas, the nation's most important geographer, to map and study the site, supplying him with military engineers and soldiers to carry out excavations. Why he chose García Cubas is not clear, but Inspector Batres was especially busy at the time, caught up in a struggle over a statue in the state of Morelos. Batres, however, found out about García Cubas's project in the press. Affronted, he complained to the Secretariat of Education that the geographer lacked a concession to excavate as well as official supervision. This was, of course, a year before the passing of the Law of Archaeological Explorations, when procedures for these contracts were less standardized. The Secretariat of Education responded that the excavation had been based on a verbal agreement between President Díaz and García Cubas and sent Batres out to supervise the geographer at the ruins. Years later, reflecting back on the incident, Batres would accuse Díaz, a man he revered, of having "broken the law."[43] Even Mexico's supreme leader was not beyond the inspector's reproach.

But instead of supervising, Batres set out to stop the "delinquents."[44] He arrived to find soldiers digging in different parts of Teotihuacán, climbed to the top of the Pyramid of the Moon to get a better view of the work, and waited for García Cubas. When the geographer arrived, Batres confronted him, questioning the legality of his agreement with President Díaz. Meanwhile, federal officials, eager to complete the project, made some sort of more formal arrangement for García Cubas. The geographer ended up excavating part of the Pyramid of the Moon and discovering some murals on the east side of the Street of the Dead. But Batres's next visit to the ruins put an end to the explorations. The inspector accused García Cubas of hacking into "various monuments to see what was in them."[45] He telegraphed the president, asking him to withdraw the troops and suspend the excavations. Not to be outdone, he also made sure one of his own studies on Teotihuacán was published in the press. García Cubas's work would be of "no consequence to archaeology," Batres declared.[46] The Congress of Americanists went on as planned; the delegates from over twenty-three countries, including Mexico, presented their research in the National Museum. They then set off on a tour of Teotihuacán, where they lunched in the massive cave at the site to a show of "dancing Indians," before making their way south to Mitla.[47]

But of all the archaeologists, it was those of the National Museum, especially the museum students, who were most often subjected to Batres's tyrannical rule. Mexico's first attempt at producing professional archaeologists took place in the museum. In 1906, the institution opened its doors to teaching. It initially taught archaeology, ethnology, and history and then gradually expanded its offerings over the years to include courses in anthropology, anthropometry, Nahuatl, and prehistory. Students could take several courses but had to specialize in one or two fields. Most of these students were white, middle- or upper-class men in their early twenties. Many of them had scholarships from the museum or worked as assistants in the institution's departments. There were only nine students in 1906, but by 1910 there were more than fifty, including a handful of women. Even so, the museum failed to grant any degrees. Although most of the students went on to have successful careers, especially in the field of education, the museum's focus on teaching was short lived; it came to a halt in 1915 when classes were transferred to the National University. Several problems plagued the project, including the archaeology professors' lack of experience with fieldwork. By then, the museum had come to acknowledge the importance of fieldwork in the training of students. As Genaro García, the institution's director in the last years of the Porfiriato, explained, archaeologists "are formed in the field, in the places where there are monuments. . . . This is where the schools of archaeology exist."[48] Nevertheless, none of the professors of archaeology—Galindo y Villa (1906), José Juan Tablada (1907), and Ramón Mena (1907–1910)—carried out much research among the ruins. Not only was it something they rarely, if ever, practiced, but they were also completely overwhelmed by their many other duties, including publishing, teaching, and managing the archaeology collection.

Another problem was Batres. If the creation of the Inspectorate made Batres the nation's number-one fieldworker, relegating the professors to the confines of the museum, Batres was determined to make this a boundary the men could not cross. While some of his conflicts with the museum men were rooted in ideological differences, many, if not most, stemmed from his territorial nature. Even though the professors were technically allowed to carry out fieldwork, and the duties of both the Inspectorate and the museum overlapped, Batres often thwarted the professors and did so with the backing of the federal government. The institutional politics were such that the government usually sided with the inspector. Perhaps the officials in the Secretariat of Education who oversaw both institutions were simply more comfortable banking on Batres, since his agency had been established with the explicit purpose of tending to the more technical aspects of archaeology, like the excavation and reconstruction of monuments. Perhaps they had less faith in the abilities of the professors, who approached archaeology as an auxiliary science, a helpmate to the study of history. The federal government, moreover, might simply have been more comfortable relying on a single figure, an official archaeologist or czar. Perhaps it boiled down to the fact that Batres was a friend of Porfirio Díaz's. In any case, Batres obstructed the professors' field activities whenever he could, quite often with the support of the government. In 1905, he discovered that the museum planned to send Galindo y Villa to the state of Puebla to remove a "tombstone" from some pyramids. Although the professors did not need permission to excavate, nor official supervision, Batres intervened nonetheless. He claimed that the removal of the tombstone would destroy the monument, resulting in "a true crime." Batres ordered the Secretariat of Education to tell the professor that he should "stick to studying the monuments without excavating them," putting an end to the plan.[49] Ironically, however, Batres also acknowledged the importance of fieldwork; as he once declared, archaeology could only be mastered through "many years of practical experience in the field."[50] While the museum professors' lack of this sort of experience cannot be blamed solely on Batres, his meddling did not help matters.

As a result, Mexico's first archaeology students went on few excursions, most of which involved no fieldwork at all. A visit to the Tepozteco pyramid in 1907, most likely led by the poet Tablada, was reduced to "a simple Tourist outing, a mere day in the country," as the students studied nothing, complained museum director García.[51] Another trip led by Professor Mena, a lawyer turned archaeologist from the state of Veracruz, saw no excavations or even pre-Hispanic sites. The class visited the Corpus Christi church of Tlalnepantla in the state of Mexico, a colonial structure that contained a few blocks of hieroglyphic-covered stones. The students photographed, measured, and made molds of the stones, spending the rest of the time listening to Mena lecture on the cosmology of the Aztecs. Mena's curriculum in the museum similarly paid no attention to fieldwork. His archaeology class focused on Mexico's ancient peoples, beginning with the most "primitive" and tracing the "evolution" of various cultures until "arriving at the Aztecs."[52] It emphasized topics such as hieroglyphics, cosmology, and calendars and taught the students how to interpret monoliths, read codices, and detect phony pieces—a subject very much in vogue at the time. Justifying the lack of hands-on research at the ruins, Mena explained that his course would be carried out "with the monuments and artifacts in view, . . . preferably in the rooms of the archaeology department of the museum, and in due time, in the actual field."[53] Faced with the predicament of being stuck with the professors in the museum, some of the students dared to venture out into the ruins on their own, where they risked running into Batres.

One of these students was Porfirio Aguirre, an archaeology student who, unlike all the other museum students, had a dark complexion and indigenous features. In October 1910, Aguirre began exploring a site near Tenancingo in the Valley of Mexico, a project that was not financed by the museum. Instead, Aguirre acted as a free agent, hiring workers with his own funds, men from the area who whittled away at the ruins with pickaxes, a tool commonly used in excavations. The young student made no maps or plans of the site; his mission was to gather ancient objects for the museum. (The exploration of a site and the search for antiquities were often synonymous.) Aguirre uncovered many figurines, tools, and other items that were eventually shipped to the museum. Batres, however, found out about Aguirre's work in the press and, without delay, ordered the local officials to stop him. He complained that Aguirre had excavated without supervision or government authorization. This was true. Aguirre had failed to obtain permission to excavate from the federal government, most likely because he did not think it necessary since he was affiliated with the museum, where the archaeologists did not have to secure this sort of approval. As punishment, Batres suggested the museum revoke Aguirre's scholarship in archaeology, a career he "had begun poorly, considering he had infringed on the current regulations regarding the conservation of archaeological monuments, regulations he is supposed to know and respect."[54] Luckily for Aguirre, the suggestion went unheeded, and he continued his studies. He soon gained the attention of Eduard Seler, an honorary professor in Mexico's museum by that point, who invited him to continue his training in Germany, an offer, for some reason, that Aguirre refused. A few years later, Aguirre became an instant celebrity when he discovered a rare turquoise-and-coral mask in the state of Guerrero. He seemed to be destined for a brilliant career—until, that is, the professors began to notice that copies of codices kept disappearing off the shelves of the museum library. It did not take them long to figure out that Aguirre had been pilfering the texts and selling them to a bookstore in downtown Mexico City. He became known as "the thief" and was forgotten in the world of archaeology.

But Batres hounded another student who did go on to have a brilliant career, the legendary Manuel Gamio. Gamio was among the first group of students in the museum, trained by the same professors who considered archaeology a tool for the study of history and nursed on the same curriculum that would lead him to dub Mexico the "American Egypt."[55] In August 1908, while working as an assistant researcher in the history department, Gamio was comissioned by the museum to explore ruins in the state of Zacatecas. The museum director notified the Secretariat of Education about the project and sent Gamio on his way with 400 pesos in his pocket. For the next three months, Gamio excavated the site of Chalchihuites with the care and "diligence of an old archaeologist," wrote the press.[56] It was a spectacular find. Gamio discovered several structures, "monuments never before seen," he exclaimed.[57] The museum reaped the benefits, filling its galleries with hundreds of artifacts, including several beautiful amphorae that looked just like "those of the Etruscans," one journalist made sure to note.[58]

But Gamio did not celebrate for long. Batres, again, found out about his work in the press and ordered the governor of Zacatecas to stop him. For some reason, the Secretariat of Education had failed to notify the inspector about the excavation, most likely because it did not think it had to since Gamio was acting on behalf of the museum. Batres complained that the excavation had gone unsupervised and that the local people had seen Gamio "destroying" the monuments. He characterized the excavation as a threat, "a dangerous attack. . . . I say attack because relics of great importance are being allowed to fall into the inexperienced hands of an amateur, a common archaeology student, who for his lack of knowledge, will let details be destroyed . . . and lost forever." It was a "crime" against the ancient peoples who had built the ruins, one that needed to be stopped "for the sake of civilization."[59]

Batres, no doubt, had already begun to feel threatened by Gamio, who was fast becoming a celebrity in the world of archaeology. While some have claimed that the inspector's actions were justified, since Gamio's lack of experience might have led to the destruction of the ruins, Gamio would prove to be a more skilled archaeologist than Batres, becoming a pioneer in stratigraphic excavation within a few short years. Even his research at Chalchihuites was more "scientific" than Batres's. In contrast to the inspector's haphazard reports, Gamio's study of the site offers a detailed description of the monuments, moving from one building to the next, noting the measurements and characteristics of the structures. It catalogues and describes the artifacts, keeping track of all the materials, even mundane ones like *comales* (earthenware griddles for the making of tortillas). It uses this data to speculate on the lives of the ancient people, noting, for instance, that the existence of so many fortifications at the site must mean the inhabitants lived in a state of "constant alert."[60] Gamio also seems to have worked with caution. To keep his workers from damaging the ruins as they hauled off the overburden—archaeology talk for soil and debris—he placed wooden planks on the ground for the carts to roll on, preventing them from making direct contact with the soil. While Chalchihuites may not have been a methodologically rigorous excavation, there was a thoroughness and control to the way Gamio went about his research.

Soon after, Gamio was introduced to Franz Boas, the so-called father of modern anthropology. Boas was head of the anthropology department at Columbia University, which offered the first PhD program in anthropology in the United States. He was looking for a Mexican student to mentor when his friend Zelia Nuttall suggested Gamio. Gamio set off to Columbia in 1909, where he eventually received a PhD, making him the first Mexican to earn a doctorate in anthropology. It was then, in 1911 at the urging of Boas, that Gamio carried out his stratigraphic work at Atzcapotzalco in Mexico City in the midst of the revolution. The excavation technique allowed him to document the succession of cultures—Archaic, Teotihuacán, and Aztec—in the Valley of Mexico, a groundbreaking find that proved the native peoples of central Mexico had evolved from simpler to more sophisticated cultures. But Gamio's interests soon began to shift toward ethnography. The Mexican revolution had given rise to an indigenismo more focused on the well-being of the contemporary Indians, a concern championed by Gamio, who believed anthropology could help integrate the Indians into the nation and unite "all Mexicans into one culture."[61] Gamio went on to publish his famous study,

The Population of the Valley of Mexico (1922), a work that draws on several disciplines to examine the indigenous past and present in central Mexico. As a result of his innovative research and his significant contributions to indigenismo and government policies, the former student in the National Museum went down in history as nothing less than the "father" of Mexican anthropology.

By contrast, history did not prove kind to Batres. He was remembered not only as a trafficker in antiquities—a traitor to his country, in other words— but as a tyrant: a man, according to Nuttall, who "discouraged all scientific archaeological research" and drove away foreign patrons and researchers like the Duke of Loubat and even his "own countrymen, Señor del Paso y Troncoso, . . . Señores Manuel Gamio and Ramon Mena, and many others."[62] Nuttall poked fun at Batres's "reign of terror" in a critique meant to mimic the voice of the inspector:

> I am Mexico's discoverer of monuments and it shall have no other but me. For I, in my person, unite many and diverse attributes[;] I am like the gods of the Indian triad, the Conservator and the Preserver; the Destroyer and the Reconstructor; the Explorer and the Exploiter; the Inspector and the Un-inspected; the Gatherer and the Distributor of all that is sacred and ancient in the land. My power extends from Ocean to Ocean, yea, unto the little islands and the fate of all ruins rests in my hands.[63]

Batres is also remembered as a disastrous archaeologist, one who destroyed more than he restored; he "altered" many sites, charged Gamio, and was oblivious of "all technique and serious methods of study," claimed the later archaeologist Ignacio Bernal.[64] Even during his tenure as inspector of monuments, Batres faced constant criticism. As one journalist declared, everyone was aware of the damage the inspector had "done to the science of archaeology through his actions, his ignorance, and his audacity which is that of an improvised savant."[65]

One of the great ironies of Mexico's archaeological project, then, was that the man in charge of supervising the work of others, an official who approached his task as a zero-sum game with room for only one archaeologist, was not necessarily the most qualified man for the job. Contemporary archaeologists such as Eduardo Matos Moctezuma have pitted Batres (the incompetent) against Gamio (the expert), portraying them as two sides of "the same coin."[66] Yet this comparison is not entirely fair, as Gamio belonged to a later generation, one that saw archaeology become a much more professional science with standardized practices. It is a mistake to search for an expert in Batres. Meticulous research was simply not the contribution he would make.

Was Batres good for Mexican archaeology? Yes and no. While his technical skills were often dubious, and he obstructed the work of others and may have even trafficked in antiquities, Batres worked tirelessly to spur the federal government into taking control of the nation's ruins. For all his failings, he played a crucial role in the creation of Mexico's ancient patrimony, in promoting the government's support of archaeology, and in forging the Inspectorate, the first agency in charge of turning the ruins into federal property and one whose creation marked a turning point in Mexican archaeology. For better or for worse, Batres laid down the institutional framework within which the state would take possession of the ruins and future archaeologists like Gamio, Bernal, and Matos Moctezuma would carry out their research. Much like Gamio, then, Batres, too, was a "pioneer."[67]

But Batres had one more trick up his sleeve, another way for the state to take charge of the ruins. He was an avid promoter of the idea that every artifact, every vase and amulet, should be transferred to the nation's capital. He considered this measure urgent, "the first step" toward ensuring the conservation of these objects, as the government turned to the task of centralizing the pre-Hispanic remains in the National Museum, Mexico's most important showcase and warehouse for the ancient objects.[68]

Figure 1. Teotihuacán's famous forgers, the Barrios brothers, pose with molds used to make masks and other items. One of the souvenir busts of Porfirio Díaz they also produced can be seen in the top of the display, second from the left (Batres, *Antigüedades mejicanas falsificadas*, plate 5).

DÉSIRÉ CHARNAY.

Figure 2. Désiré Charnay, French explorer and pioneer in photography. Etching by
E. Ronjat, after a photograph (Charnay, *Les anciennes villes du Nouveau Monde,*
front matter).

Figure 3. Edward Thompson's assistants dredge the Sacred Cenote of Chichén Itzá (photograph courtesy of the Peabody Museum of Archaeology and Ethnology, Harvard University, PM# 2004.24.3354.1, digital file #98470027).

Figure 4. Porfirio Díaz poses with the Aztec Calendar in the National Museum, 1910 (photograph courtesy of INAH). The plaque under the calendar focuses on the history of the object's location rather than its meaning, explaining that "in December of the year 1790 while the new pavement was being installed in the Plaza Mayor in this capital, this monument was discovered and then hung at the foot of the west tower of the cathedral on its west-facing side and from there it was transferred to the museum in August 1885."

Figure 5. Alfredo Chavero, historian, archaeologist, politician, and "mortal enemy" of Leopoldo Batres (Iguíniz, *Las publicaciones del Museo Nacional de Arqueología, Historia y Etnología*, 13).

Figure 6. (opposite page) Before it became a museum piece, the Aztec Calendar adorned Mexico City's Zócalo, the main plaza, embedded in a wall of the cathedral. In this interesting image, Mexicans of different ages, races, genders, and class share the same space, united under this iconic Aztec symbol (Rivera Cambas, *México pintoresco*, Vol. 1, facing page 507; photograph courtesy of *Arqueología Mexicana*, Raíces).

Figure 7. (*left*) Leopoldo Batres, inspector of monuments,
in the early twentieth century (Batres, *Visita a los monumentos
arqueológicos de "La Quemada," Zacatecas*, 3).

Figure 8. (*right*) American archaeologist Marshall Saville, 1914
(photograph courtesy of Explorers Club Research Collections, New York).

Figure 9. (*opposite page*) "An example of one of the races that currently inhabits the
ruins of Teotihuacán compared to the types of idols found at the same site (Toltec
race, Batres classification)" (Batres, *Teotihuacán; ó, La ciudad sagrada de los Toltecas*,
1889 ed., plate 9). Batres was interested in what the pre-Hispanic peoples must have
looked like. In this page from a study on Teotihuacán, one of his few and cursory
attempts at anthropometrics, the inspector compares the contemporary inhabitants
of the site to the faces found on the monuments (the Goddess of Water, in this case).
He inaccurately describes Teotihuacán's modern and ancient peoples as Toltecs.
Batres does not explain the significance of the measurements on the woman's head
but states that the Toltecs were characterized by "broad faces and flat noses,"
features he sees in both the locals and the goddess (Batres, *Teotihuacán; ó,
La ciudad sagrada de los Toltecas*, 1889 ed., 17).

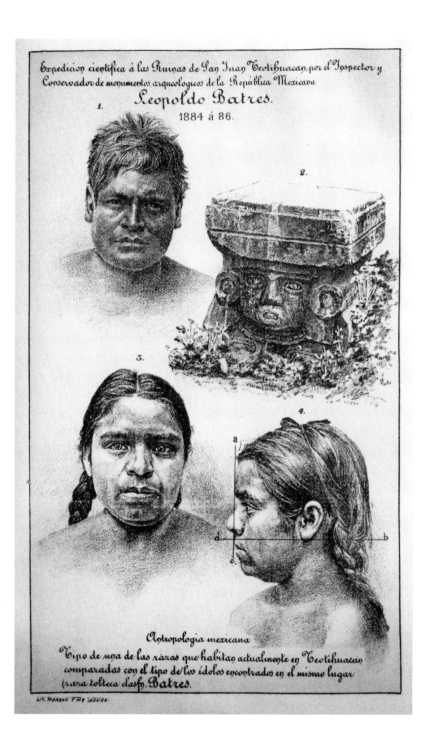

Expedicion científica á las Ruinas de San Juan Teotihuacan, por el Inspector y Conservador de monumentos arqueologicos de la República Mexicana

Leopoldo Batres.

1884 á 86.

Antropologia mexicana

Tipo de una de las razas que habitan actualmente en Teotihuacan comparadas con el tipo de los ídolos encontrados en el mismo lugar (rara tolteca clasf). Batres.

LIT. MORENO Y HO MEXICO.

143

Figure 10. Manuel Gamio, Mexico's "father" of anthropology, in the early twentieth century. (Iguíniz, *Las publicaciones del Museo Nacional de Arqueología, Historia y Etnología*, 44).

Figure 11. A man takes a break atop the Goddess of Water, Chalchiuhtlicue, in the ruins of Teotihuacán (Chabrand, *De Barcelonnette au Mexique*, facing page 324; photograph courtesy of *Arqueología Mexicana*, Raíces).

Figure 12. Workers, soldiers, and mules haul the Goddess of Water during an early stage in its move from the ruins to the National Museum (Batres, *Teotihuacán; ó, La ciudad sagrada de los Tolteca*, 1906 ed., 18).

Figure 13. The Gallery of Monoliths in Mexico's National Museum in the early twentieth century in a photograph by Alfred Saint-Ange Briquet (1833–1910?) archived at AHMNA. The Aztec Calendar hangs at the heart of the institution, the first piece visitors would have seen upon entering the museum and archaeology department. Hidden in the institution until the Porfiriato, the earth goddess Coatlicue also figures prominently in the background (photograph courtesy of *Arqueología Mexicana*, Raíces).

Figure 14. The Ahuítzotl glyph. Originally part of the Tepozteco ruins, the artifact represents Ahuítzotl, the eighth Aztec ruler, as a mythical otter-like animal. It is housed in the Mexica Room in the National Museum of Anthropology (photograph by Marco Antonio Pacheco; courtesy of *Arqueología Mexicana*, Raíces).

Figure 15. La India of Xochicalco, a monolith cherished by the locals
(Peñafiel, *Monumentos del arte mexicano antiguo*, 3:201).

Figure 16. José María Velasco's *Pyramid of the Sun*, 1878. Painted in warm and earthy hues, the image depicts Teotihuacán before its reconstruction. The pyramid looked like a gigantic hill. The rest of the ceremonial center served as farmland for the local inhabitants.

Figure 17. Reconstructing Teotihuacán's Pyramid of the Sun for the centennial celebration. Workers remove soil in ore carts set on tracks while Batres sits astride a horse, supervising the labor, in a photograph archived in INAH (photograph courtesy of *Arqueología Mexicana*, Raíces).

Figure 18. Batres's family and secretary in their home away from home in Xochicalco. The dwelling is outfitted with cups and other items from the inspector's home in Mexico City. Batres also had a daughter who is not pictured here (photograph courtesy of Elvira Pruneda Gallegos, Acervo Leopoldo Batres).

Figure 19. A conserje at Teotihuacán dressed in uniform for the centennial. The glare on the guard's chest is due to his metal badge (photograph courtesy of Elvira Pruneda Gallegos, Acervo Leopoldo Batres).

Figure 20. The historical parade during the centennial celebration, September 1910. Indians dressed as Aztecs carry Moctezuma on a litter as they reenact the momentous encounter between the Aztec emperor and the conqueror Cortés (de la Puente, *Album oficial del Comité Nacional del Comercio*; photograph courtesy of *Arqueología Mexicana*, Raíces).

Figure 21. Porfirio Díaz poses with the Cross of Palenque in the museum, a symbol of his regime's newfound (but feeble) control over Maya territory (photograph courtesy of INAH).

Figure 22. Centennial guests and members of the Congress of Americanists in front of the freshly reconstructed Pyramid of the Sun, September 1910, in a photograph published in the newspaper *El Imparcial.* Justo Sierra, the secretary of education, stands in the very center of the first row with his cane. Batres, also with a cane, is the second man to Sierra's right (photograph courtesy of *Arqueología Mexicana*, Raíces).

Figure 23. Batres in his later years (INAH; photograph courtesy of *Arqueología Mexicana*, Raíces).

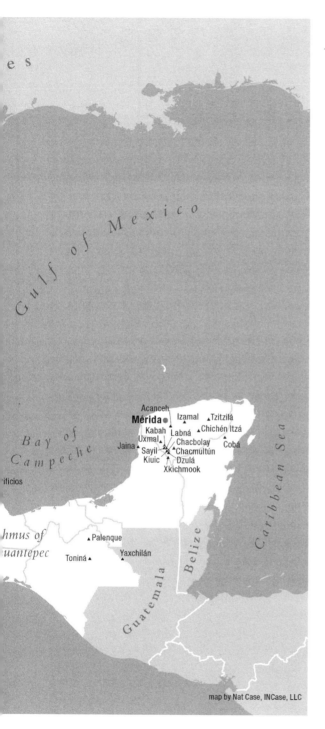

Map 1. Ancient sites during Mexico's first golden age of archaeology.

map by Nat Case, INCase, LLC

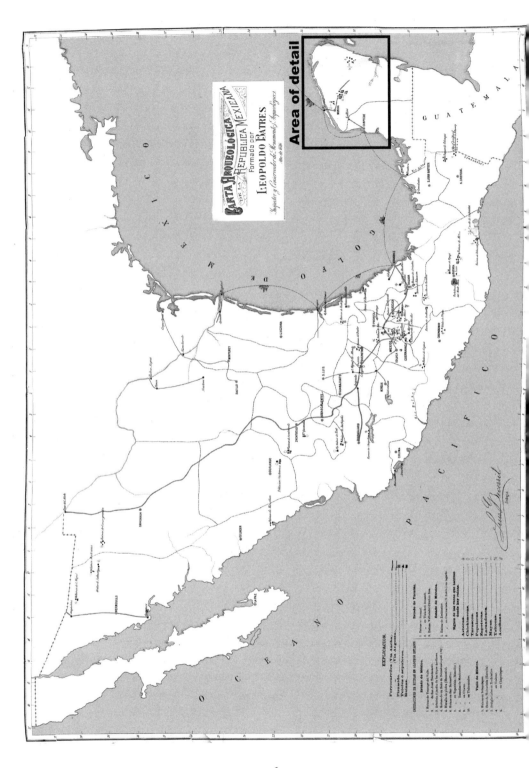

Area of detail

CARTA ARQUEOLOGICA
DE LA REPUBLICA MEXICANA
formada por
LEOPOLDO BATRES
Inspector y Conservador de Monumentos Arqueológicos
Año de 1896

GUATEMALA

GOLFO DE

MEXICO

OCEANO

PACIFICO

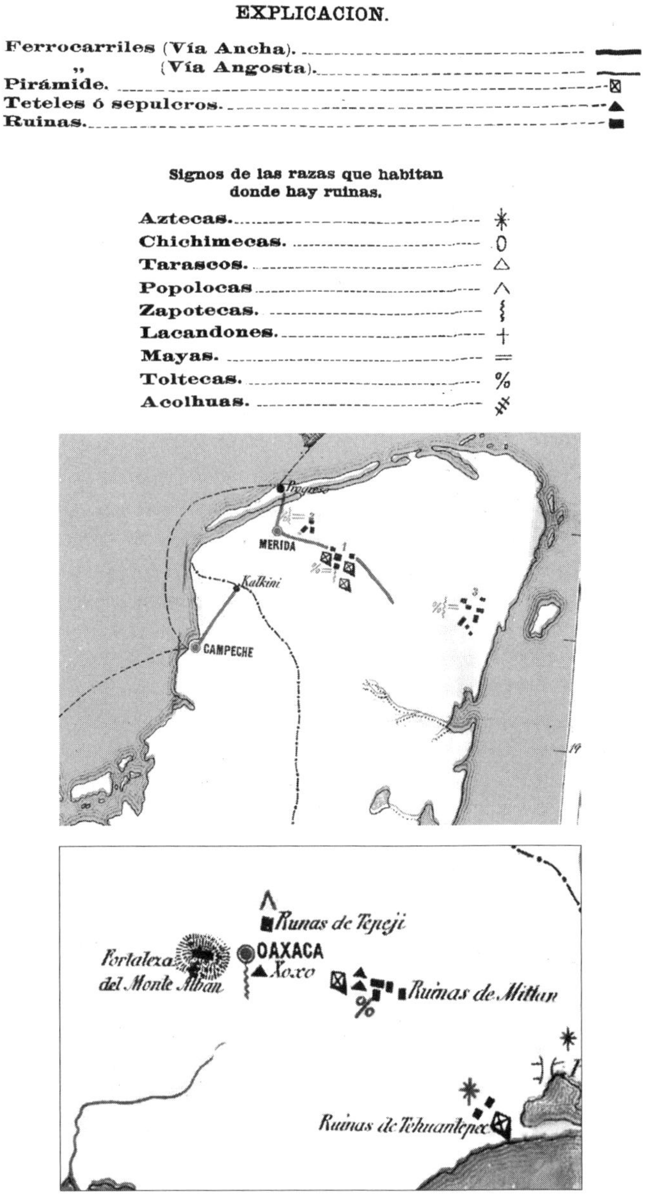

Map 2. *Archaeological Map of the Republic of Mexico* by Leopoldo Batres, 1886 (70 cm x 59 cm). Painted in the colors of the Mexican flag, with green oceans and red railway lines, Batres's curious map contains few sites; only three dot the Yucatán. It is also an ethnographic account of the nation, as the symbols stand for the contemporary "races" at the ruins rather than the ancient cultures. Many of these modern "races" are out of place, like the Toltecs—a civilization no longer in existence— whom Batres records as living in the Yucatán alongside the Maya.

161

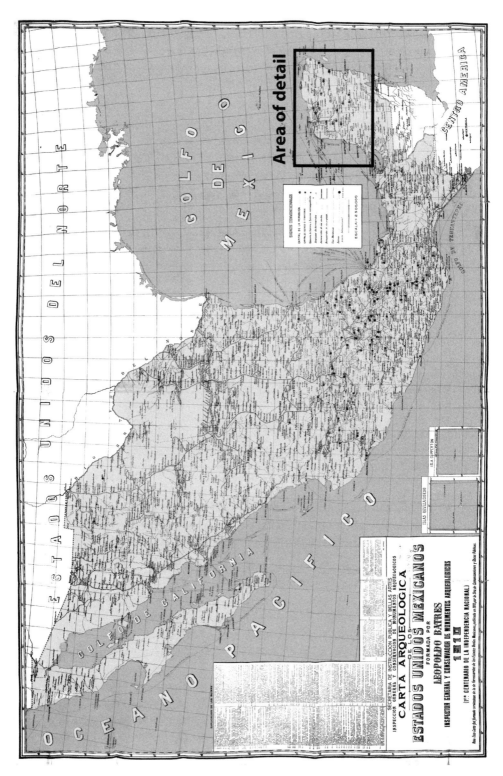

Area of detail

GOLFO DE MEXICO

ESTADOS UNIDOS DEL NORTE

GOLFO DE CALIFORNIA

OCEANO PACIFICO

CENTRO AMERICA

SECRETARIA DE INSTRUCCION PUBLICA Y BELLAS ARTES
INSPECCION GENERAL Y CONSERVACION DE MONUMENTOS ARQUEOLOGICOS

CARTA ARQUEOLOGICA
DE LOS
ESTADOS UNIDOS MEXICANOS
FORMADA POR
LEOPOLDO BATRES
INSPECTOR GENERAL Y CONSERVADOR DE MONUMENTOS ARQUEOLOGICOS
1910
(1er CENTENARIO DE LA INDEPENDENCIA NACIONAL)

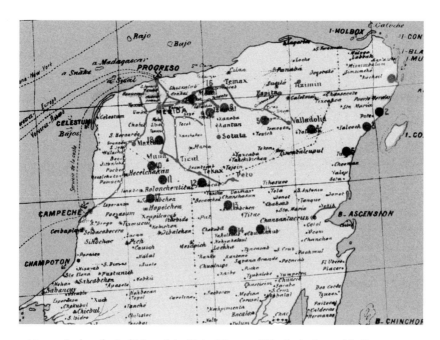

Map 3. Archaeological Map of the United States of Mexico by Leopoldo Batres, 1910 (96cm x 138cm). Batres's second archaeological map—also crafted in Mexico's national colors—has a more professional appearance than his first. It documents twice as many ancient sites and avoids any reference to the contemporary Indians.

CHAPTER SEVEN

Centralizing

⤲

ϟ IN OCTOBER 1889, BATRES SET OUT TO HAUL THE SIXTEEN-TON Goddess of Water from Teotihuacán to the National Museum. For centuries, she had been half-buried at the ruins, her head used, quite often, as a picnic table by visitors. On the day that Batres began to drag her away, the local residents gathered and shouted, "You cannot take our goddess!" The women wept and threw bouquets of yellow flowers at her feet. Batres left a sparse account of the event, but he did record that the locals were "angry" and that they chanted, "The goddess will not allow herself to be moved because she is tied to the ground with unbreakable chains." He feared they would dynamite her rather than part with her, so he placed guards on watch. The inspector spent the next two months loading the massive goddess onto what he called "the mythic carriage," an enormous cart with cables and pulleys harnessed to dozens of mules in front for traction and oxen on the sides to keep the whole contraption steady. Once loaded, the animals tugged, but the goddess would not budge. The locals roared with laughter. "Full of joy and pulque," wrote Batres, "they celebrated the failure."[1]

With the help of some sort of unspecified "mechanical" aid, Batres got the cart to roll, but it soon began falling apart, its wheels breaking under the goddess's immense weight. This led the inspector to replace the two front wheels with greased metal beams. He then put a section of train track on the ground and drew the cart along it. Once the cart reached the end of the section of track, he lifted the track and placed it in front of the cart, and the process was repeated. This is how the goddess moved from Teotihuacán to the Mexican Railroad line that was just a little over a mile away. She then traveled by train to the Buena Vista station in the nation's capital. From there, she resumed her sliding and rolling on the portable piece of track through the streets of Mexico City, moving at a snail's pace of some two hundred yards a day, giving plenty of people a chance to see her. From beginning to end, this grueling journey lasted five months. It was a difficult and dangerous process (at one point a cable snapped, crippling two workers) that remarkably cost only 300 pesos, as the government relied on the manpower of the Mexican military and free supplies from the railroads, the typical aid in these sorts of procedures. And the goddess was not alone; artifacts from all over the country were streaming into the National Museum during the age of Díaz.

Onlookers gossiped about the goddess and her meaning as she made her way to the museum. A rumor spread that she would rid the city of influenza. She became a pop icon, too. A *pulquería* took her name and so did a brand of cigarettes. Her image and "Aztec" facts were printed on the cigarette package, allowing the common people, mentioned one journalist, to assimilate "a bit of Ancient History."[2] The goddess also confounded Mexico's scholars. A debate broke out. Who was she, really? President Díaz decided to call on his wise men "to make the people's opinion uniform about the goddess."[3] He asked Batres and his enemy Chavero to form a committee, and although what became of it is not clear, its purpose was to determine the goddess's "true meaning," an apt turn of phrase, as this was, at heart, a battle over meaning. The government was making national patrimony out of objects that had other uses and meanings.

Ordinary Mexicans aided the state in its struggle to concentrate ancient objects in the capital, as the story of the Goddess of Water suggests. They not only hauled but also donated and sold artifacts to the museum. But others resisted, as the story of the goddess also makes clear. It was here, in the state's effort to take possession of Mexico's antiquities, that the different meanings of the objects came to the fore, that the making of patrimony became "a space of material and symbolic struggle," that the authoritarian, anti-Indian streak embedded in the nation's archaeological project surfaced most intensely, as the government clashed with communities that fought to keep objects important to their identities and histories.[4] Native peoples have long struggled to create their own narratives of the past, but their histories are typically dismissed as illegitimate. The official meaning assigned to ancient objects is often the only one considered valid. This was the case during the

Porfiriato, even though, as we have seen, the official history that the elites created was a selective retelling of the past, constructed for a nation that remained far from unified and pieced together by a tenuous science. The transfer of artifacts to the museum, then, allows us to question the entire nature of the state's claim to the archaeological patrimony. It allows us to ask to whom these objects belong.

As the main showcase of the objects, Mexico's National Museum played a key role in the elites' effort to build the nation. It was the most important setting for the display of Mexico as a country with deep, prestigious roots, a space where the elite version of the past—the official history—was made visible. The museum offered visitors a glimpse of the country's ancient splendor and taught Mexicans, in particular, that they shared a common national history stretching back to remote times. But there were other reasons for filling the museum with relics. Housing them there supposedly helped archaeologists, both Mexican and foreign, study the country's pre-Hispanic cultures by gathering them in one accessible spot. It helped state agencies prepare for events at which antiquities were displayed, like the Congress of Americanists held in Mexico and the world's fairs abroad. Much like the network of guards and other aspects of Mexico's archeological project, the transfer of artifacts to the capital also reflected the political centralization under way at this time, the government's effort to extend its control over the national territory. Yet if the system of guards was meant to give the state a presence in numerous sites across Mexico's vast terrain, the construction of the museum's archaeology collection had the opposite effect, drawing relics into the political center of the country and concentrating them in the institution that was thought to be the legitimate keeper of the past.

In the words of one museum professor, it brought the objects out of "isolated" pueblos and into the central showcase of the ancient past, and into a city that was being rapidly transformed into the showcase of the nation.[5] Under Díaz, Mexico City became the focus of the elite's fixation with presenting the nation as sophisticated and modern. It became a city of cable cars, paved streets, and boulevards. The antiquities were integrated into this modern setting. García Canclini has shown how the modernist design of the National Museum of Anthropology today similarly gives a contemporary treatment to Mexico's ancient patrimony. In this way, it suggests a "continuity between the past and present" and legitimizes the past as the basis of the modern nation.[6] During the Porfiriato, this modern context was supplied not only by the museum—a center of science and thus a place of modernity—but also by the capital itself. Mexico City was also being beautified, and antiquity was becoming part of the décor; the government propped up the Cuauhtémoc statue, for instance, on the newly renovated Reforma Avenue. Artifacts were like adornments, albeit housed within the museum. No one would express this more clearly than Batres, who advocated that they be brought to Mexico City to "decorate the capital."[7]

Before this time, the objects had merely trickled into the museum, leaving an archaeology collection that one observer described as "poor."[8] The Díaz regime changed this. It focused on building the collection, turning the museum into a warehouse of the ancient past. It set in motion the process that left us with the gigantic National Museum of Anthropology of today, a place so packed with artifacts people often complain that "'you can't see everything in just one visit.'"[9] Surprisingly, the effort unleashed under Díaz involved no grand innovations. The government relied on mechanisms for centralizing the artifacts that had existed since the birth of the museum, merely increasing the level of money, manpower, and support, and making what had been a sporadic, piecemeal process more systematic.

Artifacts arrived at the museum in a variety of ways, quite often as donations. Some of the most frequent donors happened to be state officials, like the general Riva Palacio, who made "significant" contributions to the archaeology collection while serving as secretary of development. Mexican newspapers and the government-sponsored *El Diario Oficial* lauded the donors. So did the museum professors: in letters that strung together words like "nation," "progress," "science," and "enlightenment," they thanked donors for "furthering the progress of science in Mexico."[10]

But museum records are also full of cases of donors without official ties. How did they know to bring the objects to the museum in the first place? One source of information was the Law of Monuments. Another source was the earlier decrees, the rulings issued throughout the nineteenth century ordering local authorities to remit any artifacts they came across to the capital. The museum also circulated its own directives, telling governors in 1840 to "collect antiquities from their departments and send them to the Museum."[11] That this information spread beyond the authorities is borne out by the many donations to the museum. In 1891, for instance, an engineer named Roberto Gayol sent a relic he had uncovered while constructing a building in Mexico City. Engineers and others who had direct contact with the soil frequently made these discoveries. There were also simply more discoveries being made, as the modern infrastructure laid down at this time, the sewers and ports, brought antiquities to light. The donors gave the objects to the museum out of a sense that they were national property or sometimes as a type of gift for President Díaz. Such was the case with José Santos Pardo, who wanted to send an "idol" from La Venta, Tabasco, to the "honorable Mr. President of the Republic, in appreciation for the peace that he has forged, which has brought us so much good and progress."[12]

Others chose to sell the antiquities to the museum instead. Some sellers were illiterate and could barely scrawl the letter "X" on their receipts, forcing the professors to add the words "because he does not know how to sign his name" in explanation. Many also made repeated sales, like a man named Juan Francisco who in February 1879 paid several visits to the museum to peddle what he called his "hancient potts to decorate the establishment."[13] Juan Francisco returned two months later and again at least four more times over the course of the year, selling close to 150 objects. It would be a mistake, though, to assume that he and other sellers were motivated purely by economic gain, since many of them could have done business with antiquities traffickers instead. Juan Francisco's pieces, in fact, were all from Teotihuacán, a site notoriously frequented by collectors. Did nationalist sentiment move him and others to sell the objects to the museum? Unfortunately, here the institution's records are mute. Juan Francisco most likely found out about the museum and its desire for antiquities through one of its professors, Jesús Sánchez, the zoologist and dabbler in archaeology. Sánchez had recently visited Teotihuacán to investigate reports that the locals were "extracting objects from the pyramids." He gathered several artifacts from the residents and from the municipal president, an "enlightened person who knows the importance of our historical monuments."[14]

More prosperous individuals also sold artifacts, a last resort for those who faced tough financial times, according to the journalist known as "Tick Tack": "Families who find themselves 'in a bad situation,'" he wrote, "get rid of the coach first; then sell the peacock; soon the birds, . . . the music box, cigar box, the silverware (in batches), the dishes, bedspread, jewels, . . . the small dog of Puebla or Chihuahua." Last on this list, after the yappy Chihuahua, came the "relics of the past," objects that were "curious because of their age, the level of civilization reached by the primitive people who had owned them, or for a multitude of other reasons."[15] The museum's bigger budget under Díaz allowed for more of these types of purchases, which came to include the collections of antiquarians such as Francisco Plancarte y Navarrete and José Dorenberg.

Collections like these were a goldmine, but they were also expensive. In 1898, the museum paid 5,000 pesos for Plancarte's assortment of over three thousand pieces, a purchase that consumed more than a fifth of its yearly budget.[16] The professors rushed to buy these collections not only because they wanted to build the museum but also because they feared the objects would end up abroad. At least one antiquarian played on this fear. In 1904, Honorato Carrasco put his nearly four-thousand-piece collection on the market, made up of artifacts he had accumulated over the course of fourteen years in the state of Puebla. Carrasco found an eager buyer in Eduard Seler. Trying to get the best deal, he presented the museum professors with a letter in which Seler claimed he wanted to purchase the collection "for the German government."[17] Although neither of the sales went through, Seler did acquire some of Carrasco's artifacts for the Ethnological Museum of Berlin.

But the museum professors did not just wait around for sellers and donors to send them artifacts—they actively demanded pieces. Mexicans were constantly discovering relics, which they publicized in the press and in letters to the museum. Sometimes, the professors or a museum assistant set out to retrieve the object, calling on the aid of the military and other government agencies, especially the Secretariat of Development, if the artifact was too heavy to move. More often, though, they exacted a type of archaeological tribute. They coaxed the discoverer into sending the piece by making appeals, once again, to the individual's patriotism and love of science and progress. In exchange, the federal government paid the shipping charges. More common still, the professors called on a local authority to send the piece, in which case, the authority usually complied. In fact, local officials were some of the most frequent contributors to the museum. One case in point was Veracruz governor Teodoro Dehesa, who sent the museum a 1,500-pound "monolith" in 1893. Dehesa wanted the monument to be installed next to the Aztec Calendar, where he thought it would "appear favorably."[18] With one stone, the governor hoped to link his state to the nation's center of power and to what happened to be the most showcased item in the museum. His donation also helped improve his own image; he was praised in the press and in a plaque that hung next to his donation.

At least one of the governors who donated artifacts identified himself as Indian. Próspero Cahuantzi, the governor of Tlaxcala, supplied the museum with relics—which later became a part of the institution's collection—for display at the 1895 Congress of Americanists. He also contributed antiquities from his state to several world's fairs. But Cahuantzi was not just a mere donor. He actively participated in the government effort to construct an ancient past. As Jaclyn Sumner has shown, the indigenous governor attended international events, including the Congress of Americanists and world's fairs. When Mexico held the congress in 1895, Cahuantzi became the head of the committee that was in charge of gathering antiquities from all over the country. He also attended the event, where he made several comments in Nahuatl and gave a speech about the importance of studying archaeological monuments. In donating artifacts and contributing to the Porfirian archaeological effort, Cahuantzi stayed "in the good graces" of Mexico's political elites.[19] He also brought the history of his tiny state of Tlaxcala to national and international attention.

At the same time, however, provincial museums throughout the country were also searching for antiquities, objects they considered part of their regional patrimony. Museums with archaeology collections could be found in Yucatán, Oaxaca, Michoacán, Colima, and San Luis Potosí.[20] According to correspondence with the National Museum, it appears that they existed in Campeche, Puebla, and Jalisco, too. Like the National Museum, these institutions circulated decrees asking local officials to send in pieces. In 1870, the Yucateco Museum in Mérida, one of the most developed of the provincial institutions, called on local officials "to gather objects of interest to enrich" the museum. That same year and again in 1886, it ordered that "councils" be established in each municipality to collect and remit antiquities.[21] Whether the national or a provincial museum ended up with a piece seems to have been based on a type of "finders, keepers" system. If the National Museum found out about an object and claimed it first, it not only got it but was also stubbornly possessive. In 1907, the interim governor of Yucatán, Enrique Muñoz Arístegui, asked to keep some relics that the National Museum had recently claimed. The governor wanted to display them in his state's "incipient and poor museum" and argued that it seemed "natural to conserve them there," since they were from Yucatán and pertained to its history. Inspector Batres, however, saw nothing "natural" about it and denied his plea, claiming it would set a "terrible precedent" if artifacts found by the authorities were diverted from their "legitimate" destination (the National Museum) and placed in the provincial museums instead.[22] When a jefe político asked to decorate the plaza of Valladolid with statues of snake heads from Chichén Itzá, he received a similarly curt reply: "Those stones belong to the Federal Government"; to forfeit them would make the government's conservation efforts seem "fruitless."[23] That there are few of these types of pleas on record, though, most likely means the provincial museums built their collections with objects that the National Museum had not found first. They had the advantage of proximity to the sites, and once a piece became a part of their collection, it usually remained there, untouched by the federal government.

One notable exception was the Chacmool of Chichén Itzá. When we last saw this statue the eccentric archaeologist Augustus Le Plongeon had hidden it in his camp outside the ruins. Le Plongeon petitioned the Mexican government for permission to transport the monolith to Philadelphia for display at the 1876 World's Fair, but his request was denied. The archaeologist protested and continued to press his claim. Meanwhile, the statue was hauled away to the regional museum of Yucatán, a move initiated by museum director Juan Peón Contreras, Governor Protasio Guerra, and Mexico's secretary of development, Riva Palacio. More than 150 Maya Indians dragged the statue along an eighteen-mile path they had cut through the jungle with machetes. The military escorted them along the way, as the peninsula's devastating Caste War raged on. Newspapers touted the move as a "triumph of science."[24] But it was also a "dangerous expedition," a foray into "enemy territory of rebel Indians," wrote Riva Palacio.[25] Onlookers compared the "barbarous" Maya rebels that were said to be lurking in the jungle to the sophisticated people of long ago, the makers of Chacmool, a monument that was "clear proof of the ancient civilization of the Mayas."[26] Chacmool, it seems, was a willing participant in the move. According to Riva Palacio, the Indian workers, full of their "superstitious fanaticism," claimed to hear the statue whisper each night, uttering the words "conex, conex," "which in their language means, let's go, let's go."[27]

Chacmool arrived in Mérida to a huge celebration; important men made speeches, school children recited poetry, and the state anthem blared. Newspapers bragged that the governor had enriched Yucatán's museum with a "priceless treasure."[28] But in less than a month, the statue was gone, whisked away to Mexico City. A newly elected governor decided to donate the piece to the National Museum as a tribute to Porfirio Díaz's victory in the Tuxtepec Revolt (1876), the uprising that brought Díaz to power. Both the governor and Riva Palacio thought the statue would "shine with more dignity" in the nation's capital, and a plaster copy was eventually set in its place in the regional museum.[29] This is how the famous Chacmool wound up in Mexico City, an offering to Díaz.

The Mexican government was not interested in just any old relic; it put a premium on artifacts like the Chacmool. It targeted what were (and are still) considered masterpieces, objects that proved the grandeur of Mexico's ancient past. While there were no specific criteria to determine what counted as a masterpiece, the objects were usually monumental, well crafted, made of precious materials, or engraved with hieroglyphics, as writing was thought to be an undeniable sign of civilization. These were the antiquities the state sought to gather into the National Museum and especially into a new room known as the Gallery of Monoliths.

Inaugurated by President Díaz on 16 September—Independence Day—1887, the gallery became the museum's main attraction. It occupied the most visible and central spot in the institution, the large hall directly facing the main entrance. A beeline walk thus took visitors from the museum's front door to the room. The purpose of the gallery was to display the finest pieces from as many of Mexico's pre-Hispanic cultures as possible. Its aim, in other words, was spatial coverage; it highlighted the presence of antiquity throughout the national territory. With artifacts lined against the walls and placed on pedestals in the center of the room in no apparent chronological order, it presented visitors with a completely ahistorical vision of the past. The gallery thus served as a type of container for the nation and its diversity. Had we entered, we would have been struck by the mix of cultures, by stones of different sizes, shapes, and colors. García Canclini has argued that today's National Museum of Anthropology similarly produces this heterogeneity. Its rooms dedicated to different cultures make it, he suggests, a "vehicle of totality," a representative or microcosm of Mexico.[30] During the Porfiriato, this melting-pot effect was produced in an even more concentrated fashion in this one room.

The gallery, in other words, gave concrete material form to the process of political centralization, to the government's attempt to control the national territory. And so, too, did the call to gather antiquities from Mexico's southern frontier, from the realm of the Maya. Chavero demanded the museum acquire more: it "truly lacks a collection of Maya antiquities. I do not need to stress the importance of such a collection, since everyone is already aware of it."[31] Chavero made this statement in 1902, a year after Mexican forces defeated the autonomous Maya in Yucatán, officially ending the Caste War, a time when the federal government had a feeble grip on the region. That he and others clamored for more Maya objects did not just reflect a concern with controlling the national territory; Mexicans also worried that failing to preserve Maya culture—what foreigners considered "the highest culture" of the New World—would give their country a bad name.[32] Maya artifacts were also some of the most exploited by foreigners. Controlling them was thought to be a sign of Mexico's strength and sovereignty. But the museum professors not only coveted the stuff of the Maya—they wanted artifacts from Mexico's northern frontier as well. This is why Gamio went to Zacatecas in 1909. The museum sponsored his expedition because it lacked antiquities from the area, and while Gamio was ultimately foiled by Batres, he succeeded in bringing back scores of relics.

How the museum visitors perceived the Gallery of Monoliths or any other exhibit is difficult to gauge, since their impressions, like those of most museum patrons, went unrecorded. From the institution's records, though, we know that most visitors were Mexican rather than foreign, that Mexican schoolchildren and military men were often taken on tours of the museum, members of two of the most important institutions for instilling a sense of nationalism in the population.[33] The professors made a distinction between the patrons, believing that Mexicans visited the museum to be taught, whereas foreigners went there to study. Although some foreigners like Nuttall and Seler did carry out research in the museum, most just went to have a look at the curious things on display. Their aims were not nearly as lofty as the professors liked to imagine.

In the eyes of the professors, the museum was also a type of civilizing institution—the men would celebrate the day when spittoons were finally installed in the galleries! Museums, after all, force visitors to leave their rowdy behavior at the door, to walk calmly through the corridors, to speak in hushed tones. They are "exemplary" spaces, writes scholar Tony Bennett, where people "learn to civilize themselves by modeling their conduct on . . . middle-class codes of behavior."[34] Still, while Mexico's museum was thought to be a place of instruction, where patrons were taught history and science as well as how to behave, the institution was hardly ever open to the public. As many scholars point out, the idea that public museums were equally accessible to all was honored more in theory than in practice. Mexico's museum was closed more often than not. In 1895, for instance, it was open to the public only "two hours a day, a few days a week, and three hours on Sundays."[35] One gets the impression that the professors and other elites involved in the Porfirian archaeological project were moved more by their own concerns than by an interest in how their efforts were actually received by the public.

The Gallery of Monoliths projected the idea that Mexico was not only an integrated nation but a nation dominated by its capital. Most of the pieces were Aztec, and the Aztec Calendar hung at the center of the room, the heart of the museum, making it the first piece visitors would see upon entering. In fact, it was under Díaz that the calendar became a part of the museum. Before this, the gigantic twenty-four-ton disk could be found on the Mexico City cathedral, where it had been embedded in the exterior of the west tower for nearly a century, a victim of the elements and of the people. Its round shape and bull's-eye like center made it a perfect target for rocks and rotten fruit. As if this were not bad enough, the monument was also a popular spot to urinate! The calendar had become "an absolute source of infection," protested one journalist.[36] The director of the National Museum, Jesús Sánchez, had his own complaint: the Mexican government would be condemned if it left the artifact exposed. In 1885, Sánchez had the calendar moved to the museum, using the manpower and supplies of a local streetcar company, the municipal government, and the Secretariat of War. The artifact went from being part of a busy street scene in the center of the capital, the symbolic heart of the nation, to a specimen in the museum, a boring, prisonlike existence according to one artist who chronicled the calendar's unhappy move in a broadside written from the monument's perspective. "To the prison of the museum, they are taking me away," mourns the calendar, as it bids farewell to the people on Mexico City's main plaza. "Goodbye to all you Mexicans—if you want to see me, I'll be doing time in the museum."[37] Today, the calendar continues to do time in the National Museum of Anthropology, where it still hangs prominently at the center of the institution.[38]

Outside of the Gallery of Monoliths, the antiquities were being constantly rearranged. This intensified toward the end of the Porfiriato, when the museum saw a major shift in the way it organized the objects. It abandoned the "typological" collection for the system that grouped artifacts by culture, the "tribal arrangement of collection" made popular by Boas. To bring about this change, it hired Seler, who was then the head of the American division at the Ethnological Museum of Berlin. Seler began the work in 1907, receiving a hefty sum to organize over ten thousand pieces in Mexico's National Museum. But the museum was unhappy with the results; it took issue with the culture and place of origin Seler attributed to some of the objects and so it decided to replace him with Batres. In the words of museum director Genaro García, one of Batres's few friends, the inspector's many years of "explorations would allow him to determine the provenance of the objects with more precision." Batres set himself to rearranging the collection, promising to avoid any "wild speculation."[39] He put labels on the pieces recording their provenance, civilization, material composition, and form. Taking full advantage of the opportunity to promote himself, he also made sure the labels were stamped with his name. And while his work was praised at the time—Secretary Sierra called the organization of the collection a "success"—one archaeologist dubbed it a "complete and serious mess," with "ridiculous" labels that gave information as useless as "Composition: Stone."[40] A more biting critique came from Batres's archenemy, Zelia Nuttall. Nuttall objected to the provenance Batres assigned to several objects and likewise condemned the labels for stating the obvious; in the category of form, she pointed out, they offered information as insightful as "this is a vase with three legs." "Mexican archaeology has received a blow" from "which it can never fully recover," she dramatically declared.[41]

For years, Batres had criticized the organization of the archaeology collection, a disapproval he often expressed in the form of violent outbursts in the museum. In 1894, he visited the museum several times; he would walk the halls and declare as loudly as possible, so that all the patrons could hear, that the professors were tricking the public with "false classifications," neglecting the archaeology collection, and spending the government's money on decorating the building instead.[42] Batres also accused the professors of hiding the museum's "treasures." The professors, he claimed, feared the patrons would steal the objects, a concern not shared by the museums of "cultured Europe," which put their finest pieces on display. Batres knew this for a fact, he stated, since he had been to the "museums of the old continent."[43] Two years after becoming inspector, the government sent him on a tour of the museums of Europe, including those of England, Spain, and France. Batres took note of the collections and recorded details like the price of admission and hours of operation. This trip, he no doubt believed, gave him the license to critique Mexico's museum, making him all the more unbearable to the professors, with whom he constantly quarreled; as a result of some sort of "grave" offense he committed in 1894, he was banned from the institution for much of the year.[44] Virtually everything was fertile ground for conflict. Batres fought with the professors over methodology (the way the archaeology collection was organized, for example), over meaning (he battled with Chavero over the identity of a statue known as Coatlinchan), and over equipment (one heated dispute involved twenty-four missing screws). He also fought with them over the installation of Chalchiuhtlicue, the Goddess of Water he had helped drag to the capital from the ruins of Teotihuacán.

Once Batres arrived at the museum with the colossal statue, the professors, for some reason, refused to let him in. "What do you want me to do with the rock?" he supposedly asked the guard at the door before heading off to lodge a complaint with President Díaz. "Do they want you to hang the boulder from the chain of a watch?" the president reportedly asked him.[45] Díaz ordered the professors to let Batres back into the museum, and Batres returned. But when he began to install the statue, most likely with a crew of soldiers, a small piece of the pedestal where the goddess was supposed to rest broke off. The professors criticized Batres's methods, which had not only damaged the pedestal but also scratched a large portion of the museum floor. Batres must have doubted the strength of the pedestal, as he decided to abandon the goddess on the ground. The helpless professors were unable to lift her, so they called in a team of engineers to determine if the pedestal could handle the goddess's vast weight. The engineers deemed the pedestal sturdy enough, and Batres returned a few days later to install the statue, maneuvering it with a teeter-totter-like system made up of several beams. Meanwhile, the press speculated about the goddess's fate. What had become of her? She had been torn from her majestic "palaces at Teotihuacán" only to be abandoned among the "tacky" "little idols" of the museum, subjected to treatment not even befitting of a third-rate goddess, wrote one observer.[46]

Although most of the mechanisms for getting antiquities to the museum had been in place for some time, two new developments made the process more efficient. One was the advent of the train: the fifteen thousand miles of track laid down during the Porfiriato not only integrated the nation but moved crates of objects and monoliths previously too heavy to transport to the capital. The other was the hiring of Batres. No one brought more artifacts to the National Museum than Batres, Mexico's great centralizer. He was the government's constant forager, a hunter, in his words, for true "treasures."[47]

Perhaps the most spectacular example of Batres's hunt for treasures was his journey to retrieve the last piece of the Cross of Palenque. This enormous limestone artifact made up of three panels adorned with hieroglyphics and human figures had originally been embedded in the chamber of Palenque's Temple of the Cross. Although the panels are now thought to depict the transfer of power from King Pakal to his son, during the Porfiriato, their meaning was unknown. Could they represent the "teachings of the Buddha?" asked Batres. "Who knows?" he went on, adding that "everything in those monuments is a mystery."[48] While a mystery, the hieroglyphics were considered proof of "how high the Maya civilization had reached . . . one of the

most industrious, intelligent, and hard-working tribes that used to populate
our territory," wrote one observer.[49] Sometime in the nineteenth century,
tomb raiders entered the chamber at Palenque and separated the three panels. The center panel was torn out of the wall and abandoned near the temple. The right panel was eventually shipped to the Smithsonian on the orders
of the American consul at Campeche in 1842. Only the left panel remained
embedded in the temple.

During the Porfiriato, the Cross of Palenque became whole again,
reunited in the National Museum. The first panel to arrive was the one abandoned outside the temple. In 1884, the Mexican government had it hauled to
the museum in order to make plaster copies of it for display at the International
Exposition in New Orleans. Next came the panel from the Smithsonian, a
move initiated by Elihu Root, US secretary of state at the time. After taking a
tour of Mexico's National Museum in 1907, Root made a promise to Sierra to
repatriate the monument. Newspapers praised Root, and the 1,350-pound slab,
the "most brilliant page of Maya scripture," noted one of the professors,
arrived in the museum the next year, the only artifact to have been repatriated
to Mexico by a foreign power during the Porfiriato.[50] Only the last panel
remained, the piece embedded in the chamber at Palenque. This was a massive hunk of fragile stone that needed to be pried out of the wall and lowered
174 feet down the length of the pyramid at a thirty-five degree incline, a complicated procedure requiring the hands of an expert, someone "well-versed in
those types of maneuvers," explained Batres, who, of course, assigned the task
to himself.[51]

Batres set out to retrieve the panel in early 1909 with Sierra on an expedition that unfolded much like a Mexican *Heart of Darkness*, only with its two
protagonists as colonizers in their own land. Newspapers even claimed that
the "famous ruins of Palenque are located in the heart of an intricate jungle
that seems African."[52] The dense forest teemed with creatures—rattlesnakes,
tarantulas, and vampire bats that emitted a "sinister" sound, wrote Batres,
"that seemed to be an omen of death." When an "eight-foot-long tiger"
threatened the group, the guard at Palenque killed it, skinned it, and offered
its pelt to Sierra as a souvenir.[53] The heat and jungle became too much for
Sierra. As one journalist remarked, "The constant climbing and descending
[of] the mounds ... had made the undertaking a difficult one for both
Mr. Sierra and Mr. Batres, both of whom are large men."[54] Batres relied on
the labor of the local Indians without recording their names, referring to
them simply as Indians or peons. He also failed to mention if they were paid,

but payment was what often seems to have motivated them. The Indians worked to pry the giant panel out of the Temple of the Cross and lower it down a ramp of bound tree trunks they had made. (An exhausted Sierra watched the whole spectacle through binoculars from the base of the pyramid.) Two workers were killed and several others seriously injured when they were crushed by a falling tree. And as they labored, observers looked on, dismissing the workers as "neglected aborigines" while celebrating the ancient peoples, the "strong and advanced race" that had built the "marvelous civilization" of Palenque.[55] Just as with the Chacmool, the removal of this artifact led onlookers to contrast the Indians of the past and present, defining them in ways that were diametrically opposed. Only here, the contemporary Indians were not the vicious rebels of the Yucatán but simply decrepit countryfolk.

And while Mexico's Indians often aided the state, they also forcefully opposed the project to gather artifacts. When one of the museum professors tried to make off with a mask used in a traditional dance in the state of Guanajuato, for instance, he succeeded, but "not without much effort." When another sought to open a tomb in Oaxaca, the villagers "demonstrated a great resistance."[56] Every now and then, a hint of opposition to the government surfaces in the official records, especially in the writings of Batres. Batres had a particularly tough time in two villages in Morelos. "Only in the state of Morelos has this Inspectorate encountered difficulties exercising its functions," he declared.[57] In both cases, indigenous communities fought to keep objects that they saw as part of their own identities and histories. In the eyes of the state, though, the people were simply destroyers, stupid Indians. As Batres would say, echoing the dominant sentiment of the day, "We need to take the antiquities to the museum; if not, they will be destroyed in the hands of the savages."[58]

The People's Claims to the Past

No place exemplifies the resistance of Indian communities better than Tepoztlán, the village near Tepozteco, the temple of the mythical chieftain who centuries earlier had defended the town from enemy attacks. When the architect and engineer Francisco Rodríguez carried out excavations at the site in 1895, he did not work alone; "a large force of Indians" aided him, voluntarily offering their services.[59] Rodríguez gathered several antiquities, including some finely carved glyphs and sculptures, which the townsfolk used to establish a municipal museum, a product of their pride and initiative. This is what contemporary archaeologists refer to as a "community museum," a museum initiated by the locals, which allows them to be the "creators of their own history."[60] Four years later, however, Batres visited the site and found the pyramid was missing the sculptures. He also discovered that the perpetrator had been Rodríguez, information he received from Bernardino Verazaluce, the master draftsman and caretaker of Tepozteco. The conserjes often served as Batres's spies, and at least this one seems to have been more loyal to his job and the federal government than to his fellow townsman, Rodríguez. Verazaluce's decision to side with the government reveals that there was not necessarily a consensus within communities about who owned the monuments. Interestingly, however, Verazaluce had been among the original group of Indians that had helped Rodríguez excavate the site. Perhaps he had had a falling out with Rodríguez. It is impossible to say. Armed with Verazaluce's information, Batres descended the hilltop pyramid as fast as his legs could take him. He burst into the museum in Tepoztlán and claimed a total of forty-six artifacts as federal property. This was unusual, as the state typically did not meddle with a provincial museum's collection. The artifacts remained there, though, in the town's museum, while the Secretariat of Education determined their fate.

Why seize the pieces? The sculptures had been pried from the pyramid, an assault on national property according to federal law. But Batres was also the state's chief treasure hunter, and one particular artifact in Tepoztlán had caught his eye: a beautiful glyph representing the eighth Aztec ruler Ahuítzotl as a mythical otter-like creature. The object obsessed him. The Gallery of Monoliths lacked a "single example of that civilization"; the glyph would fill the gap.[61]

Something else bothered Batres. After all, museums around the country were busy building their collections, often with artifacts pried from the ruins and without any government interference. The problem, it seems, was not so much the act of extracting as the extractor, Francisco Rodríguez. Months earlier, Batres had clashed with Rodríguez over a monolith known as La India in the ruins of Xochicalco. Rodríguez had been commissioned by the National Museum to retrieve La India. But this was also one of Batres's pet projects. A conflict of jurisdiction ensued that the Secretariat of Education ultimately settled, as was so often the case, by siding with Batres, authorizing him to move the statue. By the time Batres caught up with Rodríguez again, he had developed a solid grudge against him, so solid, it seems, that he interpreted the events in Tepoztlán in the following way. The town, Batres believed, had no interest in the artifacts; it had no initiative of its own. Rodríguez had manipulated the villagers. The museum was actually the architect's personal cache. In fact, it was not a museum at all, but what Batres called a "storage facility." Worst of all, Rodríguez had trespassed on what Batres considered his exclusive domain: the young upstart had the nerve to think "the Government should allow him to carry out any archaeological work in the state and especially in Tepoztlán" solely because he was "a native son of that place and . . . an architect and engineer."[62] Meanwhile, Rodríguez refused to bow to Batres's authority. Instead, he confronted the inspector on a Mexico City street and publicly scolded him.

Batres's views became especially clear after an incident at Tepozteco. One night after he had been working there, a group entered, took a stone carving, and set fire to the site. Without proof, Batres blamed Rodríguez: "The source of all these disturbances" is "an Indian from Tepoztlán named Rodríguez" who has incited the "poor natives" against the federal government and turned them into vandals.[63] Batres then reached into his repertoire of invectives and called Rodríguez a cacique, a local strongman; his behavior smacked of regionalism, Batres suggested, and was a counterweight to political centralization. Just as the dictator Díaz would consolidate his power by neutralizing caciques throughout the nation, Batres would reel in his own type of cacique, essentially anyone with plans for artifacts that countered his own. Unaware, he was making an enemy that would later haunt him.

Rodríguez was no cacique, however, nor were the Tepoztecans his followers. In 1904, Mexico's secretary of education decided the pieces would be "safer" in the National Museum and prepared to transport them. Just then, the unexpected occurred: the National Museum requested that the pieces remain in Tepoztlán and be reinstalled on the pyramid. The individual who made this plea was none other than Rodríguez. By then, Rodríguez had moved up the ranks to become director of the National Museum—one of the few Indians employed by the institution. He had received a letter in which his town asked to keep the pieces and, loyal to his roots, he offered to personally reinstall the sculptures on the pyramid. Representatives of the federal government, we should remember, come from communities and are often responsive to their needs—"state" and "local," in other words, are not mutually exclusive domains. But it is also possible that Rodríguez was moved by an ideological position that differed from that of the government. Perhaps he believed local communities had a right to keep their own patrimony. This was definitely the case when it came to his hometown. The popular and respected governor of Morelos, Manuel Alarcón, also backed Rodríguez's plan. In a letter to President Díaz, Alarcón mentioned the villagers' "disappointment" with the federal government's decision and supported their proposal to keep the antiquities.[64] But it was too late; the objects had already been shipped off to the National Museum.

Nevertheless, the town's plan remained a possibility. At one point, even President Díaz made a promise to the governor, a close ally, to return the antiquities. But then Batres intervened: to relinquish the objects would set a precedent, and "we would have to return every stone that makes up the grand archaeology collection of the museum." Besides, only a "true archaeologist" could reinstall the pieces, knowledge, he argued, that Rodríguez "completely lacks."[65] Selecting a more classist insult from his repertoire of invectives, Batres would later claim Rodríguez was no different from the museum janitor, "the *mozo* who scrubs the museum patios."[66] Batres, the dictator of Mexican archaeology, prevailed, and today the Ahuítzotl glyph can be found in the National Museum of Anthropology, a spectacular example of what Batres called the "Tepoztecan civilization." Although the Mexican government's archaeological project often floundered, this was one case in which its power proved very real.

Tepoztlán lost its battle against Batres, but another village in Morelos known as Tetlama did not. Located two and a half miles from Xochicalco, its eighty inhabitants spoke Nahuatl "almost exclusively" and preserved "many aboriginal customs and traditions," according to Marshall Saville.[67] Saville mentioned that the villagers kept a treasured object in their church, a codex depicting a map of Xochicalco, possibly a title to the land at the ruins. They also grew corn at the site, jabbing away with their digging sticks at the temples and tombs. At least this one community with a strong connection to a site seems to have had no qualms about damaging it. They simply used it as their own. And they knew it quite well; they walked through it, formed hypotheses about the structures, and even aided visiting scientists. They informed Cecilio Robelo in the 1880s, for instance, that on certain days the sun aligned perfectly over a "chimney" in one of the structures to illuminate an underground chamber, which they poetically called the "cave of the sun."[68]

The people of Tetlama also believed they were the guardians of Xochicalco. According to legend, one of their rulers in the fifteenth century, a lord they knew as Señor Tetlámatl, had defended the town against the

Aztecs, fighting bravely from the ruins.[69] Much like the Tepozteco, then, the site was associated with leaders who had opposed invaders. After the Aztec siege, the neighboring villages deemed the descendants of Señor Tetlámatl, the people of Tetlama, the keepers of the ruins. During the Porfiriato, the town was said to cherish one artifact at Xochicalco in particular: La India, the same monolith over which Batres and Rodríguez would clash, a stone carving of a human figure that the locals venerated as the goddess of marriage. According to a village elder, the people brought La India offerings. If they failed to do so, he explained, their young daughters would either not find husbands or they would find husbands who "abused them cruelly."[70] Guardians of Xochicalco, the people of Tetlama had a history of resisting central authorities. More than four hundred years after Señor Tetlámatl's battle against the Aztecs, they would fight against the state once more, struggling to keep La India, the only relic Batres would never be able to move.

On his first visit in 1886, the villagers gave Batres information. He asked why the ruins were called Xochicalco, "the place of the house of flowers," from the Nahuatl words for flower, "xóchitl," and house, "calli." The villagers answered that it was because the site became full of flowers in the spring.[71] But they were less generous with Batres when he returned in 1895 and decided to take La India to the National Museum. The Congress of Americanists was just a few months away, and again, the Gallery of Monoliths had nothing from the "special civilization of Xochicalco"; the "beautifully carved . . . goddess" would fill the gap. But she literally weighed a ton. To get her to the nearest railroad line she would have to be hauled more than six miles over rough terrain, conditions that prohibited the use of beasts of burden. Batres planned on using what he referred to as "human traction" for this task, although it is not clear which humans he had in mind.[72]

He returned and had begun to move the goddess when a Tetlama official intervened and demanded that he stop. The official had been sent by the jefe político of the district of Cuernavaca. The artifact, he warned, could not be moved until the federal government had notified Governor Alarcón, according to the typical protocol. (For some reason, the Secretariat of Education had failed to notify the governor about the project.) The Tetlama official also made it clear that Batres would not even be allowed to remain within "the perimeter of the monuments." Batres left immediately, not out of deference to either the official, the jefe político, or the governor, but because he lacked "the armed force needed" to make his "official presence respected." Meanwhile, the goddess disappeared.

A witness spotted "60 Indians" hauling her toward Tetlama. According to the witness, Jesús Moreno—the guard whose long-distance relationship to Xochicalco would eventually get him fired—the Indians told him they were acting on a "superior order" from the town government. Confused or frightened, Moreno let them take the statue away. Batres believed Governor Alarcón had ordered the move. He asked the Secretariat of Education to tell the governor that the Inspectorate was authorized to take the statue. Once Alarcón got this message, he acquiesced, and Batres returned to finish the job. But this time he could not even find the goddess. The project languished, and it was then, in 1899, that Batres would fight over the goddess with his nemesis Rodríguez.[73]

Up to this point, the historical record paints the governor and jefe político as the main sources of opposition to Batres. But what about the villagers of Tetlama? How do we explain the town's willingness to haul a one-ton goddess over miles of rough terrain? Or the sheer number of people involved? The fact that sixty inhabitants out of a town of eighty took part suggests a unified sense of purpose. Perhaps the governor *had* ordered the town to move the goddess. Alarcón did have that kind of clout. Still, it does not explain the final chapter in this story: when Batres returned to retrieve the goddess with the governor's approval, the villagers withheld her whereabouts. They were hiding her, it later turned out, in the town church.

If we search through local legends, we find that this was not the first time the villagers of Tetlama had tried to control the fate of the goddess. In one incident said to have occurred "many years ago," two villages were in the process of trying to steal the monolith when the people of Tetlama ambushed the thieves and a battle ensued.[74] The fighting continued until an important elder from Tetlama intervened. Here in the story, La India is equated with Tonantzín, Aztec mother of the gods. The elder tells the battling villages about a dream he had had in which Tonantzín appeared to him and asked to be placed in a specific spot at the ruins. He then points to the spot, and the villagers move the goddess to it.

Tetlama's desire to keep La India does surface in official records, but not until the eve of the revolution. In June 1910, Batres tried to jump-start the move of the goddess when the unpopular new governor, Pablo Escandón, warned against it. In a letter to the secretary of education, Escandón claimed that "a few years ago, someone (I think it was Mr. Batres) tried to take that idol to Mexico and was forced to abandon his project in light of the fact that the Indians of those parts were on the verge of rioting when they saw that something they considered theirs was being taken away." "At this time," he warned, "I do not think it prudent to provoke those people."[75] Either Escandón knew something Batres did not know or had failed to record, or he feared inciting an already agitated population, soon to rise up in arms. The federal government sided with the governor this time and ordered Batres to abandon the project.

But Batres shot back. He claimed that Escandón was a liar and that he was the source of the opposition; the villagers had never resisted him, and they were completely indifferent to La India's removal. Like the residents of Tepoztlán, they lacked all initiative. And just as Batres began to gear up to battle for the goddess once more, events intervened that sealed both their fates. The revolution broke out, and Batres, the Porfirian world crumbling, renounced his post. The people of Tetlama had outsmarted him, but they did not keep their goddess for long. In 1930, in circumstances unknown to this author, the governor of Morelos, Vicente Estrada Cajigal, had the goddess hauled to the Palace of Cortés in Cuernavaca, the seat of the state government. In 1974 the palace became the Cuauhnáhuac Museum, where today La India is on display, officially known as Xochiquetzal, goddess of flowers and fertility and guardian of young mothers, an identity not too distant from what the people of Tetlama had ascribed to her.

One wonders about cases of local resistance to Batres that left no paper trail. In all, Batres would record only the incidents at Tepoztlán and Tetlama and his struggle over Teotihuacán's Goddess of Water. That these occurred in Mexico's central plateau is no surprise, since this was where the government carried out most of its archaeological work. It is also unsurprising that two of the cases took place in Morelos, a state known for fiercely defending its interests. It is the region that gave birth to the Zapatista revolutionaries, and more recently, in Tepoztlán, to a movement that fought off investors' schemes to turn the area into an exclusive golf course.[76]

Today, both the Ahuítzotl of Tepoztlán and the Goddess of Water are on display in the National Museum of Anthropology. It is possible to wander through the entire institution oblivious as to how they and all the other pieces got there or how the removal of artifacts impacted local people. No label or catalogue records this information. Yet in their removal, the objects changed in significance. They were ripped out of traditional systems of meaning, what theorists refer to as their "original functional context." In placing the objects in collections dedicated to antiquity, the federal government separated them from their contemporary uses, severing the connection between the Indian present and past. While one could argue that this process protected the artifacts from destruction, it also restricted the native peoples' claims to the past, limiting their rights as curators of objects which were a part of their identities and daily lives. Museum objects are objects that by definition have "been removed from circulation," divested of their former value, and given "instructive" value instead. This new value, moreover, "'is entirely up to the subject' who has done the removing."[77] Today the National Museum of Anthropology continues to celebrate Mexico's archaeological patrimony without mentioning the "material and symbolic struggle" involved in its creation. And today, just like in the age of Díaz, this patrimony continues to be legitimized by appeals to science and nation. The claim to science and nation has functioned as an authorizing, or more precisely a *self*-authorizing, discourse with the power to silence others.

But the museum was not the only place where Mexico would shore up its ancient image in the age of Don Porfirio. As one of his last great endeavors, Inspector Batres carried out a major reconstruction of Teotihuacán, turning it into the nation's first official archaeological site for the centenario, the centennial celebration of Mexican independence in 1910. Let us imagine him standing in front of the Pyramid of the Sun, not the shaped, manicured structure we see today, but rather one encased in centuries of sediment. The year is 1905 and Batres has only five years to turn the giant hill into a pyramid worthy of international display.

CHAPTER EIGHT

Reconstructing

✢ ONE OF THE MOST FAMOUS IMAGES OF TEOTIHUACÁN BEFORE BATRES
reconstructed the site is a painting by the celebrated artist José María
Velasco. A draftsman in the National Museum, Velasco accompanied the
professors to Teotihuacán in 1877, an outing that resulted in his idyllic portrayal of the ruins. With a background dominated by clouds and Mount
Tlasinga, the landscape is illuminated by the late-morning sun in colors so
earthy the painting almost seems to emit warmth. Covered in soil, mesquite, and maguey, the Pyramid of the Sun looks nearly indistinguishable
from a hill. Few hints betray the fact that a massive monument lies underneath, much less a whole city. The uniform sides of the pyramid, the straight
lines of the Street of the Dead, and the fields of the contemporary Indians
are the only signs of a human presence. Other than these, the site, especially
the section in the foreground, appears to be completely melded with the elements, at one with nature.

Scholars have written much about landscapes, about how they serve as
metaphors for the nation. Landscapes transpose a nation's identity onto
space, a space, in the case of Velasco's painting, that has enshrouded the
ancient past in such a way that the pyramids seem to be waiting patiently to
be unearthed. Teotihuacán or "the place where the gods were conceived," a
name given to the monumental city by the Aztecs, had become so utterly
obscured by dirt and vegetation that one had to strain to imagine any sort of
monumentality, let alone any gods. Batres *had* such an imagination. Standing
before the mighty Pyramid of the Sun in early 1905, Justo Sierra supposedly

asked him if he could uncover the structure in time for the centennial celebration in September 1910. Batres's answer, of course, was yes. On 20 March
1905, the inspector began reconstructing a monument he considered "more
impressive and elegant than the pyramids of Egypt," an effort that produced
Mexico's first official archaeological site and that proved to be the culmina-
tion of his career.[1] Much like the National Museum, Teotihuacán was a place
where Mexico's official past was made visible, where visitors could witness
the country's ancient splendor, and where Mexicans could gain a sense of
themselves as a people who shared a common history rooted in antiquity. It
provided, like all the other facets of the Porfirian archaeological project, a
means of asserting and defending Mexico's national image.

It was also one of the settings during the centennial where elites sought
to project "ideal views" of the nation. In the words of Mauricio Tenorio-
Trillo, the centennial celebration was "consciously planned to be the apo-
theosis of nationalist consciousness; it was meant to be the climax of an era."
Nineteen hundred and ten was a milestone year, one that marked Mexico's
achievements since independence and that highlighted "the political and
economic success" of the Díaz regime.[2] The monthlong celebration included
public ceremonies, parades, speeches, and banquets in honor of Díaz as well
as Mexico's pantheon of heroes, especially Benito Juárez and the independence leaders José María Morelos and Miguel Hidalgo. Thousands of tourists
would be attending the event, giving Porfirian leaders a captive audience and
a perfect venue in which to showcase the nation. In preparation for the
throngs of Mexican and foreign visitors, including scholars and dignitaries
from at least twenty-eight countries, Mexico's federal, state, and municipal
governments carried out construction and beautification projects across the
nation.[3] Everything from streets and statues to penitentiaries and parks
popped up, with Mexico City as the epicenter of the most elaborate preparations and host to most of the foreign guests. The reconstruction of
Teotihuacán was one of these many projects, and an organized excursion to
the site was built into the centennial program.

The reconstruction of the site also reflected a budding interest in developing the ruins for tourism. Mexico witnessed a growth in the tourist sector
under Díaz, as a "construction fever" left behind more restaurants and hotels.[4]
The government, as we have already seen, was also keen on making the ruins
more accessible and attractive to visitors, as it cleared roads and removed
vegetation. Batres, for instance, built a bridge and staircase to the hilltop
Tepozteco pyramid in 1900. Before this, visitors had to risk their lives scaling

boulders to reach the site; a slip of the foot could send an unlucky soul on a fatal plunge some six hundred meters long. Another archaeologist who wanted to promote tourism to sites was Gamio. While a student in the museum, Gamio put together a guide to Mexico's most important ruins. Organized state by state, it gave advice on transportation to sites, from the cost of train fare to renting a mule. It offered tips on food and lodging, warning visitors to Morelos that the food was "cheap" but "bad."[5] It even suggested the best season to travel, along with the most appropriate pyramid-climbing attire. The first of Mexico's ruins to become a picture-perfect tourist attraction was Teotihuacán. As one journalist put it, the two-thousand-year-old-city had the potential to become "the most visited archaeological zone in the Americas." In the words of the Duke of Loubat, the site would draw "as many tourists to Mexico as Pompey attracts to Naples."[6]

It was bureaucrats rather than scientists who decided to reconstruct Teotihuacán. Unlike all the other centennial projects, however, the idea did not come out of the government's National Centennial Commission, the committee established in 1907 to plan the event. Instead, Justo Sierra and Ezequiel Chávez, the soon-to-be secretary and assistant secretary of education, suggested rebuilding the site in 1904, an idea that eventually was linked to plans for the centennial. Their choice of Teotihuacán reflected the government's focus on the cultures of Mexico's central plateau. And it may have also been inspired by an earlier proposal. In 1902, while serving as museum director, Alfredo Chavero recommended that the government embark on a systematic exploration of the nation's ruins, beginning with the Valley of Mexico since "the ancient people who lived there are the most important in our history." He wanted the government to start with Teotihuacán, a long-term commitment that would begin with the excavation of the two main pyramids until they were "left in prime condition."[7] While Chavero suggested the multitalented Peñafiel for the job, the plan never took off.

The government also chose Teotihuacán because it was impressive, a place the Aztecs, the original rulers of Mexico City, had also revered. Unlike other ruins that had been lost to history, the site was much too massive, monumental, and close to Mexico City to have ever been forgotten. Teotihuacán was famous, "a work of our prehistory that is of much interest to nationals and foreigners," wrote Batres.[8] A requisite stop on the itinerary of travelers, everyone who was anyone had passed through, from Bernardino de Sahagún and Alexander von Humboldt (who considered it the most important site in Mexico to see) to the nineteenth-century chronicler Fanny

Calderón de la Barca (who lamented she did not have enough time to see it). Conveniently located near the capital, the site would be just an hour's train ride away for the centennial guests.

Some of these guests were prominent archaeologists like Franz Boas and Eduard Seler, who would be in Mexico City attending the Seventeenth Congress of Americanists. The 1910 congress had originally been scheduled to take place in Buenos Aires, Argentina. Mexican delegates at the previous meeting in Austria in 1908, however, had asked that it be moved to their country. There was much opposition to the idea, since Mexicans had already hosted the conference once before, and so as a compromise the congress was split in two. The first session would be held in Argentina in May and the second in Mexico in September, allowing this important scientific event to coincide with the centennial celebrations of both nations. After the Buenos Aires congress, the delegates would travel to Mexico for the second session, touring the ruins of Peru and Bolivia along the way. The Mexican government even offered to pay some of their expenses. A proposal was also drafted to subsidize the travel of scientists coming from Europe, Canada, and the United States. Porfirian leaders clearly wanted to ensure the attendance of as many scholars as possible. As one journalist later explained, "Our land is the American Egypt, the center of research and the Mecca of pilgrimages of wise men."[9] Other congress proposals focused on lodging. To protect the hundred or so "wise men" from falling "victim" to unscrupulous hotel owners, Batres, who was made president of the Commission of Celebrations and Festivities for the congress, suggested the scientists be housed together in one huge dwelling in the center of Mexico City.[10] There, they would not only be safe but close to the National Museum, the seat of the conference.

Just as with the congress of 1895, preparations for the event in 1910 unleashed a flurry of activity in the museum, so much so that the institution had to be closed throughout the preceding year. The professors carried out a series of improvements, renovating the building and putting more artifacts on display. It was then, in preparation for the event, that they commissioned Batres to reorganize the archaeology collection and eliminated the natural history department, moving it to another location in the capital. The result was a perfect museum, claimed the press, complete with "many new objects" and tricolored curtains, the colors of the Mexican flag, draped across the shelves and cabinets.[11] That the Porfirian regime wanted to show off Mexico's ancient past during the centennial is borne out not only by its insistence on hosting the congress but by these as well as other efforts.

Outside of the museum, the regime focused on making the nation's ruins more presentable, an important task since the delegates of Mexico's first congress in 1895 had denounced the government's neglect of the sites, pointing to the shabby state of Mitla. Batres called on all the guards to clear the monuments of dirt and vegetation. The Pyramid of the Niches at El Tajín, for instance, was cleaned with "great diligence and care."[12] To facilitate excursions, Batres also designed a new map of the ruins, his *Archaeological Map of the United States of Mexico* (1910), which was distributed to the congress delegates. Rather than create the document from scratch, he used the map of the nation's railroads made by the Secretariat of Communications and Public Works. Decked out in the colors of the nation's flag, Mexico appears flanked by green oceans and crisscrossed with railway lines in bright red. Batres recorded each of the ruins with a black dot and a number, listing the name of the corresponding site in a legend on the map's left-hand side. Compared to his earlier map from a quarter of a century before, this one is more thorough: the original map contains 53 sites; the new one has 110. The new map also has a more sophisticated, standardized, and professional appearance. There are no idiosyncratic symbols or references to contemporary Indians. Its many dots and bright lines make it a busy document and also give the impression that the Mexican territory is completely under control. The ruins of antiquity and train tracks of modernity act like joined metaphors, making reference to the past and present and conveying the sense that Mexico is a nation both ancient and modern.

In preparation for the congress, Batres also paid special attention to some of the sites. In addition to taking the delegates on a tour of Teotihuacán, he planned to have them visit Xochicalco and Mitla after the conference. This meant that he would have to carry out the daunting task of reconstructing Teotihuacán while simultaneously working at Xochicalco, where in 1909 he built a road to the hilltop ruins and pieced together the famous Temple of the Feathered Serpent. Batres chose Xochicalco for its beauty and because he thought his work there would be "relatively easy."[13] He picked Mitla, in contrast, because he had already renovated the site, work he had completed while watching over Saville. What better way to counter the embarrassment of Mexico's previous congress and show off the nation's advances in the care of its ruins than to have the delegates return to the place they had once condemned?

But no site got as much attention as Teotihuacán. Batres focused on excavating and reconstructing the Pyramid of the Sun, one of the world's largest pyramids at over 200 feet tall with a base more than 730 feet long on each side. The job was "colossal," he would later explain. "I repeat, the work is gigantic, but when man sets out to accomplish something and has the strength of will . . . he defeats all obstacles and executes the task."[14] Batres did face a number of obstacles, what he called "problems."[15] There was the dirt problem, the sediment of centuries, over "1,600,000 cubic meters" of soil he needed to remove from the Pyramid of the Sun alone. There was the time problem. With the centennial just a short five years away, Batres had to work quickly—a sense of urgency permeates the records he left, as each passing day brought the event closer and closer. There was also the people problem, the locals who owned the land at the site, campesinos from the communities of San Sebastián, San Francisco Mazapa, Santa María Cuatlán, San Juan Teotihuacán, and San Martín de las Pirámides. Batres estimated they had carpeted the ruins with over 250 plots, full of crops, *pirú* trees, and maguey. If Teotihuacán were to evoke a mythical past, it had to become an empty ceremonial center, unhindered by competing interpretations of the ruins; it had to be free of residents, in other words. To turn the mounds into pristine pyramids Batres would first have to get rid of the locals.

Batres was no stranger to them. We saw him face the protests of "angry" "Indians" as he hauled away the Goddess of Water in 1889.[16] On an even earlier occasion in 1886, the villagers of San Martín supposedly "revolted" against him. The inspector had been excavating near the Temple of Agriculture when a "mob" approached him. The group took his workers hostage and tried to capture him as well. Batres claimed he escaped by striking the mob's leader in the head with the butt of his rifle, which, according to him, caused the crowd to disperse. The experience put Batres forever on guard: "Knowing the Indian as I do, I made sure they would not sense any sort of fear in me, and from that time on I walked everywhere alone, leaving work well into the night to show them that I feared nothing." A few days later, while engrossed in his work, someone threw a rock of "considerable proportions" at Batres's head. Although it is not clear what set off the hostilities, the locals most likely resented the fact that he had encroached on their lands. But Batres proved undeterred: "My brain burned thinking of future projects."[17] He returned to Teotihuacán several times over the course of the next few years, and, except for the incident with the Goddess of Water, there seem to have been no other conflicts. Perhaps Batres simply failed to record them. Or maybe the locals had gotten used to the presence of the chubby archaeologist poking about the soil, or, if he brought along police, perhaps they were just too afraid to confront him. Ultimately, a troop of seventeen armed men, a mix of military officers and rurales, were permanently stationed at Teotihuacán "to maintain order at the pyramids," explained Batres.[18]

But his visit in 1905 was different from his earlier visits—it meant the villagers would have to leave. The Law of Monuments had given the government the right to expropriate Mexico's ruins, a measure Batres would carry out at Teotihuacán. Batres, however, initially refused to compensate the locals for their land, since he believed it was not theirs in the first place: it had "belonged to the nation since the time of the Spaniards, . . . and it would set a fatal precedent to recognize monuments . . . as private property."[19] For reasons that are not entirely clear, he began working at the site before expropriating it, ordering the villagers to stop tending their fields. The first person to protest was a Sebero Reyes, the owner of the plots that encircled the base of the Pyramid of the Sun. Reyes took his case to the Secretariat of Education, requesting either the right to continue planting or compensation for his land. When Batres found out, he gave in and agreed to compensate Reyes. But Reyes, it turned out, drove a hard bargain. Although he had originally paid 10 pesos for the property, he refused to sell for less than 100. This is what the government paid for the Pyramid of the Sun—100 pesos, which, Batres complained, was "the price of gold."[20]

It was now mid-1906, time was passing, and Batres continued to work while occupying the people's land. The villagers of Santa María Cuatlán and San Francisco Mazapa protested to the Secretariat of Education. Their property, they pointed out, was "inviolable and could not be taken away unless . . . there had been previous compensation."[21] When Batres found out about the complaints, he again gave in and agreed to the idea of providing compensation, but not before he finished insulting every last villager. "His abuse has become intolerable," the locals explained. "He calls us a group of dumb Indians . . . but in words that are less tasteful, and which do not measure up to the standards of a public official." It is not clear what bothered Batres most: that the people had sought recourse from the Secretariat of Education and slowed down his work, or that the "dumb Indians" had not only understood but dared to defend their rights. Batres responded, as usual, with the claim that the people were being manipulated: in Teotihuacán, as in the rest of the nation, "the Indian race is victim to the town caciques, the *hacendados*, and the local authorities," who have incited the "poor pariahs" to "make accusations against my Office."[22]

Batres was a difficult character to be sure, but the reconstruction of Teotihuacán would probably not have occurred without him. The government depended on him, a reliance that became clear in an incident related to the expropriations. The paymaster in charge of disbursing the funds for the people's land was a Mr. Dupont, an official who Sierra described as "unbearable, a real calamity." Batres similarly disliked Dupont, so much so that he interpreted the selection of Dupont as an attack against him. The secretary of finance, José Limantour, had assigned Dupont to the task, Batres believed, solely to aggravate him, to make him "explode." In a conversation with Sierra, Batres threatened to "abandon the work at Teotihuacán" if Dupont were not replaced, a threat Sierra took very seriously. "For you men of money," Sierra wrote to the sub-secretary, "archaeology may be trivial." But the threat of Batres quitting "for me is an extremely grave matter," as the government is committed to presenting "those great works" at the centennial, a plan "that I believe would be impossible to carry out without the aid of that conniving rogue Mr. Batres."[23] Sierra, like President Díaz, shielded Batres, but he seems to have done so not because he liked him or thought he was a good man—he called him a conniving rogue!—but because he believed Batres was indispensable to the government's project.

Meanwhile, Batres went on to carve out the site of Teotihuacán from the people's plots, a process that required little more than a wire fence, some mineral lime, and a bit of his patience. Since the Law of Monuments did not specify how to carry out the expropriations or the amount of land needed to establish and conserve the ruins, Batres was forced to make up much of the process as he went along. He began by marking the boundaries of the site, raising the wire fence around the main monuments: the Pyramid of the Sun, the Pyramid of the Moon, the Street of the Dead, and the Citadel, or Ciudadela. Batres wanted to make sure the border between the site and the adjoining private land was absolutely clear and precise. So he drew a thick line of mineral lime on the ground, marking a buffer zone of more than two hundred yards outside of the fence. Next, he distributed leaflets ordering the owners of the lands within the fence and buffer zone to come to his office at what became known as Camp Pyramid of the Sun with their sale price in mind and property title in hand. He waited, but nobody came. So Batres instructed the government of the state of Mexico to order the locals to present themselves, and within days the people began filing in.

By mid-1907, most of the locals had trickled into camp Pyramid of the Sun and sold off their land. Manuel Olvera, for example, wanted 5,000 pesos for his Rancho de la Palma, but he received 520; Leandro Aguilar asked for 200 but got 12; Modesto Suárez wanted 500 but ended up with a measly 7 pesos.[24]

Batres believed the people's prices were too high, "completely exaggerated." The treasury of the state of Mexico intervened to determine the property values, which the locals were forced to accept. They had no choice. Had they refused to sell, the expropriations would have been carried out on the basis of "public use in accordance with the law."[25] As one government memorandum made clear, "The property rights possessed by the nation over the land in this case are more important than the property rights of individuals. . . . The latter are precarious and ephemeral, while those of the nation by nature are eternal."[26] The locals, moreover, lost their rights to all aspects of the land. Though the Law of Monuments had made a distinction between the surface of the land and what lay below it, allowing individuals to retain rights to the subsoil wealth found on their properties, once the government expropriated Teotihuacán, this clause was not enforced. Perhaps it was simply too impractical. Perhaps federal officials did not feel it necessary, as the people they were dealing with were nothing more than "stupid Indians." Whatever the reason, the Mexican government ended up taking possession of both the surface and the subsoil wealth at Teotihuacán. Ultimately, it paid a little over 8,200 pesos for all of the properties.[27] And so it was that the land that had once sustained hundreds of villagers became a showcase of the ancients.

Considering Batres's earlier experiences, we might have expected the people to unite as a menacing "mob," but they did not. Rather than fight for their land—which would have been futile anyway—they fought for their crops. They asked for permission to harvest for one last season. This left the government perplexed. Should it permit them? Should it compensate them for their crops? What was the protocol in such a case? Batres appears to have mellowed, letting the villagers enter the site and tend to their crops for one last time, "as long as they did not harm" the monuments.[28] After this, though, even the trees and magueys became national property, which Batres used in his reconstruction of the site in the most ingenious of ways—as the fuel to run his equipment, the "stone-breaking machine, and the pump that carried water to the top of the pyramid."[29]

Camp Pyramid of the Sun

How does one reconstruct a pyramid? There is no manual, no step-by-step guide. There is, moreover, no original pyramid to work from. As anthropologist Quetzil Castañeda reminds us, "not only has the original been lost, but the pristine and authentic original never existed." Most Mesoamerican pyramids are products of several phases of construction; they are made up of multiple layers that were set down at different points in time and that have eroded over the centuries. When in a pyramid's millennia of existence is the authentic structure to be found? Despite attempts at being faithful to some moment in the distant past, all archaeological reconstructions are a product of conjecture. They are "artifacts of . . . Western science," constructs based on "specific criteria and logics of authenticity."[30] What is considered authentic depends on who is doing the reconstructing and why. Recent approaches to archaeology acknowledge the contested nature of authenticity. Rather than reconstruction, today's goal is consolidation: archaeologists work to restore a structure and protect it from further collapse. This approach was adopted, for example, with the Great Temple in Mexico City. Archaeologists left the Aztec ruin exposed, writes one expert, but luckily did not succumb to "the temptation to rebuild the original edifice."[31]

Batres, however, worked at a time when authenticity went largely unquestioned and "reconstruction" was the operating word. Back then, the theorists of archaeological restoration ran the gamut, from those who avidly promoted this type of heavy-handed work to those who rejected it altogether, like the English architect John Ruskin, who considered restoration a "lie from beginning to end." Like many archaeologists today, Ruskin did not think a building could be returned to its original state. Instead, he advocated that it be preserved as much as possible through careful maintenance and repairs. An even more influential theorist, though, was Eugène Viollet-le-Duc, who took the opposite view. The French architect believed a monument could be returned to its pristine state. For him, the goal of restoration was to leave a structure in "mint condition," explains a later scholar, an approach that often "opened the door to imagination and whimsy."[32]

While the writings of Viollet-le-Duc circulated in Mexico, it is not clear how much they influenced the nation's archaeologists. Batres, however, seems to have leaned toward Viollet-le-Duc's way of thinking, as he sincerely believed he could restore a structure to its original state.[33] He did not always make the distinction that today's archaeologists make between an original work and modern additions. Instead, he often reassembled a structure with the goal of making his work unrecognizable. So, while today's archaeologists are careful to use materials that differ from the original stones when they cannot find those stones or are uncertain about their placement, this was not necessarily a concern for Batres. He could not be sure that the stones he gathered, say, from the people's homes at Mitla, belonged in the gaps in the ruins where he placed them, but he put them there anyway. Batres also let practicality override any sort of guiding philosophy for his work, something else evident in his reconstruction of Mitla, where he focused on protecting the murals with panes of glass at the expense of leaving huge holes in the walls. At the same time, the inspector often relied on tools such as plane tables and stadia rods—the typical tools of the trade— to measure distances and map sites and thus shape his creations with precision. And while he may not have been the most sophisticated archaeologist around, his methods were not that unusual. In most cases, he resorted to "the techniques of his time," writes a later archaeologist, the same that were being used in places such as Egypt and Mesopotamia.[34]

Although Batres did not leave behind a detailed account of how he went about reconstructing the Pyramid of the Sun, from the little information that he left we can glean this much: he began by uncovering the base of the southeast corner of the monument, where he conducted a series of "probes." With these he discovered, as he had expected, that the pyramid was made up of superimposed layers, "like the layers of an onion." Batres believed the layers were designed to give the pyramid "stability." We now know, as many suspected back then, that the layers found in Mesoamerican pyramids mark the succession of rulers, each trying to outdo his predecessor by making the structure bigger and taller. Underneath the pyramid's exterior crust of dirt and rubble lay a first layer that was "entirely ruined," according to Batres. "Four to six meters" below this, however, lay a second "well preserved" layer that, if uncovered, would reveal "the shape of the legendary temple."[35]

Here, Batres faced a dilemma: he could either leave the pyramid untouched and "mute forever" or excavate and risk destroying the first layer. Batres chose the latter, and when he began to dig, the entire layer "immediately" began falling apart, as he had expected. In his rush to uncover the massive structure, legend has it that he resorted to using dynamite, archaeology's biggest taboo. Although this claim has never been proven, Batres had worked with dynamite at ruins before, and he did have it among his supplies at Teotihuacán.[36] While many celebrated archaeologists had employed explosives in the past—Heinrich Schliemann blasted his way through much of Troy—by the time Batres set out to work in Teotihuacán, the use of dynamite in excavations was generally condemned. In any case, the inspector ended up peeling off the first layer of the pyramid on its north, south, and east sides, which left the retention walls at the top of the colossal structure exposed, which led him, in turn, to his next mistake.

Batres confused the retention walls with remnants of a terrace and proceeded to reconstruct the pyramid with an extra terrace, leaving it with five levels, when archaeologists believe there were originally just four. The much thinner terrace still found near the top of the pyramid is most likely a fabrication. While critics have charged him with falsifying it on purpose, it was probably just a mistake.[37] And if it seemed to Batres that his work could not possibly have become any more difficult, it soon did. The second, now-exposed layer was not as stable as he had thought—it was fragile, very fragile, made of adobe and stone bound with clay, so delicate that once it started to rain, the pyramid began to dissolve. To prevent the monument from disintegrating into a gigantic heap of mud, Batres covered it with a wooden framework made up of drains and gutters that channeled the water away. He then had his workers replace the clay that held the stones together with cement.

In April 1906, just as he was finishing this work on the two lower levels on the north side, President Díaz paid a visit and gave his wholehearted approval. He arrived to the sound of "cheering Indians" and tolling church bells. Díaz asked to see the pyramid's layers, correctly believing, unlike Batres, that they were markers of some important "event." It was hot and dusty as the dictator ascended the pyramid, followed by an entourage made up of military men and municipal leaders, as well as Vice President Ramón Corral, Sierra, Batres and his son Salvador, the assistant inspector. Newspapers marveled at the president's "virile stamina" during the climb; they praised him as the first leader to have "made the effort" to unearth Mexico's ruins, "monuments that are clear proof of a civilization comparable to that of Egypt."[38]

To orchestrate all the digging, lifting, and hauling involved in the reconstruction, Batres ran his camp of nearly three hundred workers with the military discipline he had learned as a young man. A cannon shot woke everyone at six in the morning, not a real cannon, recalled a worker, but "a small one, almost a toy."[39] Activities such as breakfast, digging, and dinner were highly regulated. Laborers were organized, as Batres explained, into "brigades supervised by officers and captains, under the command of a general foreman; such supervision ensured they handled their picks with complete caution so that they unearthed rather than destroyed" the pyramid.[40] The common laborers—diggers and haulers—earned little over 3.5 pesos a week, while the bricklayers who carefully inserted the cement with small spoons into the cracks between the stones earned 6.[41] Unfortunately, Batres did not record the origin of the workers. But they most likely came from the area, as was usually the case, while the more skilled laborers, like the carpenters and mechanics, were probably from Mexico City. According to Batres, the common worker was better off toiling at Teotihuacán than living as a debt peon on a hacienda. The Inspectorate had "helped tear the unhappy workers from the clutches and domination of overlords by giving them a full wage to spend where they please without onerous loans that . . . deprive them of their freedom."[42] Batres bragged that there was not even a monopoly on the sale of pulque at Camp Pyramid of the Sun, since the brigade captains brought the workers their "indispensable" alcohol daily. Along with the pulque, the camp also had a small jail for confining those who committed "infractions due to drunkenness, and other types of crimes" while they waited "to be brought before the proper authorities."[43]

It is ironic that Batres claimed the camp was better than life on a hacienda, because much like the classic landed estates, it projected an air of patrimonial benevolence amid all the hard labor. We know little about the conditions of the workers, but the camp had an infirmary, a public bathroom, and even a public bathtub. It had a spring manned by a conserje—the site ultimately had two guards—who dispensed water to the thirsty workers, relieving Batres of the need to haul in heavy barrels of the liquid, something he would have to do at Xochicalco. The camp held holiday celebrations as well. On 5 May 1905, to commemorate the nation's victory over the French at the Battle of Puebla in 1862, garlands of flowers and Mexican flags were tied to the workers' digging tools and strewn across the Pyramid of the Sun. Over eight hundred people attended the event, shouting "¡Viva México!" and cheering for the battle's famous heroes, Ignacio Zaragoza and, of course, Porfirio Díaz. One worker made a speech praising Díaz as the leader who had brought peace, civilization, and progress to the country and who had "solidified the foundations" of Mexican nationhood.[44] Batres then had the workers parade around the base of the pyramid to the sound of drums and bugles. With this curious but symbolic act, the state not only took control of the site, but incorporated the pyramid itself into Mexico's nationalist discourse and calendar of celebrations—the state was, in a sense, making the pyramid Mexican.

But nothing brought more excitement to Camp Pyramid of the Sun than the arrival of the train. Although the enormous mass of dirt and rubble was initially hauled away in wheelbarrows and, later, ore carts set on tracks, it was eventually moved by train. In 1908, tracks were extended from the nearby Mexican Railroad line to the pyramid, allowing the train to haul off rubble at the speed of one hundred tons per hour and dump it more than half a mile away. Nicknamed the Quetzalcoatl, the train, a type of metal serpent, also served the important function of transporting visitors to the site. But in the eyes of Batres, the train meant much more: it shored up Mexico's modern image: "With it we will have a truly momentous display that will live up to the expectations for the Centennial."[45] The local residents also received the train with "much enthusiasm," as it helped them get their goods more easily to market. And they benefited from the reconstruction of Teotihuacán in other ways. The site attracted so many workers that it became a town unto itself, forcing the government to build a school for the "children of the indigenous," whose grand opening was scheduled to take place during the centennial.[46]

Somehow, Batres managed all of these affairs while simultaneously working at Xochicalco (he also found the time to travel to Veracruz to put an end to the excavations of Nuttall, among other projects). To aid him in the renovation of Xochicalco, he brought along his trusty confidant, Verazaluce, the conserje of Tepozteco, who left his site in the care of his son. Batres had expected the work at Xochicalco to be easy, but it turned out to be much more complicated and costly in practice. The site lacked water and shelter for the workers; it was remote, inaccessible, and plagued by uneven, difficult terrain. The absence of transportation meant all the supplies, including heavy materials like sand and water, had to be hauled in on the backs of peons, increasing costs in a place that was already expensive (the dutiful conserje Jesús Moreno, lest we forget, took up his long-distance relationship with Xochicalco for this very reason). On top of it all, the locals kept stealing Batres's supplies, objects, he claimed, that they coveted more than any of the relics he discovered. To combat this problem, Batres ended up hiring a permanent police force for the site, yet another unforeseen expense. But he eventually got the funding he needed to finish the job. In clearing the area, he uncovered a "very rich archaeological zone, one of the biggest groups of monuments of this type ever found." He hoped the government would explore the site more thoroughly one day, as it held, he maintained, a "wealth of extraordinary discoveries."[47]

The constant shuffling back and forth between Xochicalco and Teotihuacán forced Batres to leave his son Salvador in charge of one of the sites during his absence. And while Salvador often proved to be a reliable aide, he had a considerable penchant for trouble. The assistant inspector seldom appears in official records, but when he does, he is usually out carousing, wreaking havoc, and abusing the locals. Here are some sample incidents:

July 1906: Salvador and two rurales pay a late-night visit to the home of a
mysterious Doña Delfina Ortiz in San Martín near the Pyramid of
the Moon. An "enormous scandal of bullets" shatters the silence of
the sleepy town, as the three men ride back to their camp, shooting
pistols and "shouting blasphemies" along the way.

September 1906: Salvador is "committing many arbitrary acts," "mis-
treating" and "threatening" the people of Teotihuacán, down to the
"poor widows."

Spring 1908: Salvador is in Europe studying the conservation of monuments, a government mission much like the earlier trip of his father,
and the ruins of Mexico are thus at peace. The assistant inspector
visits Italy and France, but must cut his trip short to deal with some
sort of court case pending against him back home in Mexico.

April 1910: Salvador is forcing the locals near Xochicalco to work, "insulting and threatening them with severe punishments if they do not
render all the free services he has imposed on them." To a municipal
leader who dares to defy him, he threatens: I am "the son of the
Señor Ministro," and your authority "will not be respected."[48]

When questioned about this misconduct, Batres came to his son's
defense. He reminded the government of Salvador's dedication to the
Inspectorate over the years; how Salvador severed three fingers while hauling
a statue from Monte Albán to the National Museum, how he had risked
infection from the toxic fumes that emanated from the drainage pipes as he
helped his father excavate the street of Escalerillas in Mexico City. No legal
action, it seems, was ever brought against Salvador.

Batres also often shared his camp with his wife, Josefa Castañeda y
Nájera. A photo shows the family posed in a wooden shack the inspector
lived in at Xochicalco, a type of makeshift home he seems to have set up in
Teotihuacán as well. Josefa and Batres's secretary, Antonia Clos, are seated
next to each other. Josefa stares straight at the camera, looking none too
pleased. At a distance, Batres and Salvador pose behind a table; Batres stands
while everyone else sits. The table and chairs, along with the water cooler and
cups hanging on the wall, were some of the few creature comforts in this
home away from home, objects Batres transported from his house in Mexico
City. Orderly and neat, the room attempts to bring an air of civilization to a
rustic, often-inhospitable place. There is even a gramophone and a neatly
pressed, white tablecloth on the table.

The Tourists

At Teotihuacán, Batres designed some features specifically for the tourists. He built a museum, the first state-sponsored, on-site museum in the country. With a Doric-style façade and elegant display cases filled with over eight thousand objects from his excavation, the press speculated it would "draw the attention" of Americans and Europeans.[49] To allow visitors a chance to rest during their busy tour of the ruins, which Batres estimated would take eight hours, he also planned on constructing "a tourist house and restaurant." This plan failed to materialize, however, forcing Batres to settle for a kiosk where visitors could relax and have refreshments. But his most fantastic creation at Teotihuacán was a "Japanese garden," complete with a waterfall and lake full of carp and other colorful fish. Designed by Japanese nationals living in Mexico who were experts in such matters, this feature would, Batres hoped, "eliminate the arid appearance of the region and make it more attractive to tourists."[50] Had we visited, we would have been struck not only by the lake but also by the many signs Batres had posted. While they were meant to inform, some expressed doubt at the same time, like the one in front of the Temple of Agriculture that said, "Temple of Agriculture?" Others gave bits of information Batres thought were particularly important, like the sign that explained, "This is where the rubble reached before the Pyramid of the Sun was uncovered." Or two others, with giant arrows, one pointing south that read, "this is what Monsieur Désiré Charnay discovered" and another pointing north that declared, "discovered by Leopoldo Batres."[51]

One problem the tourists faced at Teotihuacán was the sale of fake antiquities. The forgery business was booming throughout Mexico, where pieces of all kinds were being produced, from the crude and "grotesque," wrote Batres, to faithful replicas, "spectacular works in their own right."[52] Those who dedicated themselves to the industry made everything from vases to pipes, burying them in dirt and breaking off small pieces to make them look more authentic. Different parts of the country specialized in different types of objects; Oaxaca and Mexico City churned out fake artifacts made of gold, while Puebla specialized in silver. The presence of visitors at the ruins seems to have stimulated the industry, much as it does today. One group from Chicago was even said to have purchased the objects "still hot," as if straight out of the oven.[53] Tourists not only bought the forgeries but also donated them to museums back home. The problem was so rampant, observed one Mexican reporter, that several "American museums" began to distribute leaflets with warnings just in case any of their patrons were planning to take a trip south of the border.[54] Some tourists were not gullible victims of the industry but actually commissioned the locals to make the phony pieces, like the "foreigner" who placed orders with a peasant on a regular basis. The foreigner raked in a hefty profit, buying the forgeries at 6 reales a piece and selling them for close to 50 pesos. He even taught the peasant "certain curious procedures," techniques, most likely, to give the newly minted artifacts a weathered, antiqued appearance. The peasant was satisfied with the trade as well: "I've lived off of this industry for some time now," he declared, "making heads, idols, weapons, . . . and other things that I design to appear ancient, very ancient!"[55]

The "very ancient" things plagued museums around the world. Archaeologists had no way of detecting the forgeries other than examining them and comparing them with objects known to be authentic. The ability to identify the phony relics was considered a type of litmus test that separated the expert from the lesser archaeologist. Charnay, for instance, explained how even the most experienced archaeologist in Mexico fell victim to the "coarse falsifiers . . . who exploit the passion of collectors and the gullibility of the public." But Europeans, he bragged, would never be fooled by the pieces. He himself would never give the "monstrous objects" even a second glance.[56] Meanwhile, the French explorer had been busy making casts of a variety of artifacts in Mexico's National Museum. Little did he know that it would later be revealed that all three hundred vases he so painstakingly copied were fakes!

According to Batres, Mexico produced more forgeries than any other place in the Americas. This industry, he claimed, had roots stretching back to the early colonial period. And while different parts of the country had their own specialties, no place produced more fakes than Teotihuacán, "the headquarters of the traffic," wrote the American archaeologist William Henry Holmes. The locals at Teotihuacán were even masters at the art of the sale. They sauntered out to greet each passing train and, careful to avoid raising suspicions, presented the tourists with only a "limited number of pieces."[57] To add to the charade, they gave a full account of the discovery of each object, down to its exact location. The typical forger, noted Batres, was an "uncouth peasant," a drunk "who spends his time in taverns." But he could also be a criminal, like the "re-offending thief" who specialized in phony obsidian pieces and picking pockets, until he picked one too many and landed in the newly built Islas Tres Marías penitentiary.[58] At Teotihuacán, some of the most notorious forgers were the Barrios brothers from the community of San Sebastián, the two brothers who set up a "factory of false

idols" where they manufactured ceramic masks and statues along with souvenir busts of Porfirio Díaz. Batres took a practical and benevolent approach
to the brothers who, like other forgers, he considered victims of unscrupulous middlemen. Rather than shut down their business, he convinced them
to be honest about the origin of the objects and present them to customers as
a "local industry."[59] With this, the illicit artifacts became handicrafts, passing from one type of commodity to another, a transformation that highlights
the flexible meaning of the objects. Teotihuacán's tourists could now go
home both with their souvenirs and undeceived.

Batres claimed he fought long and hard against the forgery business, an
industry he thought caused "incalculable damage, not only to the pockets of
the unwary . . . but to history."[60] He wrote a book exposing it, his *Falsified
Mexican Antiquities* (1910). He also built an exhibit in the National Museum
that taught the public how to detect phony pieces. Designed with objects he
had come across while organizing the archaeology collection, the exhibit
displayed the "evolution" of the industry, beginning with the most crudely,
"poorly cooked" ceramic pots and progressing to the finer items made of
obsidian and gold. The collection had a "rigorous classification," remarked
one observer, with labels just like those found on the "real" antiquities,
recording the object's culture and place of origin, as well as the type of artifact it sought to imitate. According to Batres, the only way to tell a fake from
an original was to have a "well-trained eye."[61] He, of course, possessed such
an eye and could detect the forgeries based on their craftsmanship and form,
while his rivals like Chavero and Saville, he insisted, were frequently duped.

The Centennial

As the centennial approached and Batres tended to some of the finishing
touches, he decided to make the two conserjes at Teotihuacán more presentable by dressing them in uniform. Their "humble Indian clothes," he
explained, made the "tourists look upon them with even more disdain."[62] Off
went their traditional *calzón de manta* (comfortable hot-weather clothing)
and on came their new attire: red pants, a grey wool jacket with gold buttons,
and a helmet and badge engraved with the word "conserje." Mexico during
the age of Díaz saw several similar attempts to modernize the Indians and
lower classes through the regulation of dress, an effort that reached "extreme
levels" during the centennial as officials prepared to show off the nation.[63]

Batres also ordered German pistols and sabers for each of the guards, to give them "the appearance that befits them as authorities of the place." He planned to have all the caretakers at "the principal ruins dressed in uniform" during the centennial, but this never happened.[64]

Here, as on other occasions, the irony of what Batres was doing did not come into question: as the ruins of the ancient Indians were being unveiled, the contemporary Indians, the "savages," were being expelled from the site and concealed. This contradiction was apparent not only in the making of Teotihuacán but in the centennial festivities, as officials in Mexico City did everything possible to hide the Indians from public view, forcing them to exchange the calzón de manta for "trousers, sombreros for felt hats, and sandals for shoes."[65] At the same time, hundreds of Indians were made to dress up as Aztecs for the historical parade, complete with Moctezuma, the last Aztec emperor before the Spanish conquest, carried on an elaborate litter, surrounded by an entourage made up of ancient warriors, lords, virgins, and priests. Over two hundred thousand spectators watched the event, a reenactment of the momentous encounter between Moctezuma and the conqueror Cortés.

Meanwhile, just a few feet away in the museum, the professors scurried about, taking care of the final preparations for the Congress of Americanists. Days before the event, President Díaz arrived to inaugurate the newly renovated museum. Like others, he too thought it had been "perfectly" refurbished. As he toured each department, he integrated his own life history into what he saw on display. He stopped at the portrait of José María Arteaga, the general who had fought beside him against the French, and remarked that it "did not look anything" like him. He paused in the patio near the plaster casts of Mitla that Batres had made and recalled how he had played among the ruins as a young child. Gazing at the objects in the archaeology collection, Díaz commented that the ancient Indians had been "very developed."[66] Then he took his famous photograph in front of the Aztec Calendar. Mexico's supreme leader posed with the Cross of Palenque, too, the massive artifact Batres and Sierra had recently hauled out of the jungles of Chiapas, a symbol of the regime's newfound control over Maya territory. The National Museum was set for the congress.

The weeklong event began on 7 September 1910, presided over by the conference president, Eduard Seler, and vice president, Franz Boas. Over sixty delegates presented papers, almost all of which examined Mexico's ancient Indians, especially the dominant cultures like the Aztecs and Maya.

Topics ranged from trepanation—the practice of drilling holes into human skulls—to a discussion of whether the Indians had worn ponytails, an idea thought to demonstrate a connection between the ancient Mexicans and the Chinese. But most of the papers treated what one delegate called "higher knowledge," Indian languages, cosmology, religion, and the measurement of time. The congress reinforced the idea that Mexico possessed a sophisticated, ancient past. And it also drove home the notion that Mexico was scientific and modern, "the archaeological capital of the American continent," as Sierra declared. In his inaugural address at the event, Sierra emphasized these points when he welcomed the delegates to Mexico, a country "with an ardor for the future, an ardor for growth, a desire to reach new heights," and full of "passion for its history."[67]

The congress delegates not only exchanged ideas but some, including Seler and Boas, took advantage of the occasion to discuss the foundation of what became known as the International School of American Archaeology and Ethnology. Housed in the National Museum, this international effort at scientific cooperation was sponsored by the governments of Mexico and Prussia as well as Columbia University, the University of Pennsylvania, and Harvard. The school opened in Mexico in early 1911 and carried out most of its work after the fall of Díaz. Its purpose was to develop the different fields of anthropology in the Americas, especially in Mexico, by focusing on the training of students, an emphasis that most likely reflected the interests of Boas, who was not only one of the founders but a teacher of anthropology and anthropometrics at the school. Boas saw the institution as an opportunity to spread his scientific methods in Mexico and to "train professional archaeologists on his own terms."[68] The aim of the school, then, was to teach field methods to students. And it had one major success, as it was under its guidance that Gamio carried out his famous stratigraphic excavations in central Mexico. But overall, the institution was a failure. It produced no great discoveries and closed abruptly when Mexico's political instability forced the last director, Alfred Tozzer of Harvard, to flee the country in 1914, less than four years after the delegates at the Congress of Americanists had met to establish the school.

One of the highlights of the congress was the excursion to Teotihuacán. The scientists, a group of over two hundred, including Mexican officials and a delegation led by the ambassadors of the United States, Japan, China, and Spain, arrived at the site on the Quetzalcoatl train.[69] Batres acted as tour guide and gave a systematic recounting of all his work in French. The visitors walked around the Pyramid of the Sun; some climbed to the top for a breathtaking view of the Valley of Mexico and the capital in the distance. They also toured the new museum at the site, which was opened on that day. Just as they had done during the 1895 congress, they lunched in the impressive nearby cave, which was now called the Porfirio Díaz Grotto. An orchestra played Mexican and foreign melodies throughout the meal, bursting into the anthems of the representative nations and forcing the visitors to stand at attention every now and then. Mexico's secretary of foreign relations, Enrique Creel, gave a toast to all the "cultured nations" that had sent representatives. Sierra made a speech praising Teotihuacán as one of "humanity's great works," a site that proved "the grandeur of a people."[70] Seler and Boas commended Batres on his reconstruction. Batres was satisfied as well. He had unveiled the city of the "Greeks of the yellow American race," the "Rome of the Toltecs," and considered it a "happy success." In addition to rebuilding the Pyramid of the Sun, he uncovered the Temple of Agriculture, the so-called Subterranean Buildings, and parts of the Ciudadela. Years later, Batres would explain that this work had been part of his larger effort to ensure Mexicans were not judged "as illiterates in the realm of science."[71] In fact, his reconstruction was considered such a success that the press speculated that the Pyramid of the Moon would be next.

But no sooner had the centennial come and gone than the country erupted in revolution. President Díaz's formula for order and progress had brought benefits to only a few—for most Mexicans, it was much "too costly and constraining to bear."[72] Like wildfires, revolts spread throughout the country. Díaz fled to Europe, for a comfortable exile in Paris; before he died, he got a glimpse of the pyramids of Egypt, monuments Mexicans had always compared to their own. One month after Díaz's departure, in July 1911, Batres resigned as inspector. He too left for Europe. He lived in Barcelona for a year and then returned to Mexico, only to be forever condemned for his work. He had "disfigured" the Pyramid of the Sun, declared Gamio. His excavation failed to produce much "useful information," charged the later archaeologist Ignacio Bernal. His reconstruction was nothing more than a "stupendous monument to self-assertion and incompetence," wrote the Englishman Maudslay. The reconstructed Pyramid of the Sun was much smaller than the original, and it had an added terrace; what is more, the cement used to hold it together gave it "an alien, modern appearance," according to the later critic Sigvald Linné.[73] Today, this use of cement remains under attack. While the cement was meant to stabilize the pyramid, it prevents the evaporation of water. As a result, the north side of the structure is more dense, and the south side, where the sun hits the hardest, is drying out. At the time of this writing, archaeologists are looking for ways to keep the pyramid from crumbling apart like a gigantic, dried-up sand castle. A couple of archaeologists have come to Batres's defense, however. One, for instance, considers his reconstruction of Xochicalco a "faithful and accurate job." Even the critic Linné acknowledges that while Batres used "far too heavy a hand" at Teotihuacán, the Pyramid of the Sun is "more or less accurate."[74] Overall, however, reactions to Batres's work tend to be negative, even though he had used the techniques of his time and even though some of his contemporaries who are now held in high regard, scientists like Seler and Boas, had praised him. What is more, reconstructions carried out later in Mexico into the 1970s and beyond were often not much better than those of Batres, "despite the improvements in archaeological techniques and despite the advances" made in restoration theory and practice.[75] Nevertheless, to this day, Batres is not taken seriously in the world of archaeology.

While Batres was not the best of archaeologists, he also found himself on the wrong end of the political spectrum. He was a symbol of the old order. Like Díaz, he too went down as a villain in the annals of history, which, until recently, had exalted the revolution and disparaged anything associated with the Porfirian government. The inspector was much too wedded to the ancien régime to be treated objectively by later scholars, and his lack of scientific rigor only aggravated matters. Unlike most of Mexico's archaeologists, he would not weather the transition to the new revolutionary regime, a circumstance shaped in large part by his constant conflicts with others. Instead, the dictator of Mexican archaeology who had hindered the work of so many of his peers was banished from the world of science, and his reconstruction of Teotihuacán became the focus of the critiques leveled against him. The work was fanciful, some said; he used dynamite; he allowed the train tracks to cut right through the ruins. The list of accusations goes on and on, and Batres would spend the rest of his life defending himself from the charges.

But while all of these critiques are valid, they fail to take into account the context of the reconstruction and its aim. The aim had never been to carry out a painstakingly accurate archaeological restoration and study of Teotihuacán. Instead, the overriding concerns had been political and ideological. The aim had been to quickly turn the ruins into an official site to showcase Mexico as a great, modern nation with a prestigious ancient past—in time for the centennial and the many guests. If we keep this in mind, Batres's work was truly a "happy success."

Epilogue

❧

❧ LEOPOLDO BATRES'S LAST YEARS MUST HAVE BEEN DIFFICULT. HE resigned as Mexico's inspector of monuments only to be replaced by his dreaded enemy, Francisco Rodríguez, the archaeologist with whom he had battled over the Tepozteco artifacts and the statue of La India. Batres also faced a slew of attacks. In addition to having his archaeological expertise critiqued time and again and facing charges of trafficking, he was accused of falsifying antiquities, an allegation that had surfaced much earlier—the Frenchman Boban made the claim in the 1880s—but that reemerged with a vengeance once Batres stepped down from his powerful office. After years of perfecting his "falsification techniques," he left the country full of forgeries, wrote archaeology professor Ramón Mena, another scientist who had tangled with Batres over the years to the point of becoming one of his most bitter rivals.[1]

But other charges against Batres were new. Critics claimed he had embezzled funds, appropriated artifacts from Teotihuacán, and used the expropriation of the site to acquire lands of his own. They also accused him of using government-paid peons to carry out work in his home in Mexico City and of pilfering federal property—when he resigned, some equipment and horses, among other things, were reportedly found missing. His most dogged accuser was Rodríguez, the "most jealous and brutal of my enemies," Batres complained.[2] The new inspector rounded up peons from Teotihuacán and other sites to testify against Batres, while the old inspector gathered peons of his own, who attested to his "rigorous and unyielding honesty." Just as he had done years before, Batres claimed Rodríguez was manipulating the "simple Indians," riling the people of "little intelligence" against him.[3] The locals at

Teotihuacán, he said, were simply angry with him for having taken away their lands during the expropriation. Batres had a response for each of the accusations made against him, and he was never formally charged with anything. Instead, the official archaeologist of the Porfirian regime spent his last years shunted from the world of archaeology, hammering away at his typewriter writing emotional tracts in his defense, taking on each allegation, and making lists of people. He divided all the people he knew into three categories: "my enemies," "the jealous ones," and "my defenders." And he summed up his troubles in one statement: "Everybody kicks you when you're down."[4]

Once in a while, Batres would visit the National Museum bearing antiquities and other objects to donate or sell, much as he had done years before. Only now he complained about the "tiny sum" he received in exchange. He had no choice; he was forced to sell the items for "economic reasons."[5] Meanwhile, the professors undertook every effort to erase any trace of him from the museum. They dismantled the Gallery of Monoliths, the layout of which "revealed an absolute lack of knowledge and even common sense," charged his enemy Mena. (Much of it had been driven by a desire to make the pieces look uniform by matching them in height.) Batres pleaded with the professors to keep his projects intact, but they did not. Instead, they tore down his falsification exhibit, transferring the objects to the ethnography department, where they became examples of contemporary indigenous crafts. They removed the plaster casts of Mitla he had set up in the patio and, according to Batres, put them in storage in the janitors' bathroom. Adding insult to injury, they destroyed one of Batres's greatest points of pride, his classification of the archaeology collection. The "ridiculous captions" on the labels were removed and the antiquities regrouped, even though the professors would continue to struggle over how to arrange them.[6] "The museum is now free of the archaeological and artistic attacks perpetrated by Mr. Leopoldo Batres," pronounced Mena.[7] Batres's past, it seems, had finally caught up with him.

Francisco Rodríguez served as inspector of monuments until mid-1913, when the position was divided up among four men, at least three of whom were enemies of Batres: Mena, Gamio, Aguirre—the former archaeology student whose excavations Batres had thwarted and who would eventually be known as "the thief"—and Juan Martínez Hernández, a Mayanist and lawyer. The new inspectors were now accountable directly to the museum, a change designed to quell the rivalry between the Inspectorate and the museum. With Batres gone, the professors hoped to rein in the Inspectorate.

They thought the two agencies would finally be able to work in tandem: the museum would serve as the intellectual guide, and the Inspectorate would carry out its orders in the field. Each of the new inspectors took charge of a different archaeological zone in the country: Aguirre oversaw the north; Gamio, central Mexico; Mena, the Isthmus of Tehuantepec; and Martínez, Chiapas and the Yucatán Peninsula.[8] But Gamio dominated the new system. Not only did he control central Mexico, the area considered most important, but he was made chief inspector. This arrangement, however, soon fell apart. Within months, the Inspectorate separated from the museum, a result of both personality conflicts and the long-standing differences between the two institutions' practical and theoretical approaches to archaeology. The Inspectorate was placed, once again, under the jurisdiction of the Secretariat of Education, where it remained in the hands of four archaeologists. But this, too, did not last long. By 1918 the Inspectorate had changed names and jurisdictions: it was now called the Directorate of Anthropology and was overseen by the Secretariat of Agriculture and Development. And it was also back to having just one inspector; not surprisingly, this was Gamio.

Although he was cast aside by the changing of the guard, Batres still had a lot of fight left in him. When President Alvaro Obregón granted the Carnegie Institution its famous concession to carry out excavations in Yucatán in the early 1920s, Batres was livid. The concessions, he said, only exposed Mexico to a "filibusterism that goes by the name of science and that has damaged our wealth of monuments, sacking and devastating them without mercy." The American archaeologists were nothing but "Yankee vampires," not to be trusted.[9] Batres also had enough fight left in him to go to battle against Gamio, an enemy who was not even worthy of such a title; instead, Batres placed him in the category of "the jealous ones." (He put Rodríguez and Mena in the same category, too.) When Gamio criticized Batres's reconstruction of Teotihuacán in his seminal work _The Population of the Valley of Mexico_, Batres snapped back. He accused Gamio of being a liar, a man with neither a conscious nor scientific credentials who had moved up in the world of archaeology only because he had been shielded by the official establishment (which was, of course, the same argument that had always been used against Batres). The tension between the two men was fierce. In one incident, Gamio supposedly went to visit Batres at his home in order to apologize for having bad-mouthed him. Batres's dutiful son Salvador got involved. He seized Gamio and, dragging him by the ear, forced him to beg for forgiveness at his father's feet.[10]

Amazingly, all of these changes to Mexico's archaeological infrastructure (and all of this drama!) took place in the midst of war. And as on so many other occasions in the nation's history, the monuments did not go unscathed. When the revolution broke out, federal and rebel troops swept through the ruins, using them as shelters and forts. They set fire to Xochicalco. They ransacked the museum of Tepoztlán. Peasants also took action. At Teotihuacán, they tore down the fence that marked the archaeological zone and reclaimed the land. But no one at the sites suffered more than the guards. At Mitla, for instance, rebel forces robbed the conserje of his life savings, money he had gathered at the cost of "true sacrifices." Some of the guards abandoned their posts, leaving the ruins at the mercy of sackers; when the caretaker of Tepozteco took off, the site "lost one of its best pieces." But others stayed on, living in constant fear. Life "in those places is very difficult," wrote one of the men. "The situation is very dangerous, and I am constantly being pursued," said another. "I risk my life and that of my peon, both of us unarmed, how can we defend ourselves?" It was far worse at night, so much so that the guard at Teotihuacán took to sleeping in the nearby caves. The cold was brutal, he pointed out, but it was the only way to save his "skin."[11] Nearby, in Mexico City, the National Museum likewise did not go unscathed. When the revolution shook the capital during the Ten Tragic Days in February 1913, hundreds of people stormed the museum in search of shelter. Outside, bullets flew, damaging much of the building. Everyone involved in Mexico's archaeological establishment—from the professors to the inspectors to the guards—not only saw their share of violence but faced interruptions in work and went unpaid, often for years. The situation was so unstable that between 1915 and 1916 the position of museum director changed hands an astonishing seven times.

Yet far from unraveling, the infrastructure Batres and Mexican elites had created to control the past stayed intact. It not only stayed intact but also thrived, once the chaos of the revolution subsided, forming the basis of Mexico's archaeological establishment in the twentieth century. All of the debates, all the wrangling, all the lugging around of statues had not been for naught. While scholars have tended to see Mexico's embrace of the Indian past as a product of the revolution, when archaeologists began erecting site after pristine site and famous artists began paying homage to antiquity in huge murals on government buildings, the effort to take charge of the past took root much earlier, during the long reign of Porfirio Díaz. The revolution in this sense brought more continuity than change. It reinforced some well-entrenched patterns: the artifacts continued to be funneled into the museum, archaeological laws were made stronger, more ruins were reconstructed, and the guards continued (or not) to remain at their sites, as the government intensified its claim to the Indian past through the INAH, the grandchild of the Inspectorate created in 1939, which is still in existence today. But Leopoldo Batres would not live to see this last change. He died in 1926 and was buried in a tomb he had designed in imitation of the ruins of Mitla, his most beloved of sites, complete with replicas of the elaborate friezes he had carefully pieced back together on the ruins so many years before.

Just like Batres and his carefully constructed friezes, Mexico during the age of Díaz pieced together an ancient past a stone at a time, with a relic here, another there. The country's leaders did not uncover a past as much as they constructed one, making choices about what to emphasize and what to ignore. But the story of archaeology in Mexico is not just a reminder that all modern nations need histories and work hard to produce them. It also highlights the problem inherent in the way the relationship between nations and indigenous peoples has been imagined. It points to the exclusionary nature of modern states. All over the world, the nation-state and modernity itself are generally perceived to be at odds with aboriginal peoples, who are cast as too backward, too traditional, or too lacking in one way or another to fit in. Mexico responded to this tension in large part by retreating into a bygone past. Like so many other countries across the globe, it appropriated bits and pieces of indigenous culture, creating a romanticized account of native people while marginalizing them at the same time.

Notes

Introduction

1. Coe and Koontz, *Mexico*, 111.
2. Diehl, *Tula*, 27.
3. *El Monitor Republicano*, 12 September 1879, in Lombardo de Ruiz, *El pasado prehispánico*, 1:67.
4. Archivo Histórico del Museo Nacional de Antropología, Museo Nacional de Antropología (hereafter cited as AHMNA), vol. 1, exp. 40, fol. 92. All translations are mine unless otherwise noted.
5. Bernal, *A History of Mexican Archaeology*, 116.
6. Quoted in Castillo Ledón, *El Museo Nacional*, 24.
7. Rivera Cambas, *México pintoresco*, 1:179. For the history of archaeology in Mexico from the colonial period to the Porfiriato, see García Mora, ed., *La antropología en México*, vol. 1.
8. MacLachlan and Beezley, *El Gran Pueblo*, 152.
9. Archivo Leopoldo Batres, Mexico City, Subdirección de Documentación, Biblioteca Nacional de Antropología e Historia (hereafter cited as ALB), fols. 292 and 294.
10. Anderson, *Imagined Communities*, 6, 163.
11. Earle, "*Sobre héroes y tumbas*," 379.
12. For the elite fixation with European goods and culture, see Bauer, *Goods, Power, History*, Tenorio-Trillo, *Mexico at the World's Fairs*, and Beezley, *Judas at the Jockey Club*.
13. An analysis of *Mexico through the Centuries* (*México a través de los siglos*) can be found in Tenorio-Trillo, *Mexico at the World's Fairs*, and Florescano, *Imágenes de la patria a través de los siglos*.
14. For the place of Latin America in postcolonial theory, see Thurner and Guerrero, *After Spanish Rule*, and Moraña, Dussel, and Jáuregui, eds., *Coloniality at Large: Latin America and the Postcolonial Debate*.
15. Nora, "Between Memory and History," 9.

16. *El Monitor Republicano*, 31 May 1890, in Lombardo de Ruiz, *El pasado prehispánico*, 1:186; ALB, fol. 517.

17. García Canclini, *Hybrid Cultures*, 115; García Canclini, "El patrimonio de México y la construcción imaginaria de lo nacional," 63.

18. Lomnitz, *Deep Mexico, Silent Mexico*, 230.

19. Trigger, *A History of Archaeological Thought*, 174.

20. Earle, *The Return of the Native*, 134; Benavides, *Making Ecuadorian Histories*, 13.

21. Bonfil Batalla, "Nuestro patrimonio cultural," 46.

22. Esposito, *Funerals, Festivals, and Cultural Politics in Porfirian Mexico*, 4.

23. Appadurai, introduction to *The Social Life of Things*, 5.

24. Bonfil Batalla, "Nuestro patrimonio cultural," 37-38.

25. García Canclini, "El patrimonio de México y la construcción imaginaria de lo nacional," 61. Other studies that analyze the creation of patrimony as contested terrain in Mexico include Ferry, *Not Ours Alone*, and Breglia, *Monumental Ambivalence*. Outside of Mexico, there is a large body of research with this same focus; see, for example, Gathercole and Lowenthal, eds., *The Politics of the Past*, Bender, *Stonehenge*, and Greenspan, *Creating Colonial Williamsburg*.

26. Earle, *The Return of the Native*, 171.

27. Knight, "Racism, Revolution, and *Indigenismo*," 79.

28. Brading, *The Origins of Mexican Nationalism*, 1.

29. Knight, "Popular Culture and the Revolutionary State in Mexico," 431.

30. See, for example, Tenenbaum, *Mexico and the Royal Indian*, Tenenbaum, "Streetwise History," Widdifield, *The Embodiment of the National*, Tenorio-Trillo, *Mexico at the World's Fairs*, Florescano, *Imágenes de la patria a través de los siglos*, and Earle, *The Return of the Native*.

31. Schiffman, *The Birth of the Past*, 2.

Chapter One

1. *El Imparcial*, 16 February 1898, in Lombardo de Ruiz, *El pasado prehispánico*, 2:56.

2. ALB, fol. 412.

3. *El Imparcial*, 30 March 1910, in Lombardo de Ruiz, *El pasado prehispánico*, 2:586; ibid., 29 August 1909, in Lombardo de Ruiz, *El pasado prehispánico*, 2:549; ALB, fol. 276.

4. Archivo General de la Nación, Instrucción Pública y Bellas Artes (hereafter cited as AGN, IPBA), caja 152, exp. 49, fol. 2.

5. *El Monitor Republicano*, 13 May 1883, in Lombardo de Ruiz, *El pasado prehispánico*, 1:106.

6. Ibid., 19 June 1880, in Lombardo de Ruiz, *El pasado prehispánico*, 1:74.

7. *El Imparcial*, 3 June 1899, in Lombardo de Ruiz, *El pasado prehispánico*, 2:76.

8. *El Monitor Republicano*, 7 May 1890 and 2 July 1893, in Lombardo de Ruiz, *El pasado prehispánico*, 1:179, 246.

9. *El Imparcial*, 3 June 1899, in Lombardo de Ruiz, *El pasado prehispánico*, 2:76.

10. Saville, "The Temple of Tepoztlan, Mexico," 223.

11. For some of these legends, see Lomnitz, *Deep Mexico*. The celebration and the temple's significance are discussed in Redfield, *Tepoztlán*.

12. Charnay, *Ciudades y ruinas americanas*, 190.

13. *El Imparcial*, 9 December 1910 and 27 February 1906, in Lombardo de Ruiz, *El pasado prehispánico*, 2:664, 274.

14. AHMNA, vol. 9, exp. 46, fol. 144; Saville, "The Cruciform Structures of Mitla," 165; *El Monitor Republicano*, 19 May 1892, in Lombardo de Ruiz, *El pasado prehispánico*, 1:225.

15. Appadurai, introduction to *The Social Life of Things*, 15.

16. Brodie, Doole and Watson, *Stealing History*, 12.

17. Black, *On Exhibit*, 17.

18. Bazin, *The Museum Age*, 193.

19. Conn, *Museums and American Intellectual Life*, 9.

20. Black, *On Exhibit*, 4.

21. Bataille, "Museum," 64.

22. Black, *On Exhibit*, 9.

23. Conn, *Museums and American Intellectual Life*, 81.

24. Aguirre, *Informal Empire*, 28 and xiii.

25. Penny, *Objects of Culture*, 27.

26. Ames, *Museums, the Public and Anthropology*, 10.

27. Donato, "The Museum's Furnace," 223.

28. Clifford, "Objects and Selves," 237, 244.

29. Ministère de l'Instruction Publique, *Archives de la Commission Scientifique du Mexique*, 14. For a comparison of how the French and British took possession of pre-Hispanic antiquities see Aguirre, *Informal Empire*, xvii. See also Boone, ed., *Collecting the Pre-Columbian Past*, and Hocquenghem, Tamasi, and Villain-Gandossi, eds., *Pre-Columbian Collections in European Museums*.

30. Edison "Conquest Unrequited," 459, 468. Other works that examine the French Scientific Commission and French archaeology include Schávelzon, "La arqueología y el imperialismo" and "La Comisión Científica Francesa a México (1864–1867) y el inicio de la arqueología en América."

31. Bazin, *The Museum Age*, 210.

32. Williams, "Art and Artifact at the Trocadero," 148.

33. Penny, *Objects of Culture*, 10, 44.

34. Larson, *Our Indigenous Ancestors*, 56–57.

35. Penny, *Objects of Culture*, 52.

36. Rutsch, *Entre el campo y el gabinete*, 54.

37. Clifford, "Objects and Selves," 242.

38. Charnay, "Mis descubrimientos en México y en la América Central," 274; Williams, "Art and Artifact at the Trocadero," 159.
39. AHMNA, vol. 9, exp. 46, fol. 144.
40. The skull was made on a rotary wheel, a tool unknown to the Aztecs, and the quartz most likely came from Brazil, well out of the reach of Mesoamerican networks of trade. For the detective work that confirmed the piece is a fake, see Sax et al, "The Origins of Two Purportedly Pre-Columbian Mexican Crystal Skulls." For an account of Boban's role in peddling and producing fake skulls, see Maclaren Walsh, "Crystal Skulls and Other Problems."
41. AHMNA, vol. 9, exp. 12, fols. 37–38. Kunz brought the ax to world attention, but for years its culture of origin remained a mystery. Shaped like a "were-jaguar," a creature part jaguar and part human, the ax "had no features that could be linked with known Mesoamerican cultures, yet it had surely been made" in Mesoamerican antiquity. It was not until 1955, with radiocarbon dating and a series of excavations at La Venta, Tabasco, that archaeologists came to realize that the ax is Olmec. Today the piece belongs to the American Museum of Natural History in New York City. See Miller, *The Art of Mesoamerica*, 18–19.
42. Aguirre, *Informal Empire*, 19. This section draws heavily on Aguirre's work.
43. Lombardo de Ruiz and Solís Vicarte, *Antecedentes de las leyes sobre monumentos históricos*, 39. A subsequent ruling in 1832 similarly gave the state the power to forbid the exportation of "objects of art and science" (Lombardo de Ruiz and Solís Vicarte, *Antecedentes de las leyes sobre monumentos históricos*, 45).
44. Charnay, *Ciudades y ruinas americanas*, 89, 227.
45. Edison, "Patrimony on the Periphery," 495.
46. Ruiz, "Insiders and Outsiders," 4.
47. Edison, "Patrimony on the Periphery," 499–500.
48. See Desmond, *Yucatán through Her Eyes*. Le Plongeon most likely derived his dwarf theory from local lore, as many people in the Yucatán credited dwarves with building temples, including the Pyramid of the Dwarf or Pyramid of the Magician in Uxmal. Like other native cultures, the Maya often depicted dwarves in their art and held them in high esteem. They considered them the children of Chacs, or rain gods, and believed they had the power to bring rain.
49. The citations in this passage are from Desmond's *Yucatán through Her Eyes*, 135, 110, 111, 98, and 127.
50. Aguirre, *Informal Empire*, xxiii.
51. Maudslay, *Archaeology*, 42–43.
52. In *Alfred Maudslay and the Maya*, biographer Ian Graham claims that the Mexican government was unaware of the existence of Yaxchilán at the time, but this was not the case, as the site was listed on a government-sponsored map from 1886. Designed by Leopoldo Batres, the inspector of monuments, the map places the ruins in Mexico. It records Yaxchilán as the "City of Lorillard," a name invented by Charnay, an early explorer of the site, in honor of his patron, the tobacco tycoon

Pierre Lorillard. See the *Carta arqueológica de la República Mexicana, formada por Leopoldo Batres, ynspector y conservador de monumentos arqueológicos, año de 1886*, AGN, IPBA, caja 147, exp. 6, fol. 14. Batres's map is examined in chapter 5.

53. Willard, *The City of the Sacred Well*, 103, 118.

54. Ibid., 104.

55. Ibid., 127, 131, 149.

56. Thompson, "Forty Years of Research and Exploration in Yucatan," 48. For the objects found in the cenote by Thompson as well as by other archaeologists, see Coggins and Shane III, *Cenote of Sacrifice*.

57. Hinsley, "From Shell-Heaps to Stelae," 51.

58. Thompson, "Forty Years of Research and Exploration in Yucatan," 46–47.

59. García Moll, "El saqueo de Yaxchilán," 32.

60. Hinsley, "From Shell-Heaps to Stelae," 71.

61. Sigaux, *History of Tourism*, 82.

62. Feifer, *Going Places*, 193 and 195.

63. AGN, IPBA, caja 149, exp. 3, fol. 6.

64. *El Imparcial*, 19 December 1907, in Lombardo de Ruiz, *El pasado prehispánico*, 2:403.

65. Smith and Brent eds., *Hosts and Guests Revisited*, 4.

66. *El Imparcial*, 18 July 1897, in Lombardo de Ruiz, *El pasado prehispánico*, 2:48.

67. The graffiti was recorded by Alice Dixon Le Plongeon; see Desmond, *Yucatán through Her Eyes*, 178 and 144.

68. AGN, IPBA, caja 171, exp. 4, fol. 2.

69. Clifford, "Objects and Selves," 241.

70. Stewart, *On Longing*, 135–48.

71. *El Monitor Republicano*, 13 September 1896, in Lombardo de Ruiz, *El pasado prehispánico*, 1:299.

72. AGN, IPBA, caja 167 bis, exp. 66, fol. 30.

73. AHMNA, vol. 3, exp. 26, fol. 97.

74. *El Monitor Republicano*, 24 May 1888, in Lombardo de Ruiz, *El pasado prehispánico*, 1:147–48.

75. Hollowell, "Moral Arguments on Subsistence Digging," 74, 77.

76. Ibid., 88.

77. Brodie, Doole, and Watson, *Stealing History*, 13.

78. *El Monitor Republicano*, 22 May 1880, in Lombardo de Ruiz, *El pasado prehispánico*, 1:73.

79. *El Imparcial*, 25 April 1907 and 6 April 1904, in Lombardo de Ruiz, *El pasado prehispánico*, 2:347, 208–9.

Chapter Two

1. Tenorio-Trillo, *Mexico at the World's Fairs*, 245.

2. Esposito, *Funerals, Festivals, and Cultural Politics*, 6.

3. Florescano, *Imágenes de la patria a través de los siglos*, 206.

4. Tenorio-Trillo, *Mexico at the World's Fairs*, 69.

5. *El Imparcial*, 5 April 1910, in Lombardo de Ruiz, *El pasado prehispánico*, 2:587–88; Tenorio-Trillo, *Mexico at the World's Fairs*, 66.

6. AGN, IPBA, caja 167, exp. 34, fol. 3.

7. Chavero, *Historia antigua y de la conquista*, 76.

8. AGN, IPBA, caja 167 bis, exp. 53, fol. 1. Mexico's revolutionary archaeologists would echo Chavero's claim. Alfonso Caso, for instance, spoke of the Aztecs as "our closest genetic root, . . . our identifiable grandparent" (quoted in del Villar, "La construcción del Museo Nacional de Antropología," 21).

9. See Rius, *Un siglo de caricatura en México*, 13.

10. Orozco y Berra, "Dedicación del Templo Mayor de México," 68–71.

11. *El Monitor Republicano*, 9 June 1888, in Lombardo de Ruiz, *El pasado prehispánico*, 1:151.

12. Quoted in Earle, *The Return of the Native*, 107.

13. Tenorio-Trillo, *Mexico at the World's Fairs*, 242.

14. Widdifield, *The Embodiment of the National*, 11.

15. *El Monitor Republicano*, 19 November 1891, 13 January 1892, and 20 July 1881, in Lombardo de Ruiz, *El pasado prehispánico*, 1:215, 219, and 81.

16. AGN, IPBA, caja 152, exp. 67, fol. 5; *El Imparcial*, 8 April 1905 and 4 February 1909, in Lombardo de Ruiz, *El pasado prehispánico*, 2:239, 483; Díaz y de Ovando, *Memoria de un debate*, 20.

17. *El Monitor Republicano*, 22 April 1879, in Lombardo de Ruiz, *El pasado prehispánico*, 1:64; Peñafiel, *Teotihuacán*, 8; *El Imparcial*, 18 July 1897, in Lombardo de Ruiz, *El pasado prehispánico*, 2:46.

18. *El Imparcial*, 25 January 1898, in Lombardo de Ruiz, *El pasado prehispánico*, 2:53–54.

19. Ibid., 16 May 1900, in Lombardo de Ruiz, *El pasado prehispánico*, 2:85–86.

20. Tenorio-Trillo, *Mexico at the World's Fairs*, 94. See Tenorio-Trillo, *Mexico at the World's Fairs*, especially 64–80 and 92–95, for an analysis of the Aztec palace.

21. Mendoza, "Complemento al erudito artículo del señor Orozco y Berra," 225.

22. *El Monitor Republicano*, 5 April 1890, in Lombardo de Ruiz, *El pasado prehispánico*, 1:177.

23. *El Imparcial*, 5 April 1910, in Lombardo de Ruiz, *El pasado prehispánico*, 2:588.

24. Chavero, *Historia antigua y de la conquista*, 102.

25. AGN, IPBA, caja 152, exp. 49, fol. 2.

26. *El Imparcial*, 6 April 1904, in Lombardo de Ruiz, *El pasado prehispánico*, 2:207 and 209; AHMNA, vol. 4, exp. 1, fol. 10.

27. Rivera Cambas, *México pintoresco*, 1:179.

28. AGN, IPBA, caja 150, exp. 2, fol. 3, and caja 169, exp. 8, fol. 4.

29. Ruiz, "Insiders and Outsiders," 8.

30. AGN, IPBA, caja 111, exp. 31, fol. 19.

31. AHMNA, vol. 6, exp. 47, fol. 169; AGN, IPBA, caja 165, exp. 57, fol. 3.

32. ALB, fol. 278. Batres would make this claim later, in 1918.

33. Edison, "Patrimony on the Periphery," 495.

34. For the 1827 and 1868 decrees, see Lombardo de Ruiz and Solís Vicarte, *Antecedentes de las leyes sobre monumentos históricos*, 39, 62. In some instances, the Mexican government did not resort to a contract but simply wrote up a letter of introduction for the archaeologist to present to local officials that requested their assistance, especially with rounding up labor.

35. The above citations from this debate can be found in Díaz y de Ovando, *Memoria de un debate*, 60–89.

36. Edison, "Patrimony on the Periphery," 459–95.

37. Sierra, *Epistolario y papeles privados*, 290.

38. Sierra, *Obras completas*, 9:128–29.

39. Stabb, "Indigenism and Racism in Mexican Thought," 407.

40. Ibid., 408.

41. Sierra, *Obras completas*, 5:213; Sierra, *The Political Evolution of the Mexican People*, 368.

42. Keen, *The Aztec Image in Western Thought*, 435.

43. Lomnitz, *Death and the Idea of Mexico*, 20.

44. Kourí, "Interpreting the Expropriation of Indian Pueblo Lands in Porfirian Mexico," 103, 102.

45. Keen, *The Aztec Image in Western Thought*, 434.

46. *El Monitor Republicano*, 14 January 1877, in Lombardo de Ruiz, *El pasado prehispánico*, 1:51.

47. de la Cadena, *Indigenous Mestizos*, 4.

48. Stabb, "Indigenism and Racism in Mexican Thought," 417.

49. Kourí, "Interpreting the Expropriation of Indian Pueblo Lands in Porfirian Mexico," 87.

50. Pilcher, *¡Que vivan los tamales!*, 84.

51. Sierra, *Obras completas*, 8:256.

52. See Keen, *The Aztec Image in Western Thought*, 435–36.

53. Mendoza, "Las pirámides de Teotihuacan," 189, 191.

54. Earle, "Nineteenth-Century Historia Patria and the Pre-Columbian Past."

Chapter Three

1. For del Paso's mission in Europe, see Zavala, *Francisco del Paso y Troncoso, su misión en Europa*.

2. Rutsch, *Entre el campo y el gabinete*, 142.

3. Earle, *The Return of the Native*, 152.

4. Quoted in Castillo Ledón, *El Museo Nacional*, 60.

5. See, for instance, Anderson, "Census, Map, Museum," in *Imagined Communities*, 163–85, and Crimson, "Nation-building, Collecting and the Politics of Display."

6. Earle, *The Return of the Native*, 139.

7. AHMNA, vol. 8, exp. 6, fol. 70.

8. Florescano, "La creación del Museo Nacional de Antropología," 158. For the museum budget during the Porfiriato, see Rutsch, *Entre el campo y el gabinete*. Other studies that look at the museum during the Díaz years include Suárez Cortes, "Las interpretaciones positivistas del pasado y el presente (1880–1910)," Fernández, *Historia de los museos de México*, Rico Mansard, *Exhibir para educar*, Garrigan, "Secretos y revelaciones del archivo," and Garrigan, *Collecting Mexico*.

9. AHMNA, vol. 3, exp. 15 fol. 75. The museum would ultimately be dedicated exclusively to the anthropological sciences. In 1944, the history department was relocated to the Chapultepec castle. The National Museum was then renamed the National Museum of Anthropology, and twenty years later, in 1964, it was moved to its present-day setting in Chapultepec Park. This means that the National Museum of Anthropology of today is the closest descendent of the original National Museum, a lineage that underscores the importance of the anthropological sciences in the nation.

10. Sierra, *Epistolario y papeles privados*, 290.

11. Ruiz, "Insiders and Outsiders," 4.

12. Hamy, *Mémoires d'archéologie et d'ethnographie américaines*, 94.

13. Kohl, "Nationalism and Archaeology," 226–40.

14. Kuhn, *The Structure of Scientific Revolutions*.

15. Rutsch, *Entre el campo y el gabinete*, 79.

16. Peñafiel, *Teotihuacán*, 43.

17. ALB, fols. 292 and 517.

18. According to Benjamin Keen, the Indian past was a safer topic of study. At a time when "Porfirista policy in favor of . . . great landowners and against the Indian tended to make protest against that policy futile and possibly even dangerous," scholars "found it more profitable to confine their attention to Indians who had been dead for a number of centuries" (*The Aztec Image*, 417).

19. Bernal, *Historia de la arqueología en México*, 139–40. For del Paso's expedition, see Galindo y Villa, "Las ruinas de Cempoala y del Templo del Tajín."

20. AGN, IPBA, caja 150, exp. 22, fol. 5.

21. See Lyman and O'Brien, "Americanist Stratigraphic Excavation and the Measurement of Cultural Change," 72. Lyman and O'Brien provide a more technical definition of stratigraphic excavation: the procedure involves "removing artifacts and sediments from vertically discrete three-dimensional units of deposition and keeping those artifacts in sets based on their distinct vertical recovery proveniences for the purpose of measuring time either synchronically or diachronically" (59–60).

22. Galindo y Villa, "Las ruinas de Cempoala y del Templo del Tajín," clx.

23. Peñafiel, *Teotihuacán*, 8.

24. AHMNA, vol. 13, exp. 13, fol. 98.

25. Aguirre, *Informal Empire*, 26.

26. AHMNA, vol. 10, exp. 13, fol. 49; Galindo y Villa, "En la apertura de clases de historia correspondientes al curso de 1911–1912," 22; AHMNA, vol. 4, exp. 39, fol. 236.

27. Mendoza, "Idolo Azteca de Tipo Japonés," 91.

28. *El Monitor Republicano*, 18 December 1878, in Lombardo de Ruiz, *El pasado prehispánico*, 1:62.

29. Mendoza and Sánchez, "Catálogo de las colecciones histórica y arqueológica del Museo Nacional de México," 445.

30. Archivo Histórico Institutional, Serie Museo Nacional de Arqueología, Historia y Etnografía, Subserie Departamento de Arqueología, Subdirección de Documentación, BNAH, caja 1, exp. 78, fol. 1. (hereafter cited as AHI, MNAHE, Subserie Depto. de Arq.)

31. Chavero, "Discurso pronunciado el 24 de septiembre de 1904," 388.

32. Mendoza, "Discurso acerca de la piedra llamada Calendario Mexicano pronunciado por el profesor Philipp Valentini," 241; *El Monitor Republicano*, 15 September 1877, in Lombardo de Ruiz, El pasado prehispánico, 1:54–55.

33. Robelo, "Xochicalco," 9.

34. Lowenthal, "Fabricating Heritage," 6–7.

35. *El Monitor Republicano*, 31 May 1890, in Lombardo de Ruiz, *El pasado prehispánico*, 1:186.

36. García Canclini, "El patrimonio de México y la construcción imaginaria de lo nacional," 70, 85.

37. Kohl, "Nationalism and Archaeology," 224.

38. ALB, fol. 287.

Chapter Four

1. In 1918 the Inspectorate became the Office of Anthropology under the guidance of Manuel Gamio. In 1925, this institution was divided into the General Inspectorate of Monuments, which oversaw historical monuments, and the Office of Archaeology, which dealt with pre-Hispanic ruins. In 1930, the two agencies merged to become the Department of Artistic, Archaeological, and Historic Monuments, which became the INAH in 1939. See Olivé Negrete and Urteaga, *INAH*, 7–17. The original decree generated by the Secretariat of Education outlining the inspector's duties can be found in AHMNA, vol. 7, exp. 30, fol. 214.

2. AGN, caja 167 bis, exp. 78, fol. 1.

3. "Autobiografía: por Leopoldo Batres y memorias del mismo," in ALB, fols. 340 and 341.

4. Conklin, *In the Museum of Man*, 31.

5. Batres, "Estudio sobre los Toltecas," plate 9. The inspector dedicated only one substantial work to anthropometry, his *Anthropologie mexicaine*. This study examines the skulls and bones of dead Indians, both from antiquity and recent times. Batres obtained the bones from "ancient tombs" as well as the San Andrés Hospital in Mexico City.

6. Williams, "Art and Artifact at the Trocadero," 159, 161.

7. ALB, fol. 379.

8. Ibid., fol. 292.

9. AGN, IPBA, caja 165, exp. 44, fol. 3.

10. See Lombardo de Ruiz, *El pasado prehispánico*, 1:39.

11. Based on family lore, this story was told to me by Batres's great-grandniece, Elvira Pruneda, during an interview in Cuernavaca, Mexico, in March 2007.

12. Manrique, "Leopoldo Batres," 246; ALB, fol. 303.

13. Rutsch, *Entre el campo y el gabinete*, 90.

14. Camp, *Reclutamiento político en México*, 85.

15. Rutsch, "Natural History, National Museum and Anthropology in Mexico," 106.

16. Manrique, "Leopoldo Batres," 244.

17. Vázquez León, "Mexico: The Institutionalization of Archaeology," 72.

18. AGN, IPBA, caja 167 bis, exp. 78, fol. 1.

19. *El Monitor Republicano*, 3 September 1895, in Lombardo de Ruiz, *El pasado prehispánico*, 1:282.

20. Bernal, *A History of Mexican Archaeology*, 150.

21. AGN, IPBA, caja 111, exp. 24, fol. 8.

22. Ibid., caja 171, exp. 23, fol. 4.

23. Ibid., caja 171, exp. 19, fol. 4.

24. Rutsch, *Entre el campo y el gabinete*, 71; for an analysis of the Inspectorate and museum budgets, see 71–101. For Vázquez's claim, see Vázquez León, *El leviatán arqueológico*.

25. See, for instance, Cleere, ed., *Approaches to the Archaeological Heritage*.

26. See Lombardo de Ruiz and Solís Vicarte, *Antecedentes de las leyes sobre monumentos históricos*, 48–62. Mexico's archaeological legislation during the nineteenth century is clustered around the early independence period and the end of the century, a pattern, according to Rebecca Earle, typical of Latin American nations. But Mexico was different because it also enacted laws nearly every decade of the century.

27. The Law of Monuments can be found in Lombardo de Ruiz and Solís Vicarte, *Antecedentes de las leyes sobre monumentos históricos*, 68.

28. Suarez-Potts, *The Making of Law*. For more on property rights, see Haber, Razo, and Maurer, *The Politics of Property Rights*.

29. Mexico, *Diario*, 1:572 and 542.

30. Ibid., 1:537. The Veracruz politician Adalberto Esteva and a Leonardo Fortuño were also members of the committee.

31. Ibid., 567. See also "Ley sobre ocupación y enajenación de terrenos baldíos," 26 March 1894, in Olivé Negrete and Cottom, *INAH*, 3:236.

32. Lombardo de Ruiz and Solís Vicarte, *Antecedentes de las leyes sobre monumentos históricos*, 68.

33. Ibid., 62.

34. Mexico, *Diario*, 1:567.

35. Federal ownership of portable artifacts came about in a gradual, piecemeal fashion over the course of the twentieth century, but it was not until 1972 that Mexico would unequivocally claim ownership over all of the archaeological remains in the country with the Federal Law on Archaeological, Artistic, and Historic Monuments and Zones. Article 27 of the ruling declares that archaeological "monuments, movable and immovable, are the inalienable and imprescriptible property of the nation." Today, Mexican law continues to allow for the private possession of antiquities but requires that they be registered with the government, among other conditions.

36. See Merryman, Elsen, and Urice, *Law, Ethics, and the Visual Arts*.

37. Mexico, *Diario*, 1:613–14; *El Monitor Republicano*, 5 December 1896, in Lombardo de Ruiz, *El pasado prehispánico*, 1:309.

38. Mexico, *Diario*, 3:154.

39. Edison, "Patrimony on the Periphery," 502.

40. Ibid., 499.

41. Mexico, *Diario*, 3:154.

42. AGN IPBA, caja 166, exp. 59, fols. 1–5.

43. ALB, fol. 292.

44. AHMNA, vol. 7, exp. 30, fol. 214.

Chapter Five

1. Scott, *Seeing Like a State*, 57, 87.

2. Craib, *Cartographic Mexico*, 34, 37. Batres's map was hung in the National Museum and distributed among Mexican and foreign archaeologists. The *Carta Arqueológica de la República Mexicana*, or *Archaeological Map of the Republic of Mexico* can be found here on pages 160–61.

3. For a list of all the sites with conserjes see AGN, IPBA, caja 111, exp. 9, fol. 1, and caja 112, exp. 115, fol. 1. Cajas 150 and 153 also contain numerous files recording the hiring of guards. For the first conserjes to be appointed, see Baranda, *Memoria*, 380.

4. Fewkes, "Mural Relief Figures of el Casa del Tepozteco," 147–48.

5. AGN, IPBA, caja 150, exp. 10, fol. 34, and caja 151, exp. 2, fol. 3.

6. Ibid., caja 149, exp. 2, fols. 2–3.

7. Ibid., caja 152, exp. 52, fol. 6.

8. Ibid., caja 152, exp. 50, fols. 5, 8.

9. Ibid., caja 152, exp. 58, fol. 3.
10. Robelo, "Xochicalco," 9, 13.
11. AGN, IPBA, caja 120, exp. 23, fol. 1.
12. Ibid., caja 167, exp. 24, fol. 1.
13. Ibid., caja 167, exp. 2, fol. 1.
14. Tenorio-Trillo, "1910 Mexico City," 93.
15. AGN, IPBA, caja 148, exp. 19, fol. 1.
16. Ibid., caja 167 bis, exp. 54, fol. 2.
17. Fewkes, "Mural Relief Figures of el Casa del Tepozteco," 147.
18. Saville, "The Temple of Tepoztlan, Mexico," 222.
19. González Casanova, "El ciclo legendario del Tepoztécatl," 27.
20. AGN, IPBA, caja 171, exp. 19, fol. 2.
21. According to Rutsch, the pay scale was standardized in 1911, when all the conserjes began to earn an annual wage of 492 pesos. For more on the conserje and Inspectorate wages, see Rutsch, *Entre el campo y el gabinete*, 91.
22. AGN, IPBA, caja 154, exp. 60, fol. 5.
23. Ibid., caja 148, exp. 20, fol. 18.
24. Ibid., caja 120, exp. 15, fol. 3.
25. Ibid., caja 149, exp. 3, fol. 6, and caja 166, exp. 34, fol. 5.
26. Ibid., caja 149, exp. 3, fols. 1–19.
27. Ibid., caja 150, exp. 60, fol. 3.
28. Ibid., caja 167, exp. 13, fol. 66, and caja 150, exp. 11, fol. 2.
29. Ibid., caja 154, exp. 60, fol. 7.
30. Ibid., caja 148, exp. 20, fol. 18.
31. Ibid., caja 149, exp. 55, fol 39.
32. Ibid., caja 171, exp. 1, fol. 13.
33. Ibid., caja 171, exp. 4, fol. 11; *El Imparcial*, 21 December 1906, in Lombardo de Ruiz, *El pasado prehispánico*, 2:333.
34. AGN, IPBA, caja 116, exp. 5, fol. 15. Batres used the guards' reports as the basis of his own yearly report to the Secretariat of Education on the state of the ruins. Both his report and those of the guards were also frequently published in the press.
35. AGN, IPBA, caja 150, exp. 14, fol. 8.
36. Ibid., caja 167, exp. 24, fol. 1.
37. Ibid., caja 149, exp. 17, fol. 2.
38. Ibid., caja 149, exp. 17, fol. 1.
39. *El Monitor Republicano*, 8 July 1893, in Lombardo de Ruiz, *El pasado prehispánico*, 1:253.
40. AGN, IPBA, caja 148, exp. 41, fol. 4.
41. The details of this story can be found in AGN, IPBA, caja 150, exp. 10, fols. 1–35.
42. Ibid., caja 148, exp. 41, fol. 3.
43. Ibid., caja 150, exp. 60, fol. 3.

44. Ibid., caja 148, exp. 19, fol. 1.
45. Ibid., caja 150, exp. 32, fol. 1.
46. Saville, *Bibliographic Notes on Palenque, Chiapas*, 156.
47. See Schávelzon, "Saqueo y destrucción del patrimonio nacional (1821–1911)." See also Molina Montes, "Palenque."
48. AGN, IPBA, caja 150, exp. 50, fol. 5, and caja 150, exp. 14, fol. 25.
49. Burke, "The Man Who Owned Chichén Itzá"; Burke, "Envoy," 3.
50. *El Imparcial*, 2 February 1906, in Lombardo de Ruiz, *El pasado prehispánico*, 2:265. For Mérida's public works, see Wells and Joseph, "Modernizing Visions, 'Chilango' Blueprints, and Provincial Growing Pains." For Maler's take on Bolio, see Ramírez Aznar, *El saqueo del cenote sagrado de Chichén Itzá*, 25–58.
51. ALB, fols. 515–16.
52. AGN, IPBA, caja 150, exp. 50, fol. 8.
53. Burke, "Envoy," 6. According to Burke, the Peabody returned some of the gold and copper cenote artifacts to Mexico in 1959 in exchange for other objects. In 1976, it also gave Mexico several jade items as a gift.
54. Beals, *Porfirio Díaz*, 338.
55. Nuttall, "The Island of Sacrificios," 279, 282.
56. Batres, *La isla de sacrificios*, 3.
57. AHMNA, vol. 10, exp. 29, fol. 89. See ALB 529 for Batres's defense.
58. AGN, IPBA, caja 167, exp. 38, fol. 4.

Chapter Six

1. ALB, fol. 310.
2. Saville, *Bibliographic Notes on Palenque*, 156, 167.
3. ALB, fol. 310. See also ALB, fol. 557.
4. Though the law does not seem to have had a name at the time, scholars have dubbed it the Law of Archaeological Explorations. See, for instance, López Camacho, "El caso particular de la legislación sobre monumentos arqueológicos."
5. Saville, "The Work of the Loubat Expedition in Southern Mexico," n.p.
6. AGN, IPBA, caja 149, exp. 11, fol. 1.
7. Ibid., caja 169, exp. 42, fol. 8.
8. Ruiz Martínez, "La construcción del conocimiento en ruta," 227.
9. The quotations in this paragraph and the next are from AGN, IPBA, caja 169, exp. 8, fols. 3–4.
10. Ruiz, "Insiders and Outsiders," 110, 108; Ruiz Martínez, "La construcción del conocimiento en ruta," 231.
11. Saville, *Bibliographic Notes on Palenque*, 163.
12. Batres, *Explorations of Mount Alban*, 8, 19. This is one of the only works Batres published in English.

13. Saville, "The Cruciform Structures of Mitla," 168.
14. AGN, IPBA, caja 167, exp. 13, fol. 68.
15. Saville, "The Cruciform Structures of Mitla," 189. There was long a debate over which culture had built the site, but archaeologists now believe Mitla is Zapotec with some Mixtec influence.
16. AGN, IPBA, caja 166, exp. 34, fols. 1–2.
17. Ibid., caja 167, exp. 21, fol. 1. A more detailed analysis of Mitla's colonial remodeling can be found in Robles García, Leonardo Magadán, and Moreira Quirós, *Reconstrucción colonial en Mitla, Oaxaca.*
18. Batres, *Reparación y consolidación.* The following account is derived from this work.
19. AGN, IPBA, caja 167, exp. 21, fol. 1.
20. Robles García "Historia de la arqueología de Mesoamérica," 115; Batres, *Reparación y consolidación,* 3–4.
21. AGN, IPBA, caja 149, exp. 55, fol. 40.
22. This plaque is recorded in Matos Moctezuma, *Las piedras negadas,* 55.
23. AGN, IPBA, caja 167, exp. 16, fol. 1; caja 168, exp. 36, fol. 12. For the protests of the priest, see *El Imparcial,* 25 April 1907, in Lombardo de Ruiz, *El pasado prehispánico,* 2:350.
24. Saville, "The Work of the Loubat Expedition," n.p.
25. AGN, IPBA, caja 167, exp. 13, fols. 68–69.
26. Saville, "The Work of the Loubat Expedition," n.p.
27. Batres, *Explorations of Mount Alban,* 28, 30.
28. "Mexico Indian Remains Returned from NY for Burial: Cross-Border Effort Wins Proper Burial for Mexican Indian Remains after 100 Years in NY Museum," Associated Press, 17 November 2009, https://www.victoriaadvocate.com/news/2009/nov/17/bc-lt-mexico-warriors-homecoming/.
29. ALB, fol. 77.
30. *El Imparcial,* 4 November 1902, in Lombardo de Ruiz, *El pasado prehispánico,* 2:174–75.
31. Ruiz, "Insiders and Outsiders," 305.
32. ALB, fol. 526.
33. *El Imparcial,* 28 October 1902, in Lombardo de Ruiz, *El pasado prehispánico,* 2:174.
34. ALB, fol. 79.
35. Graham, *Alfred Maudslay and the Maya,* 215.
36. *El Monitor Republicano,* 23 June 1895, in Lombardo de Ruiz, *El pasado prehispánico,* 1:275.
37. AHMNA, vol. 9, exp. 88, fol. 234.
38. Fewer visitors venture onto the contemporary museum's second floor. Only 57 percent of them see the ethnographic collections, which they attribute to a "lack of time," after being overwhelmed by the massive archaeology collection on the ground floor (García Canclini, *Hybrid Cultures,* 131).

39. AHMNA, vol. 9, exp. 88, fol. 236.
40. Ibid., vol. 9, exp. 85, fol. 216.
41. Ibid., vol. 10, exp. 13, fol. 49, and vol. 9, exp. 87, fol. 225.
42. Ibid., vol. 203, exp. 99, fol. 237.
43. ALB, fol. 473.
44. Ibid.
45. AGN, IPBA, caja 167, exp. 24, fol. 1.
46. ALB, fol. 474.
47. *El Monitor Republicano*, 6 November 1895, in Lombardo de Ruiz, *El pasado pre-hispánico*, 1:291.
48. AGN, IPBA, caja 168, exp. 1, fol. 2.
49. Ibid., caja 170, exp. 36, fols. 20–21.
50. Ibid., caja 167, exp. 24, fol. 1.
51. Ibid., caja 168, exp. 1, fol. 2.
52. AHMNA, vol. 11, exp. 23, fol. 189.
53. Ibid., vol. 12, exp. 11, fol. 41.
54. AGN, IPBA, caja 112, exp. 100, fol. 1.
55. Ibid., caja 152, exp. 67, fol. 5.
56. *El Imparcial*, 8 November 1908, in Lombardo de Ruiz, *El pasado prehispánico*, 2:453.
57. AGN, IPBA, caja 168, exp. 38, fol. 5.
58. *El Imparcial*, 22 November 1908, in Lombardo de Ruiz, *El pasado prehispánico*, 2:465.
59. AGN, IPBA, caja 168, exp. 38, fol. 7.
60. Gamio, "The Chalchihuites Area, Zacatecas," 70.
61. Dawson, *Indian and Nation in Revolutionary Mexico*, 6.
62. Nuttall, "The Island of Sacrificios," 280.
63. Quoted in Ruiz, "Insiders and Outsiders," 308.
64. For Gamio's critiques see Matos Moctezuma, *Teotihuacán*, 29; Bernal, *Historia de la arqueología en México*, 141.
65. Quoted from a 2 June 1910 article in *El Tiempo*, in Nuttall, "The Island of Sacrificios," 281.
66. Matos Moctezuma, *Las piedras negadas*, 79.
67. Bernal, *Historia de la arqueología en México*, 141.
68. ALB, fol. 292.

Chapter Seven

1. ALB, fols. 391–93. As on most occasions, Batres did not bother to record who these people were, referring to them simply as "indios." They most likely came from five villages located on or near the site: San Sebastián, San Francisco Mazapa, Santa María Cuatlán, San Juan Teotihuacán, and San Martín de las Pirámides.

2. *El Monitor Republicano*, 12 November 1890, in Lombardo de Ruiz, *El pasado prehispánico*, 1:198.

3. AGN, IPBA, caja 147, exp. 40, fol. 2.

4. García Canclini, "El patrimonio de México y la construcción imaginaria de lo nacional," 61.

5. AHMNA, vol. 2, exp. 29, fol. 110.

6. García Canclini, *Hybrid Cultures*, 116.

7. AGN, IPBA, caja 167, exp. 46, fol. 25. On the modernization of the capital see Tenorio-Trillo, "1910 Mexico City," and Lear, "Mexico City."

8. Rivera Cambas, *México pintoresco*, 1:176.

9. García Canclini, *Hybrid Cultures*, 127.

10. AHMNA, vol. 7, exp. 2, fol. 8, and vol. 203, exp. 68, fol. 168.

11. Ibid., vol. 1, exp. 5, fol. 13.

12. AGN, IPBA, caja 151, exp. 40, fol. 1.

13. AHMNA, vol. 4, exp. 6, fol. 99.

14. Ibid., vol. 3, exp. 26, fols. 97–99. One of Mexico's most prized possessions, the famous obsidian vessel shaped in the form of a monkey also became part of the museum thanks to a peasant. In the 1920s a peasant showed up at the museum door with the antiquity, which he exchanged with the institution's director for a sack of corn. In 1985 thieves stole the piece from the Aztec room in the National Museum of Anthropology, along with over a hundred other artifacts, in one of the single largest heists of precious objects in history. Happily, though, the monkey and nearly all of the other objects were recuperated a few years later.

15. *El Imparcial*, 10 April 1904, in Lombardo de Ruiz, *El pasado prehispánico*, 2:213.

16. For the purchase of the collection, see AHMNA, vol. 204, exp. 141, fols. 314–17; for the budget, see *El Imparcial*, 12 April 1910, in Lombardo de Ruiz, *El pasado prehispánico*, 2:591. Sometimes the museum got lucky and was able to buy a collection with another government agency. For example, it purchased the antiquities of José Dorenberg, the Belgian consul in Puebla, with the Junta Colombina, the Mexican organization in charge of preparations for the Columbian Exposition in Spain. The museum paid 3,000 pesos of the 7,500 total but got to keep the objects once the exposition ended. See AHMNA, vol. 9, exp. 35, fol. 81.

17. AHMNA, vol. 11, exp. 15, fol. 136.

18. Ibid., vol. 9, exp. 53, fol. 165.

19. Sumner, "National Autocracy, Regional Governance," 82.

20. Fernández, *Historia de los museos de México*, 174.

21. Ríos Meneses, "Museo regional de antropología de Yucatán," 601.

22. AGN, IPBA, caja 168, exp. 2, fols. 12 and 11. Compared to Batres, the museum professors had a less possessive attitude toward the antiquities. They were more willing to relinquish artifacts to regional museums, perhaps because they were accustomed to the idea of museums functioning as trading houses for the objects. When Juan Peón Contreras, the director of the Yucateco Museum and a frequent

donor to the National Museum, decided to establish a museum in Campeche, he asked the professors for "duplicates and even triplicates" of antiquities. They agreed, on the condition that he send them objects from Campeche in exchange (AHMNA, vol. 8, exp. 13, fol. 91).

23. AGN, IPBA, caja 150, exp. 14, fols. 37 and 32.

24. *El Monitor Republicano*, 30 March 1877, in Lombardo de Ruiz, *El pasado prehispánico*, 1:52.

25. Quoted in Sánchez, "Estudio acerca de la estatua llamada Chac-Mool ó Rey Tigre," 272 and 270.

26. *El Monitor Republicano*, 30 March 1877, in Lombardo de Ruiz, *El pasado prehispánico*, 1:53.

27. Sánchez, "Estudio acerca de la estatua llamada Chac-Mool ó Rey Tigre," 272.

28. *El Monitor Republicano*, 30 March 1877, in Lombardo de Ruiz, *El pasado prehispánico*, 1:53.

29. Sánchez, "Estudio acerca de la estatua llamada Chac-Mool ó Rey Tigre," 272.

30. García Canclini, *Hybrid Cultures*, 127. The gallery's collection more than doubled during the Porfiriato. In 1895, a year for which data exists, the room housed over three hundred antiquities, including some of Mexico's most famous: the Chacmool of Chichén Itzá, the Aztec Xochipilli, Coatlicue, and the Stone of Tizoc. By the end of the period, in 1908, the same room contained over seven hundred pieces.

31. AGN, IPBA, caja 167, exp. 48, fol. 1.

32. Hinsley, "From Shell-Heaps to Stelae," 71.

33. The professors' attendance records are spotty. In 1904 more than 240,000 Mexicans and close to 11,500 foreigners visited the museum. Four years later, some 233,000 Mexicans and almost 3,400 foreigners visited; see *El Imparcial*, 13 January 1905, in Lombardo de Ruiz, *El pasado prehispánico*, 2:232, and AHMNA, vol. 12, exp. 16, fol. 218. About the elusive nature of museum patrons Steven Conn explains that they "left little trace of themselves and did not register with any specificity in the official records of most museums. Some museums kept attendance figures, some kept records of visitor comments, and occasionally individual visitors turn up in the record because they caused some kind of trouble" (*Museums and American Intellectual Life*, 19).

34. Bennett, *The Birth of the Museum*, 28. Also see Carol Dunce, *Civilizing Rituals*. For a look at the struggle over "proper" behavior in other public settings, see John Kasson, *Rudeness and Civility*.

35. Garrigan, "Secretos y revelaciones del archivo," 74.

36. *El Monitor Republicano*, 18 December 1878, in Lombardo de Ruiz, *El pasado prehispánico*, 1:62.

37. The broadside by popular artist Manuel Manilla can be found in López Luján, "'El adiós y triste queja del gran Calendario Azteca,'" 80. While Batres is often credited with hauling the calendar to the museum, he does not appear in the records related to the event. In addition to highlighting the Aztecs through its

attention to the calendar, the museum also emphasized the Aztecs by centering its curriculum around the group and by making the study of Nahuatl mandatory for all students.

38. When the current National Museum of Anthropology was under construction, archaeologist Alfonso Caso insisted on placing the Aztec exhibition at the center of the institution, telling museum architect Pedro Ramírez Vázquez it was "essential that everyone see that gallery." Today, visitors must ascend a ramp to enter the gallery. The ramp forces them to slow down and creates a dramatic entrance that helps to emphasize the dominance of the Aztecs in the museum: "I want them to enter slowly and with respect. This is why I raised the floor 70 cm with a marble ramp," Ramírez Vázquez explained in an interview, adding devilishly that "either they move slowly, or they fall." See del Villar, "La construcción del Museo Nacional de Antropología," 18.

39. AGN, IPBA, caja 169, exp. 71, fol. 3; Batres, *La isla de sacrificios*, 6. For the shift from typological to cultural collections, see Jacknis, "Franz Boas and Exhibits."

40. AHMNA, vol. 17, exp. 25, fols. 229 and 234. For Sierra's remark, see Rutsch, *Entre el campo y el gabinete*, 125.

41. Nuttall, "The Island of Sacrificios," 284, 287.

42. AGN, IPBA, caja 166, exp. 23, fol. 1.

43. Ibid., caja 170, exp. 33, fol. 2, and caja 147, exp. 6, fol. 15. The report on his trip can be found in AHMNA, vol. 9, exp. 9, fols. 26–30 and in Batres, *Informe*. Mexicans were not the only ones who studied the museums of other countries. When the Trocadéro was being established, for instance, E. T. Hamy took a trip to Scandinavia to investigate the ethnology museums of Copenhagen, Stockholm, and Oslo.

44. AGN, IPBA, caja 166, exp. 23, fol. 1.

45. ALB, fol. 395.

46. *El Monitor Republicano*, 10 May 1890, in Lombardo de Ruiz, *El pasado prehispánico*, 1:180.

47. AGN, IPBA, caja 167 bis, exp. 78, fol. 1.

48. Ibid., caja 111, exp. 21, fol. 2.

49. *El Imparcial*, 30 March 1908, in Lombardo de Ruiz, *El pasado prehispánico*, 2:425. Museum professor Jesús Sánchez accurately predicted the mysterious characters would one day be deciphered and reveal "many points that are now completely dark and unknown about the history of the American continent" (AHMNA, vol. 6, exp. 45, fol. 159). It would take a century to prove him right. For a fascinating account of the decipherment of Maya hieroglyphics, see Coe, *Breaking the Maya Code*.

50. AGN, IPBA, caja 168, exp. 20, fol. 12.

51. Ibid., caja 167 bis, exp. 56, fol. 6. An earlier attempt to bring back the last panel ended in failure. In the 1880s, the secretary of development called on the governor of Chiapas to remit the piece. The governor agreed and requested 1,000 pesos to pay for the opening of a road along with the oxen, carts, and Indians to

transport the panel. Once he realized the magnitude of the project, however, he withdrew his support.

52. *El Imparcial*, 5 March 1909, in Lombardo de Ruiz, *El pasado prehispánico*, 2:503.

53. AGN, IPBA, caja 111, exp. 21, fol. 2, and exp. 31, fol. 9 bis.

54. Ibid., caja 111, exp. 31, fol. 9 bis. Sierra often made fun of the fact that he and Batres were large, comparing his "huge stomach" with Batres's trade-mark belly and joking that "Batres eats ten times more than I" (Sierra, *Epistolario y papeles privados*, 475, 256). At Palenque, Batres's men did more than remove the panel. After setting up camp in one of the structures, they cleared a road to the town of Palenque, removed debris from the Temple of the Cross, and sketched, photographed, and made molds of the monuments. Batres also corrected maps of the ruins he had made a decade earlier during his trip with Saville. All of this work, along with other expedition activities, were recorded in a film.

55. *El Imparcial*, 7 March 1909, in Lombardo de Ruiz, *El pasado prehispánico*, 2:512.

56. AGN, IPBA, caja 170, exp. 36, fol. 15, and caja 150, exp. 22, fol. 17.

57. Ibid., caja 166, exp. 75, fol. 29.

58. Ibid., caja 167, exp. 31, fol. 3.

59. Saville, "The Temple of Tepoztlan, Mexico," 221.

60. Camarena Ocampo and Morales Lersch, "Museos comunitarios de Oaxaca," 72. In his classic study of the village, anthropologist Oscar Lewis mentions that the museum was founded by "a small group of Tepoztecan intellectuals" (*Life in a Mexican Village*, xxv). It is possible, however, that more people were involved in its creation. When professors from the National Museum visited the institution in 1905, they noted that it contained "various idols and curiosities gathered by the Indians of the place" (*El Imparcial*, 12 June 1905, in Lombardo de Ruiz, *El pasado prehispánico*, 2:246).

61. AGN, IPBA, caja 167 bis, exp. 60, fol. 15.

62. Ibid., caja 166, exp. 75, fols. 29–30.

63. Ibid., caja 166, exp. 75, fol. 29.

64. Ibid., caja 170, exp. 49, fol. 2.

65. Ibid., caja 167 bis, exp. 60, fol. 15.

66. Batres, *Memorandum*, 9.

67. Saville, *Bibliographic Notes on Xochicalco, Mexico*, 186.

68. Robelo, "Xochicalco," 7.

69. For the legend, see Robelo, *Geografía del estado de Morelos*, 6. Señor Tetlámatl eventually escaped the Aztecs using one of the many tunnels under the site. During the Porfiriato, locals claimed to still see him roaming the tunnels, dressed in animal skins and golden feathers.

70. The elder's statement was recorded in 1888 by Peñafiel in *Monumentos del arte mexicano antiguo*, 1:44.

71. The site's name is still a mystery. Many scholars believe it refers to the ornately decorated Pyramid of the Plumed Serpent. The "name communicates the special

esteem that pre-Hispanic peoples had for this locale and is a literal metaphor for 'regal house' or 'revered place'" (Hirth, *Archeological Research at Xochicalco*, 1:3).

72. AGN, IPBA, caja 166, exp. 52, fol. 1. Batres possibly planned to use military troops.

73. The above citations for this discussion can be found in ibid., caja 166, exp. 52, fols. 3, 5.

74. Peñafiel, *Monumentos del arte mexicano antiguo*, 1: 45.

75. AGN, IPBA, caja 112, exp. 77, fol. 4.

76. See Rosas, *Tepoztlán*.

77. Conn, *Museums and American Intellectual Life*, 23.

Chapter Eight

1. Batres, *Teotihuacán: Memoria*, 21.

2. Tenorio-Trillo, "1910 Mexico City," 75–76.

3. Six countries attended the centennial with special diplomatic missions (Japan, France, Germany, Italy, Spain and the United States), and eighteen with special envoys (Argentina, Bolivia, Brazil, Chile, Costa Rica, Cuba, El Salvador, Guatemala, Honduras, Panama, Peru, Uruguay, Austria, Belgium, Holland, Portugal, Russia and Norway). Three countries appointed residents in Mexico to represent them (Colombia, Venezuela, and Switzerland), while Nicaragua's envoy was the poet Rubén Darío. Great Britain missed the event due to the death of King Edward VII. See Tenorio-Trillo, "1910 Mexico City," 90. For an analysis of the event, see also Gonzales, "Imagining Mexico in 1910."

4. Romero, *Crónica mexicana del turismo*, 170. See also Berger and Wood, *Holiday in Mexico*.

5. AGN, IPBA, caja 153, exp. 48, fol. 2.

6. *El Imparcial*, 10 April 1906, in Lombardo de Ruiz, *El pasado prehispánico*, 2:283; AGN, IPBA, caja 149, exp. 6, fol. 2.

7. AGN, IPBA, caja 167 bis, exp. 53, fol. 2.

8. ALB, fol. 214.

9. *El Imparcial*, 23 January 1911, in Lombardo de Ruiz, *El pasado prehispánico*, 2:687.

10. Ibid., 20 April 1910, in Lombardo de Ruiz, *El pasado prehispánico*, 2:593.

11. Ibid., 29 August 1910, in Lombardo de Ruiz, *El pasado prehispánico*, 2:613–617.

12. Ibid., 25 February 1910, in Lombardo de Ruiz, *El pasado prehispánico*, 2:579.

13. AGN, IPBA, caja 112, exp. 82, fol. 13.

14. ALB, fol. 215.

15. Ibid., fol. 219.

16. Ibid., fol. 391.

17. ALB, fols. 489–93.

18. AGN, IPBA, caja 171, exp. 18, fol. 60.

19. Ibid., caja 152, exp. 19, fol. 6.

20. ALB, fol. 216.

21. AGN, IPBA, caja 171, exp. 2, fol. 1.
22. Ibid., caja 171, exp. 2, fols. 8, 11.
23. Sierra, *Obras completas*, 14:289–90.
24. AGN, IPBA, caja 338, exp. 2, fol. 35. Unfortunately, we do not know the dimensions of the plots since they were recorded by name rather than size.
25. Ibid., caja 338, exp. 2, fols. 14 and 4.
26. Ibid., caja 338, exp. 2, fol. 6.
27. Lombardo de Ruiz and Solís Vicarte, *Antecedentes de las leyes sobre monumentos históricos*, 82. That the government came to control the surface of the land *and* the subsoil wealth at Teotihuacán may have been the result of a ruling enacted after the Law of Monuments. Passed in 1902, the Decree on the Clasification and Regulation of Federal Immovable Property made the ruins the property of the nation without differentiating between the surface and subsoil rights, giving the government ownership of both. See Lombardo de Ruiz and Solís Vicarte, *Antecedentes de las leyes sobre monumentos históricos*, 75.
28. AGN, IPBA, caja 338, exp. 3, fol. 6.
29. Ibid., caja 338, exp. 10, fol. 3.
30. Castañeda, *In the Museum of Maya Culture*, 104–5.
31. Coe, *Archaeological Mexico*, 19.
32. Molina Montes, "Archaeological Buildings," 125. On Viollet-le-Duc's influence in Mexico, see Schávelzon, "Historia social de la restauración arquitectónica en México."
33. For more on Batres's thoughts on restoration, see ALB, fol. 294.
34. Manrique, "Leopoldo Batres," 253.
35. ALB, fols. 217–20.
36. See AGN, IPBA, caja 168, exp. 11, fol. 5. Batres had used dynamite at Tepozteco, for instance, to clear roads, but not to remove debris from the structures.
37. Archaeologist Rémy Bastien accuses Batres of deliberately falsifying the terrace in his "La pirámide del sol en Teotihuacán."
38. *El Imparcial*, 9–10 April 1906, in Lombardo de Ruiz, *El pasado prehispánico*, 2:275–89.
39. Manrique, "Leopoldo Batres," 252.
40. ALB, fol. 222.
41. AGN, IPBA, caja 168, exp. 11, fol. 1.
42. Ibid., caja 171, exp. 2, fol. 11.
43. ALB, fol. 157.
44. *El Imparcial*, 6 May 1905, in Lombardo de Ruiz, *El pasado prehispánico*, 2:241.
45. AGN, IPBA, caja 171, exp. 18, fol. 54.
46. *El Imparcial*, 31 May 1908, in Lombardo de Ruiz, *El pasado prehispánico*, 2:438.
47. AGN, IPBA, caja 112, exp. 82, fols. 14–15.
48. Ibid., caja 152, exp. 11, fol. 1, caja 152, exp. 21, fols. 1–2, caja 155, exp. 35, fols. 1–32, and caja 112, exp. 96, fol. 1.

49. *El Imparcial*, 26 December 1909, in Lombardo de Ruiz, *El pasado prehispánico*, 2:567.
50. AGN, IPBA, caja 171, exp. 18, fol. 54.
51. ALB, fol. 162; AGN, IPBA, caja 120, exp. 27, fol. 37.
52. Batres, *Antigüedades mexicanas falsificadas*, 4.
53. Díaz y de Ovando, *Memoria de un debate*, 35.
54. *El Imparcial*, 13 January 1906, in Lombardo de Ruiz, *El pasado prehispánico*, 2:256.
55. *El Monitor Republicano*, 8 July 1887, in Lombardo de Ruiz, *El pasado prehispánico*, 1:139.
56. Charnay, "Mis descubrimientos en México," 271–78.
57. Holmes, "The Trade in Spurious Mexican Antiquities," 171.
58. Batres, *Antigüedades mexicanas falsificadas*, 14–15.
59. ALB, fol. 225; Batres, *Antigüedades mexicanas falsificadas*, 13.
60. Batres, *Antigüedades mexicanas falsificadas*, 13.
61. ALB, fol. 258; *El Imparcial*, 30 October 1908, in Lombardo de Ruiz, *El pasado prehispánico*, 2:452–53; Batres, *Antigüedades mexicanas falsificadas*, 7.
62. AGN, IPBA, caja 111, exp. 27, fol. 1.
63. Tenorio-Trillo, "1910 Mexico City," 91. As Michael J. Gonzales explains, attempts were made throughout Mexico to regulate dress during the event and everywhere "proved unenforceable" ("Imagining Mexico in 1910," 510). For the more general "hats and pants laws" requiring men to wear trousers and employees to wear uniforms during the Porfiriato, see Beezley, *Judas at the Jockey Club*.
64. AGN, IPBA, caja 112, exp. 84, fol. 3, and caja 111, exp. 60, fol. 3.
65. Gonzales, "Imagining Mexico in 1910," 510.
66. *El Imparcial*, 29 August 1910, in Lombardo de Ruiz, *El pasado prehispánico* 2:613–15.
67. Congreso Internacional de Americanistas, *Reseña de la segunda sesión*, 17.
68. Ruiz, "Insiders and Outsiders," 173.
69. For an account of the excursion and the centennial, see García, *Crónica oficial de las fiestas del Primer Centenario de la Independencia de México*.
70. *El Imparcial*, 11 September 1910, in Lombardo de Ruiz, *El pasado prehispánico*, 2:634–35.
71. ALB, fol. 502; AGN, IPBA, caja 165, exp. 75, fol. 1; ALB, fols. 264, 271.
72. Wells and Joseph, "Modernizing Visions," 214.
73. Gamio, *La población de Teotihuacán* (1922), 109; Bernal, *Historia de la arqueología en México*, 141; Graham, *Alfred Maudslay and the Maya*, 252; Linné, *Archaeological Researches at Teotihuacán, Mexico*, 32.
74. Hirth, *Archaeological Research at Xochicalco*, 2:40; Linné, *Archaeological Researches at Teotihuacán*, 32.
75. Molina Montes, "Archaeological Buildings," 129.

Epilogue

1. AHI, MNAHE, Subserie Depto. de Arq., caja 1, exp. 88, fol. 1.
2. ALB, fol. 199.
3. Ibid., fol. 237; Batres, *Memorandum*, 6.
4. Batres, *Memorandum*, 22–23; ALB, fol. 199.
5. AHI, MNAHE, Subserie Depto. de Arq., caja 2, exp. 128, fol. 1.
6. AGN, IPBA, caja 160, exp. 89, fol. 1; AHI, MNAHE, Subserie Depto de Arq., caja 1, exp. 72, fol. 1.
7. AGN, IPBA, caja 160, exp. 89, fol. 1.
8. It was Gamio who came up with the idea of dividing the country into four archaeological "zones": zone 1 included Yucatán, Campeche, Tabasco, Chiapas, and the territory of Quitana Roo, and was overseen by Martínez; zone 2 included Oaxaca, Veracruz, and Guerrero, and was overseen by Mena; zone 3 included Michoacán, Colima, Jalisco, Sonora, Sinaloa, Durango, Coahuila, Chihuahua, Tamaulipas, Nuevo León, Zacatecas, Aguascalientes, San Luis Potosí, Querétaro, Guanajuato, and the territory of Tepic, and was overseen by Aguirre; and zone 4 included Mexico, Hidalgo, Morelos, Puebla, Tlaxcala, and the Federal District, and was overseen by Gamio. Gamio based his scheme on what he believed were the four main cultural divisions in the nation. Zone 1, the "peninsular" territory, was essentially Maya. Zone 2, the "Isthmus" region, included the Mixtecs and Zapotecs but also the Totonacs of Veracruz, since this last culture "had contact" with the two others in antiquity. Zone 3, "the northern zone," was the most complex, but here, Gamio decided that the dominant culture was "Tarascan." The final zone, "the center," the most uniform area, was dominated by the cultures of "the mountain, of Teotihuacán, and of the Aztecs." See Gamio's "Ensayo de clasificación cultural de los monumentos de la República Mexicana," AGN, IPBA, caja 113, exp. 3, fols. 4–5.
9. ALB, fol. 307.
10. Ibid., fol. 543.
11. AGN, IPBA, caja 113, exp. 55, fol. 2, caja 120, exp. 1, fol. 9, caja 113, exp. 58, fol. 1, and caja 113, exp. 60, fol. 5; ALB, fol. 208; AGN, IPBA, caja 161, exp. 25, fol. 4.

Bibliography

Archival Sources (Mexico City)

Archivo General de la Nación, Instrucción Pública y Bellas Artes

Archivo Histórico del Museo Nacional de Antropología, Museo Nacional de Antropología

Archivo Histórico de la Dirección General del Instituto Nacional de Antropología e Historia, Subdirección de Documentación, dependiente de la Biblioteca Nacional de Antropología e Historia

Archivo Leopoldo Batres

Serie Francisco del Paso y Troncoso

Serie Museo Nacional de Arqueología, Historia y Etnografía, Subserie Departamento de Arqueología

Serie Museo Nacional de Arqueología, Historia y Etnografía, Subserie Dirección

Published Sources

Aguirre, Robert D. *Informal Empire: Mexico and Central America in Victorian Culture.* Minneapolis: University of Minnesota Press, 2005.

Alcantara-Russell, Keitlyn. "Renditions of Remains: The Implications of an Archaeologically Reconstructed Identity: A Case in Mexico." MA Thesis, University of Chicago, 2011.

Altamirano Piolle, María Elena. *José María Velasco (1840–1912), National Homage.* 2 vols. Mexico City: Consejo Nacional para la Cultura y las Artes, 1993.

Ames, Michael M. *Museums, the Public and Anthropology: A Study in the Anthropology of Anthropology.* Vancouver: University of British Columbia Press, 1986.

Anderson, Benedict. *Imagined Communities: Reflections on the Origin and Spread of Nationalism.* London: Verso, 1991.

Appadurai, Arjun. Introduction. *The Social Life of Things: Commodities in Cultural Perspective*, edited by Arjun Appadurai, 3–63. Cambridge, UK: Cambridge University Press, 1986.

Appelbaum, Nancy P., Anne S. Macpherson, and Karin Alejandra Rosemblatt, eds. *Race and Nation in Modern Latin America*. Chapel Hill: University of North Carolina Press, 2003.

Associated Press. "Mexico Indian Remains Returned from NY for Burial: Cross-Border Effort Wins Proper Burial for Mexican Indian Remains after 100 Years in NY Museum." November 17, 2009.

Atwood, Roger. *Stealing History: Tomb Raiders, Smugglers, and the Looting of the Ancient World*. New York: St. Martin's Press, 2004.

Bahn, Paul. *Archaeology: A Very Short Introduction*. Oxford, UK: Oxford University Press, 1996.

Baranda, Joaquín. *Memoria que en cumplimiento del precepto constitutional presenta al Congreso de la Union el C. Lic. Joaquin Baranda, Secretario de Estado y del despacho de Justicia é Instrucción pública*. Mexico City: Imprenta del Gobierno, 1887.

Barkan, Leonard. *Unearthing the Past: Archaeology and Aesthetics in the Making of Renaissance Culture*. New Haven: Yale University Press, 1999.

Bastien, Rémy. "La pirámide del sol en Teotihuacán." Thesis, Escuela Nacional de Antropología e Historia, 1947.

———. "The Pyramid of the Sun in Teotihuacan: A New Interpretation." In vol. 1 of *The Civilizations of Ancient America: Selected Papers of the 29th International Congress of Americanists*, edited by Sol Tax, 62–67. Chicago: University of Chicago Press, 1951.

Bataille, Georges. "Museum." In *Encyclopaedia Acephalica: Comprising the Critical Dictionary and Related Texts*, edited by Georges Bataille, Isabelle Waldberg, and Robert Lebel, translated by Iain White, 64–65. London: Atlas, 1995.

Batres, Leopoldo. *Anthropologie mexicaine: Ostéologie*. Mexico City: La Europa, 1900.

———. *Antigüedades mejicanas falsificadas: Falsificación y falsificadores*. Mexico City: Fidencio S. Soria, 1910.

———. *Antropología mexicana, clasificación del tipo étnico de las tribus Zapoteca del estado de Oaxaca y Acolhua del Valle de México*. Mexico City: Imprenta del Gobierno Federal en el Ex-Arzobispado, 1890.

———. *Arqueología mexicana: Civilización de algunas de las diferentes tribus que habitaron el territorio, hoy mexicano, en la antigüedad*. Mexico City: Imprenta del Gobierno Federal en el Ex-Arzobispado, 1888, 1891.

———. *Cartilla histórica de la ciudad de México, escrita por Leopoldo Batres, inspector y conservador de los monumentos arqueológicos de la república mexicana, aprobado como texto por el Consejo Superior de Instrucción del Distrito Federal*. Mexico City: Gallegos Hermanos, 1893.

———. *Civilización prehistórica de las riberas del Papaloapam y costa de Sotavento, estado de Veracruz.* Mexico City: Buznego y León, 1908.

———. *El Sr. Lic. Chavero y El Monolito de Coatlinchán.* Mexico City: Fidencio S. Soria, 1904.

———. "Estudio sobre los Toltecas." In Joaquín Baranda, *Memoria que en cumplimiento del precepto constitutional presenta al Congreso de la Union el C. Lic. Joaquin Baranda, Secretario de Estado y del despacho de Justicia é Instrucción pública,* 382–93. Mexico City: Imprenta del Gobierno, 1887.

———. *Exploraciones arqueológicas en la calle de las Escalerillas, año de 1900.* Mexico City: La Europa, 1902.

———. *Exploraciones de Monte Albán.* Mexico City: Gante, 1902.

———. *Exploraciones y consolidación de los monumentos arqueológicos de Teotihuacán.* Mexico City: Buznego y León, 1908.

———. *Explorations of Mount Alban, Oaxaca, Mexico.* Mexico City: Gante, 1902.

———. *Informe que rinde el inspector y conservador de los monumentos arqueológicos de la República Mexicana, Leopoldo Batres, acerca de la comisión que llevó a Europa para visitar los museos, según el orden de 6 de octubre de 1887,* part 1, edited by Sabás A. y Munguía. Mexico City: Imprenta del Gobierno Federal en el Ex-Arzobispado, 1888.

———. *La isla de sacrificios, la señora Zelia Nuttall de Pinard y Leopoldo Batres.* Mexico City: Tipografía Económica, 1910.

———. *Memorandum dirigido al Sr. Lic. D. Miguel Díaz Lombardo, Ministro de Instrucción Pública y Bellas Artes.* Barcelona: Viuda de J. Cunill, 1911.

———. *Reparación y consolidación del edificio de las columnas en Mitla por Leopoldo Batres.* Mexico City: Buznego y León, 1908.

———. *Teotihuacán: Memoria que presenta Leopoldo Batres, inspector general y conservador de los monumentos arqueológicos de la República Mexicana al XV Congreso Internacional de Americanistas que deberá reunirse en Quebec el mes de Septiembre 1906.* Mexico City: Fidencio S. Soria, 1906.

———. *Teotihuacán; ó, La ciudad sagrada de los Toltecas.* Mexico City: Talleres de la Escuela Nacional de Artes y Oficios, 1889.

———. *Teotihuacán; ó, La ciudad sagrada de los Tolteca.* Mexico City: Hull, 1906.

———. *Visita a los monumentos arqueológicos de "La Quemada," Zacatecas.* Mexico City: Francisco Díaz de León, 1903.

———. "Visit to the Archaeological Remains of La Quemada, Zacatecas, Mexico." In *The North American Frontier,* edited by Basil C. Hedrick, J. Charles Kelley, and Carroll L. Riley, 1–20. Carbondale: Southern Illinois University Press, 1971.

Baudez, Claude, and Sidney Picasso. *Lost Cities of the Ancient Maya.* New York: Abrams, 1987.

Bauer, Arnold J. *Goods, Power, History: Latin America's Material Culture.* Cambridge, UK: Cambridge University Press, 2001.

Bazin, Germain. *The Museum Age.* Translated by Jane van Huis Cahill. New York: Universe Publishers, 1967.

Beals, Carleton. *Porfirio Díaz: Dictator of Mexico.* Philadelphia: Lippincott, 1932.

Beezley, William H. *Judas at the Jockey Club and Other Episodes of Porfirian Mexico.* Lincoln: University of Nebraska Press, 1987.

Beezley, William H, Cheryl English Martin, and William E. French, eds. *Rituals of Rule, Rituals of Resistance: Public Celebrations and Popular Culture in Mexico.* Wilmington, DE: Scholarly Resources, 1994.

Benavides, Hugo, O. *Making Ecuadorian Histories: Four Centuries of Defining Power.* Austin: University of Texas Press, 2004.

Bender, Barbara. *Stonehenge: The Making of Space.* Oxford, UK: Berg, 1999.

Bennett, Tony. *The Birth of the Museum: History, Theory, Politics.* London: Routledge, 1995.

Berger, Dina, and Andrew Grant Wood. *Holiday in Mexico: Critical Reflections on Tourism and Tourist Encounters.* Durham, NC: Duke University Press, 2010.

Bernal, Ignacio. *Cien obras maestras del museo nacional de antropología.* Mexico City: José Bolea, 1969.

———. *Historia de la arqueología en México.* Mexico City: Porrúa, 1992.

———. *A History of Mexican Archaeology: The Vanished Civilizations of Middle America.* London: Thames and Hudson, 1980.

———. *Museo Nacional de Antropología de México: Arqueología.* 3rd ed. Mexico City: Aguilar, 1972.

———. *100 Great Masterpieces of the Mexican National Museum of Anthropology.* New York: Harry N. Abrams, 1969.

Berrin, Kathleen, and Esther Pasztory, eds. *Teotihuacan: Art from the City of the Gods.* New York: Thames and Hudson, 1993.

Bethell, Leslie, ed. *Mexico since Independence.* Cambridge, UK: Cambridge University Press, 1991.

Black, Barbara J. *On Exhibit: Victorians and Their Museums.* Charlottesville: University of Virginia Press, 2000.

Blanning, T. C. W. "The Commercialization and Sacralization of European Culture in the Nineteenth Century." In *The Oxford Illustrated History of Modern Europe,* edited by T. C. W. Blanning. Oxford, UK: Oxford University Press, 1996.

———, ed. *The Oxford Illustrated History of Modern Europe.* Oxford, UK: Oxford University Press, 1996.

Blom, Franz. *Las ruinas de Palenque, Xupá y Finca Encanto.* Mexico City: INAH, 1923.

Boas, Franz. *Anthropological Essays Presented to Frederic Ward Putnam in Honor of His Seventieth Birthday, April 16, 1909, by His Friends and Associates.* New York: G. E. Stechert, 1909.

Bonfil Batalla, Guillermo. "Nuestro patrimonio cultural: Un laberinto de significados." In vol. 1 of *El patrimonio nacional de México,* 2 vols., edited by Enrique

Florescano, 28–56. Mexico City: Consejo Nacional para la Cultura y las Artes/ Fondo de Cultura Económica, 1997.

Boone, Elizabeth Hill, ed. *Collecting the Pre-Columbian Past: A Symposium at Dumbarton Oaks, 6th and 7th October 1990.* Washington, DC: Dumbarton Oaks, 1993.

———, ed. *Falsifications and Misreconstructions of Pre-Columbian Art: A Conference at Dumbarton Oaks, October 14th and 15th, 1978.* Washington, DC: Dumbarton Oaks, 1982.

Boytner, Ran, Lynn Swartz Dodd, and Bradley J. Parker, eds. *Controlling the Past: Owning the Future: The Political Uses of Archaeology in the Middle East.* Tucson: University of Arizona Press, 2010.

Brading, David A. *The First America: The Spanish Monarchy, Creole Patriots and the Liberal State, 1492–1867.* Cambridge, UK: Cambridge University Press, 1991.

———. *The Origins of Mexican Nationalism.* Cambridge, UK: Cambridge University Press, 1985.

Breglia, Lisa C. "Docile Descendants and Illegitimate Heirs: Privatization of Cultural Patrimony in Mexico." PhD diss., Rice University, 2003.

———. *Monumental Ambivalence: The Politics of Heritage.* Austin: University of Texas Press, 2006.

Brodie, Neil, Jenny Doole, and Peter Watson. *Stealing History: The Illicit Trade in Cultural Material.* Cambridge, UK: McDonald Institute, 2000.

Brodie, Neil, and Kathryn Walker Tubb. *Illicit Antiquities: The Theft of Culture and the Extinction of Archaeology.* London: Routledge, 2002.

Brunhouse, Robert L. *Frans Blom, Maya Explorer.* Albuquerque: University of New Mexico Press, 1976.

———. *In Search of the Ancient Maya: The First Archaeologists.* Albuquerque: University of New Mexico Press, 1973.

———. *Pursuit of the Ancient Maya: Some Archaeologists of Yesterday.* Albuquerque: University of New Mexico Press, 1975.

———. *Sylvanus G. Morley and the World of the Ancient Maya.* Norman: University of Oklahoma Press, 1971.

Bueno, Christina. "*Forjando Patrimonio*: The Making of Archaeological Patrimony in Porfirian Mexico." *Hispanic American Historical Review* 90, no. 2 (2010): 215–46.

———. "Teotihuacan: Showcase for the Centennial." In *Holiday in Mexico: Critical Reflections on Tourism and Tourist Encounters*, edited by Dina Berger and Andrew Grant Wood, 54–76. Durham, NC: Duke University Press, 2010.

Burke, Spencer. "Envoy: From Deep to Dark." *Harvard Advocate* (May 2011).

———. "The Man Who Owned Chichén Itzá." Unpublished manuscript.

Cabello Carro, Paz. *Coleccionismo americano indígena en la España del siglo XVIII.* Madrid: Ediciones de Cultura Hispánica, 1989.

Camarena Ocampo, Cuauhtémoc, and Teresa Morales Lersch. "Museos comunitarios de Oaxaca: memoria comunal para combatir el olvido." *Arqueología Mexicana* 12, no. 72 (2005): 72–77.

Camp, Roderic Ai. *Reclutamiento político en México.* Mexico City: Siglo XXI, 1996.

Castañeda, Quetzil E. "The Aura of Ruins." In *Fragments of a Golden Age: The Politics of Culture in Mexico Since 1940,* edited by Gilbert M. Joseph, Anne Rubenstein, and Eric Zolov, 452–67. Durham, NC: Duke University Press, 2001.

———. *In the Museum of Maya Culture: Touring Chichén Itzá.* Minneapolis: University of Minnesota Press, 1996.

Castillo Ledón, Luis. *El Museo Nacional de Arqueología, Historia y Etnografía, 1825–1925, Reseña histórica escrita para la celebración de su primer centenario.* Mexico City: Talleres gráficos del Museo Nacional de Arqueología, Historia y Etnografía, 1924.

Castro-Klarén, Sara. "The Nation in Ruins: Archaeology and the Rise of the Nation." In *Beyond Imagined Communities: Reading and Writing the Nation in Nineteenth-Century Latin America,* edited by Sara Castro-Klarén and John Charles Chasteen, 161–96. Baltimore: Johns Hopkins University Press, 2003.

Castro-Klarén, Sara, and John Charles Chasteen, eds. *Beyond Imagined Communities: Reading and Writing the Nation in Nineteenth-Century Latin America.* Baltimore: Johns Hopkins University Press, 2003.

Chabrand, Émile. *De Barcelonnette au Mexique.* Paris: Plon, Nouritt, 1892.

Charnay, Désiré. *The Ancient Cities of the New World: Voyages and Explorations in Mexico and Central America.* Translated by J. Gonino and Helen S. Conant. New York: Harper and Brothers, 1887.

———. *Ciudades y ruinas americanas.* Translated by Rocío Alonzo. Mexico City: Consejo Nacional para la Cultura y las Artes, 1994.

———. *Les anciennes villes du Nouveau Monde: Voyages d'explorations au Mexique et dans l'Amérique Centrale.* Paris: Hachette, 1885.

———. "Mis descubrimientos en México y en la América Central." In *América pintoresca: Descripción de viajes al nuevo continente por los más modernos exploradores,* edited by Charles Weiner, 265–340. Barcelona: Montaner y Simon, 1884.

Chavero, Alfredo. "Discurso pronunciado el 24 de septiembre de 1904 en el Congreso de Artes y Ciencias de la Exposición Universal de San Luis Missouri." *Anales del Museo Nacional* 2, ser. 2 (1905): 387–400.

———. *Historia antigua y de la conquista.* Vol. 1 of *México a través de los siglos: Historia general y completa del desenvolvimiento social, político, religioso, militar, artístico, científico y literario de México desde la antigüedad más remota hasta la época actual,* edited by Vicente Riva Palacio. Barcelona: Espasa, 1887–89.

———. *Monolito de Coatlinchán: Disquisición arqueológica presentada al XIV Congreso de Americanistas por Alfredo Chavero.* Mexico City: Imprenta del Museo Nacional, 1904.

Christensen, Andrew L., ed. *Tracing Archaeology's Past: The Historiography of Archaeology.* Carbondale: Southern Illinois University Press, 1989.

Cleere, Henry, ed. *Approaches to the Archaeological Heritage: A Comparative Study of World Cultural Resource Management Systems.* Cambridge, UK: Cambridge University Press, 1984.

Clifford, James. "Objects and Selves—An Afterword." In *Objects and Others: Essays on Museums and Material Culture,* edited by George W. Stocking Jr., 236-46. Madison: University of Wisconsin Press, 1985.

———. *Routes: Travel and Translation in the Late Twentieth Century.* Cambridge, MA: Harvard University Press, 1997.

Coe, Andrew. *Archaeological Mexico: A Traveler's Guide to Ancient Cities and Sites.* Emeryville, CA: Avalon, 2001.

Coe, Michael D. *Breaking the Maya Code.* New York: Thames and Hudson, 1999.

Coe, Michael D., and Rex Koontz. *The Maya.* 6th ed. New York: Thames and Hudson, 1999.

———. *Mexico: From the Olmecs to the Aztecs.* 5th ed. New York: Thames and Hudson, 2002.

Coggins, Clemency Chase, and Orrin C. Shane III, eds. *Cenote of Sacrifice: Maya Treasures from the Sacred Well at Chichén Itzá.* Austin: University of Texas Press, 1984.

Cole, Douglas. *Captured Heritage: The Scramble for Northwest Coast Artifacts.* Norman: University of Oklahoma Press, 1985.

Congreso Internacional de Americanistas. *Reseña de la segunda sesión del XVII Congreso Internacional de Americanistas efectuada en la ciudad de México durante el mes de septiembre de 1910 (Congreso del centenario).* Nendeln, Liechtenstein: Kraus, 1968.

Conklin, Alice. *In the Museum of Man: Race, Anthropology, and Empire in France, 1850–1950.* Ithaca, NY: Cornell University Press, 2013.

Conn, Steven. *Museums and American Intellectual Life, 1876–1926.* Chicago: University of Chicago Press, 1998.

Corner, William. "Mitla: An Archaeological Study of the Ancient Ruins and Remains in that Pueblo." *Journal of the Anthropological Institute of Great Britain and Ireland* 29, nos. 1-2 (1899): 29-50.

Coronado, Jorge. *The Andes Imagined: Indigenismo, Society, and Modernity.* Pittsburgh, PA: University of Pittsburgh Press, 2009.

Cosío Villegas, Daniel. *Historia moderna de México: El Porfiriato.* Mexico City: Hermes, 1957.

Craib, Raymond B. *Cartographic Mexico: A History of State Fixations and Fugitive Landscapes.* Durham, NC: Duke University Press, 2004.

Crimson, Mark. "Nation-building, Collecting and the Politics of Display: The National Museum of Ghana." *Journal of the History of Collecting* 13, no. 3 (2001): 231-50.

Davis, Keith F. *Désiré Charnay: Expeditionary Photographer*. Albuquerque: University of New Mexico Press, 1981.

Dawson, Alexander S. *Indian and Nation in Revolutionary Mexico*. Tucson: University of Arizona Press, 2004.

de la Cadena, Marisol. *Indigenous Mestizos: The Politics of Race and Culture in Cuzco, Peru, 1919–1991*. Durham, NC: Duke University Press, 2000.

de la Puente, Gómez. *Album oficial del Comité Nacional del Comercio: Primer centenario de la independencia de México, 1810–1910*. Mexico City: Gómez de la Puente, 1910.

del Río de Icaza, Lorenza. *Espacio y tiempo del Museo Regional Cuauhnáhuac: Palacio de Cortés*. Mexico City: Consejo Nacional para la Cultura y las Artes, 2001.

del Villar, Mónica. "La construcción del Museo Nacional de Antropología: Entrevista con Pedro Ramírez Vázquez." *Arqueología Mexicana* 4, no. 24 (1997): 12–21.

Desmond, Lawrence Gustave. *Yucatán through Her Eyes: Alice Dixon Le Plongeon, Writer and Expeditionary Photographer*. Albuquerque: University of New Mexico Press, 2009.

Díaz y de Ovando, Clementina. *Memoria de un debate (1880): La postura de México frente al patrimonio arqueológico nacional*. Mexico City: UNAM, 1990.

Diehl, Richard A. *Tula: The Toltec Capital of Ancient Mexico*. London: Thames and Hudson, 1983.

Donato, Eugenio. "The Museum's Furnace: Notes Toward a Contextual Reading of *Bouvard and Pécuchet*." In *Textual Strategies: Perspectives in Post-Structuralist Criticism*, edited by Josué Harari, 213–38. Ithaca, NY: Cornell University Press, 1979.

Dublán, Manuel, and José María Lozano. *Legislación Mexicana o colección completa de disposiciones legislativas expedidas desde la independencia de la República*. Vol. 2. Mexico City: Dublán y Chávez, 1876.

Dunce, Carol. *Civilizing Rituals: Inside Public Art Museums*. London: Routledge, 1995.

Earle, Rebecca. "Monumentos y museos: la nacionalización del pasado precolombino durante el siglo XIX." In *Galerías del progreso: Museos, exposiciones y cultura visual en América Latina*, edited by Beatriz González Stephan and Jens Alderman, 27–56. Rosario, Argentina: Beatriz Viterbo, 2006.

———. "Nineteenth-Century Historia Patria and the Pre-Columbian Past." Paper presented at the Institute of Latin American Studies, London, June 2003.

———. "'Padres de la Patria' and the Ancestral Past: Commemorations of Independence in Nineteenth-Century Spanish America." *Journal of Latin American Studies* 34, no. 3 (2002): 775–805.

———. *The Return of the Native: Indians and Myth-Making in Spanish America, 1810–1930*. Durham, NC: Duke University Press, 2007.

———. "*Sobre Héroes y Tumbas*: National Symbols in Nineteenth-Century Spanish America." *Hispanic American Historical Review* 85, no. 3 (2005): 375–416.

Edison, Paul. "Conquest Unrequited: French Expeditionary Science in Mexico, 1864–1867." *French Historical Studies* 26, no. 3 (2003): 450–95.

————. "Patrimony on the Periphery: French Archaeologists in Nineteenth-Century Mexico." In *Proceedings of the Annual Meeting of the Western Society for French History*, vol. 24, edited by Barry Rothaus, 494–505. Boulder: University Press of Colorado, 1997.

Eriksen, Thomas Hylland, and Finn Sivert Nielsen. *A History of Anthropology*. London: Pluto, 2001.

Esposito, Matthew D. *Funerals, Festivals, and Cultural Politics in Porfirian Mexico*. Albuquerque: University of New Mexico Press, 2010.

Evans, R. Tripp. *Romancing the Maya: Mexican Antiquity in the American Imagination, 1820–1915*. Austin: University of Texas Press, 2004.

Feifer, Maxine. *Going Places: The Ways of the Tourist from Imperial Rome to the Present*. London: Macmillan, 1985.

Fernández, Miguel Angel. *Historia de los museos de México*. Mexico City: Promotora de Comercialización Directa, 1987.

Ferry, Elizabeth Emma. *Not Ours Alone: Patrimony, Value, and Collectivity in Contemporary Mexico*. New York: Columbia University Press, 2005.

Fewkes, Jesse Walter. "Mural Relief Figures of el Casa del Tepozteco." In *Proceedings of the Davenport Academy of Sciences*, vol. 10, 146–52. Davenport, IA: Davenport Academy of Sciences, 1907.

Florescano, Enrique. "The Creation of the Museo Nacional de Antropología of Mexico and Its Scientific, Educational, and Political Purposes." In *Collecting the Pre-Columbian Past: A Symposium at Dumbarton Oaks, 6th and 7th October 1990*, edited by Elizabeth Hill Boone, 81–103. Washington, DC: Dumbarton Oaks, 1993.

————. "El patrimonio nacional: Valores, usos, estudios y difusión." In vol. 1 of *El patrimonio nacional de Mexico*, 2 vols., edited by Enrique Florescano, 15–27. Mexico City: Consejo Nacional para la Cultura y las Artes/Fondo de Cultura Económica, 1997.

————. *Imágenes de la patria a través de los siglos*. Mexico City: Taurus, 2005.

————. "La creación del Museo Nacional de Antropología." In vol. 2 of *El patrimonio nacional de México*, 2 vols., edited by Enrique Florescano, 147–71. Mexico City: Consejo Nacional para la Cultura y las Artes/Fondo de Cultura Económica, 1997.

————. "México a través de los siglos: Un nuevo modelo para relatar el pasado." *La Jornada*, suplemento mensual, 9 March 2001. http://www.jornada.unam.mx/2001/03/09/suple.html.

Galindo y Villa, Jesús. "En la apertura de clases de historia correspondientes al curso de 1911–1912." *Boletín del Museo Nacional de Historia y Etnología* 1, ser. 3a, nos. 1–12 (1911–12): 22–26.

————."Las ruinas de Cempoala y del Templo del Tajín (Estado de Veracruz) exploradas por el director del Museo Nacional de Arqueología, Historia y Etnología, in misión en Europa, Francisco del Paso y Troncoso: Notas arregladas por Jesús Galindo y Villa en homenaje al XVIII Congreso Internacional de Americanistas que se reunirá en Londres, el mes de mayo de 1912." *Anales del Museo Nacional de Arqueología, Historia y Etnología* 3, ser. 3 (1912): 97–161.

Gallegos Ruiz, Roberto, José Roberto Gallegos Téllez Rojo, and Gabriel Miguel Pastrana Flores. *Antología de documentos para la historia de la arqueología de Teotihuacán*. Mexico City: INAH, 1997.

Gamio, Manuel. "The Chalchihuites Area, Zacatecas." In *The North American Frontier*, edited by Basil C. Hedrick, J. Charles Kelley, and Carroll L. Riley, 50–72. Carbondale: Southern Illinois University Press, 1971.

———. *La población del valle de Teotihuacán*. Vol. 1:1. Mexico: Dirección de Talleres Gráficos, 1922.

Gänger, Stephanie. "Conquering the Past: Post-War Archaeology and Nationalism in the Borderlands of Chile and Peru, c. 1880–1920." *Comparative Studies in Society and History* 51, no. 4 (2009): 691–714.

García, Genaro. *Crónica oficial de las fiestas del Primer Centenario de la Independencia de México*. Mexico City: Talleres del Museo Nacional, 1911.

García Canclini, Néstor. "El patrimonio de México y la construcción imaginaria de lo nacional." In vol. 1 of *El patrimonio nacional de Mexico*, 2 vols., edited by Enrique Florescano, 57–86. Mexico City: Consejo Nacional para la Cultura y las Artes/ Fondo de Cultura Económica, 1997.

———. *Hybrid Cultures, Strategies for Entering and Leaving Modernity*. Translated by Christopher L. Chiappari and Silvia L. López. Minneapolis: University of Minnesota Press, 1995.

García Icazbalceta, Joaquín. *Don Fray Juan de Zumárraga*. Mexico City: Andrade y Morales, 1881.

García Moll, Roberto. "El saqueo de Yaxchilán." *Arqueología Mexicana* 4, no. 21 (1996): 32.

García Mora, Carlos, ed. *La antropología en México*. 15 vols. Mexico City: INAH, 1987.

Garrigan, Shelley. *Collecting Mexico: Museums, Monuments, and the Creation of National Identity*. Minneapolis: University of Minnesota Press, 2012.

———. "Secretos y revelaciones del archivo: Monumentalidad y ciudadanía en la capital mexicana." In *Galerías del progreso: Museos, exposiciones y cultura visual en América Latina*, edited by Beatriz González Stephan and Jens Alderman, 65–88. Rosario, Argentina: Beatriz Viterbo, 2006.

Gathercole, Peter, and David Lowenthal, eds. *The Politics of the Past*. London: Unwin Hyman, 1999.

Gazin-Schwartz, Amy, and Cornelius J. Holtorf, eds. *Archaeology and Folklore*. London: Routledge, 1999.

Gertz Manero, Alejandro. *Defensa jurídica y social del patrimonio cultural*. Mexico City: Fondo de Cultura Económica, 1976.

Gillingham, Paul. *Cuauhtémoc's Bones: Forging National Identity in Modern Mexico*. Albuquerque: University of New Mexico Press, 2011.

Glick, Thomas A., Miguel Angel Puig-Samper, and Rosaura Ruiz. *The Reception of Darwinism in the Iberian World*. Dordrecht: Kluwer, 2001.

Glyn, Daniel. *A Short History of Archaeology*. London: Thames and Hudson, 1981.

Gonzales, Michael J. "Imagining Mexico in 1910: Visions of the *Patria* in the Centennial Celebration in Mexico City." *Journal of Latin American Studies* 39, no. 3 (2007): 495–533.

González Casanova, Pablo. "El ciclo legendario del Tepoztécatl." *Revista Mexicana de Estudios Históricos* 2, no. 1 (1928): 18–63.

González Phillips, Graciela. "Antecedentes coloniales." In vol. 1 of *La antropología en México*, 15 vols., edited by Carlos García Mora, 213–59. Mexico City: INAH, 1987.

Graham, Ian. *Alfred Maudslay and the Maya: A Biography*. London: British Museum Press, 2002.

Graham, Richard, ed. *The Idea of Race in Latin America, 1870–1940*. Austin: University of Texas Press, 1990.

Greenspan, Anders. *Creating Colonial Williamsburg*. Washington, DC: Smithsonian Institution Press, 2002.

Haber, Stephen, Armando Razo, and Noel Maurer. *The Politics of Property Rights: Political Instability, Credible Commitments, and Economic Growth in Mexico, 1876–1929*. Cambridge, UK: Cambridge University Press, 2003.

Hale, Charles A. *The Transformation of Liberalism in Late Nineteenth-Century Mexico*. Princeton, NJ: Princeton University Press, 1989.

Hamy, Ernest-Théodore. *Les origines du Musée d'Ethnographie*. Paris: Jean-Michel Place, 1988.

———. *Mémoires d'archéologie et d'ethnographie américaines*. Graz, Austria: Akademische Druck, 1971.

Harari, Josué, ed. *Textual Strategies: Perspectives in Post-Structuralist Criticism*. Ithaca, NY: Cornell University Press, 1979.

Hinsley, Curtis. "From Shell-Heaps to Stelae: Early Anthropology at the Peabody Museum." In *Objects and Others: Essays on Museums and Material Culture*, edited by George W. Stocking Jr., 49–74. Madison: University of Wisconsin Press, 1985.

———. *The Smithsonian and the American Indian: Making a Moral Anthropology in Victorian America*. Washington, DC: Smithsonian Institution Press, 1981.

Hirth, Kenneth. *Archaeological Research at Xochicalco*. 2 vols. Salt Lake City: University of Utah Press, 2000.

Hobsbawn, Eric, and Terence Ranger, eds. *The Invention of Tradition*. Cambridge, UK: Cambridge University Press, 1983.

Hocquenghem, Anne-Marie, Peter Tamasi, and Christiane Villain-Gandossi, eds. *Pre-Columbian Collections in European Museums*. Budapest: Akademiai Kiado, 1987.

Hoffman, Barbara T., ed. *Art and Cultural Heritage: Law, Policy, and Practice*. Cambridge, UK: Cambridge University Press, 2006.

Hollowell, Julie. "Moral Arguments on Subsistence Digging." In *The Ethics of Archaeology: Philosophical Perspectives on the Practice of Archaeology*, edited by Geoffrey Scarre and Chris Scarre, 69–94. Cambridge, UK: Cambridge University Press, 2006.

Holmes, William Henry. *Monuments of Chiapas, Oaxaca, and the Valley of Mexico.* Vol. 2 of *Archaeological Studies among the Ancient Cities of Mexico.* Field Columbian Museum Anthropological Series, vol. 1, no. 1, Archaeological Studies. Chicago: Publications of the Field Museum of Natural History, 1897.

———. "The Trade in Spurious Mexican Antiquities." *Science 7*, no. 159 (1886): 170–72.

Iguíniz, Juan B. *Las publicaciones del Museo Nacional de Arqueología, Historia y Etnología, apuntes histórico-bibliográficos.* Mexico: Imprenta del Museo Nacional de Arqueología, Historia y Etnología, 1912.

International Congress of Americanists. *Actas del Congreso Internacional de Americanistas: Actas de la Undécima Reunión, Mexico, 1895.* Nendeln, Liechtenstein: Kraus-Thomson, 1968.

———. *Proceedings of the International Congress of Americanists, 13th Session, New York, 1902.* Nendeln, Liechtenstein: Kraus-Thomson, 1968.

Jacknis, Ira. "Franz Boas and Exhibits: On the Limitations of the Museum Method in Anthropology." In *Objects and Others: Essays on Museums and Material Culture,* edited by George W. Stocking Jr., 75–111. Madison: University of Wisconsin Press, 1985.

Kasson, John. *Rudeness and Civility: Manners in Nineteenth-Century Urban America.* New York: Hill and Wang, 1990.

Katz, Friedrich. "The Liberal Republic and the Porfiriato, 1867–1910." In *Mexico since Independence,* edited by Leslie Bethell, 49–124. Cambridge, UK: Cambridge University Press, 1991.

Keen, Benjamin. *The Aztec Image in Western Thought.* New Brunswick, NJ: Rutgers University Press, 1971.

Kelly, Joyce. *Archaeological Guide to Mexico's Yucatán Peninsula.* Norman: University of Oklahoma Press, 1993.

Knight, Alan. "Popular Culture and the Revolutionary State in Mexico, 1910–1940." *Hispanic American Historical Review 74*, no. 3 (1994): 383–444.

———. "Racism, Revolution, and *Indigenismo*: Mexico, 1910–1940." In *The Idea of Race in Latin America, 1870–1940,* edited by Richard Graham, 71–113. Austin: University of Texas Press, 1990.

Koch, Peter O. *John Lloyd Stephens and Frederick Catherwood: Pioneers of Mayan Archaeology.* Jefferson, NC: McFarland, 2013.

Kohl, Philip L. "Nationalism and Archaeology: On the Constructions of Nations and the Reconstructions of the Remote Past." *Annual Review of Anthropology 27* (1998): 223–46.

Kourí, Emilio H. "Interpreting the Expropriation of Indian Pueblo Lands in Porfirian Mexico: The Unexamined Legacies of Andrés Molina Enríquez." *Hispanic American Historical Review 82*, no. 1 (2002): 69–118.

Krech, Shepard, III, and Barbara Hail. *Collecting Native America, 1870–1960.* Washington, DC: Smithsonian Institution Press, 1999.

Kuhn, Thomas S. *The Structure of Scientific Revolutions*. Chicago: University of Chicago Press, 1996.

Larson, Carolyne R. *Our Indigenous Ancestors: A Cultural History of Museums, Science, and Identity in Argentina, 1877–1943*. University Park: Pennsylvania State University Press, 2015.

Lear, John. "Mexico City: Space and Class in the Porfirian Capital, 1884–1910." *Journal of Urban History* 22, no. 4 (1996): 454–92.

Léon y Gama, Antonio. "Descripción histórica y cronológica de las dos piedras." In *Trabajos arqueológicos en el centro de México*, edited by Eduardo Matos Moctezuma, 43–95. Mexico City: INAH, 1979.

————. *Descripción histórica y cronológica de las dos piedras que con ocasión del nuevo empedrado que se está formando en la plaza principal de México, se hallaron en ella el año de 1790*. Mexico City: Felipe de Zúñiga y Ontiveros, 1792.

Lewis, Oscar. *Life in a Mexican Village: Tepoztlán Restudied*. Chicago: University of Illinois Press, 1951.

"Ley sobre ocupación y enajenación de terrenos baldíos." In vol. 3 of *INAH: Una historia*, 3 vols., edited by Julio César Olivé Negrete and Bolfy Cottom, 236. Mexico City: Consejo Nacional para la Cultura y las Artes, INAH, 1995.

Linné, Sigvald. *Archaeological Researches at Teotihuacan, Mexico*. Tuscaloosa: University of Alabama Press, 2003.

Litvak King, Jaime, Luis González R., and María del Refugio González, eds. *Arqueología y derecho en México*. Mexico City: UNAM, 1980.

Lombardo de Ruiz, Sonia. *El pasado prehispánico en la cultura nacional: Memoria hemerográfica, 1877–1911*. 2 vols. Mexico City: INAH, 1994.

Lombardo de Ruiz, Sonia, and Ruth Solís Vicarte. *Antecedentes de las leyes sobre monumentos históricos, 1536–1910*. Mexico City: INAH, 1988.

Lomnitz, Claudio. *Death and the Idea of Mexico*. New York: Zone, 2005.

————. *Deep Mexico, Silent Mexico: An Anthropology of Nationalism*. Minneapolis: University of Minnesota Press, 2001.

López Camacho, María de Lourdes. "El caso particular de la legislación sobre monumentos arqueológicos." Biblioteca Jurídica Virtual del Instituto de Investigaciones Jurídicas de la UNAM, n.d.

López Luján, Leonardo. "'El adiós y triste queja del gran Calendario Azteca': El incesante peregrinar de la Piedra del Sol." *Arqueología Mexicana* 16, no. 91 (2008): 78–83.

Lorenzo, José Luis. *La arqueología y México*. Ed. Lorena Mirambell Silva and Jaime Litvak King. Mexico City: INAH, 1998.

Lowenthal, David. "Fabricating Heritage." *History and Memory* 10, no. 1 (1998): 5–24.

Lyman, R. Lee, and Michael J. O'Brien. "Americanist Stratigraphic Excavation and the Measurement of Cultural Change." *Journal of Archaeological Method and Theory* 6, no. 1 (1999): 55–108.

Lynott, Mark J., and Alison Wylie. *Ethics in American Archaeology: Challenges for the 1990s*. Washington, DC: Society for American Archaeology, 1995.

MacLachlan, Colin M., and William H. Beezley. *El Gran Pueblo: A History of Greater Mexico*. Upper Saddle River, NJ: Pearson Prentice Hall, 2004.

Maclaren Walsh, Jane. "Crystal Skulls and Other Problems; or, 'Don't Look It in the Eye.'" In *Exhibiting Dilemmas: Issues of Representation at the Smithsonian*, edited by Amy Henderson and Adrienne L. Kaeppler, 116–39. Washington, DC: Smithsonian Institution Press, 1997.

Manrique Castañeda, Leonardo. "Leopoldo Batres." In vol. 9 of *La antropología en México*, 15 vols., edited by Carlos García Mora and Lina Odena Güemes, 242–57. Mexico City: INAH, 1987.

Matos Moctezuma, Eduardo. *Las piedras negadas: De la Coatlicue al Templo Mayor*. Mexico City: Consejo Nacional para la Cultura y las Artes, 1997.

———. *Manuel Gamio: La arqueología mexicana*. Mexico City: UNAM, 1983.

———. *Teotihuacán: The City of Gods*. New York: Rizzoli, 1990.

———, ed. *Trabajos arqueológicos en el centro de México*. Mexico City: INAH, 1979.

Mauch Messenger, Phyllis. *The Ethics of Collecting Cultural Property: Whose Property? Whose Culture?* Albuquerque: University of New Mexico Press, 1999.

Maudslay, Alfred Percival. *Archaeology: Biologia Centrali-Americana*. Vol. 5. New York: Milpatron, 1974.

Méndez-Gastelumendi, Cecilia. "Incas Sí, Indios No: Notes on Peruvian Creole Nationalism and Its Contemporary Crisis." *Journal of Latin American Studies* 28, no. 1 (1996): 197–225.

Mendoza, Gumesindo. "Complemento al erudito artículo del señor Orozco y Berra escrito por el señor Gumesindo Mendoza, Director del Museo." *Anales del Museo Nacional de México* 1, ser. 1 (1877): 217–25.

———. "Discurso acerca de la piedra llamada Calendario Mexicano pronunciado por el profesor Philipp Valentini." *Anales del Museo Nacional de México* 1, ser. 1 (1877): 226–41.

———. "Idolo Azteca de Tipo Japonés." *Anales del Museo Nacional de México* 1, ser. 1 (1877): 91.

———. "Las pirámides de Teotihuacan." *Anales del Museo Nacional de México* 1, ser. 1 (1877): 186–95.

Mendoza, Gumesindo, and Jesús Sánchez. "Catálogo de las colecciones histórica y arqueológica del Museo Nacional de México." *Anales del Museo Nacional de México* 2, ser. 1 (1882): 445–86.

Merryman, John Henry, Albert Edward Elsen, and Stephen K. Urice. *Law, Ethics, and the Visual Arts*. Netherlands: Kluwer, 2007.

Mexico. *Diario de los debates de la Cámara de Diputados, Decimaoctava Legislatura Constitutional de la Unión*. Vol. 1. Mexico City: El Partido Liberal, 1896.

———. *Diario de los debates de la Cámara de Diputados, Decimanovena Legislatura Constitutional de la Unión*. Vol. 3. Mexico City: Central, 1899.

Meyer, R. M. Alejandro. "Alfredo Chavero." In vol. 9 of *La antropología en México*, 15 vols., edited by Carlos García Mora and Lina Odena Güemes, 588–601. Mexico City: INAH, 1987.

Miller, Mary, and Karl Taube. *An Illustrated Dictionary of the Gods and Symbols of Ancient Mexico and the Maya*. London: Thames and Hudson, 1993.

Miller, Mary Ellen. *The Art of Mesoamerica: From Olmec to Aztec*. Rev. ed. London: Thames and Hudson, 1996.

Millon, René. *Urbanization at Teotihuacán, Mexico*. 3 vols. Austin: University of Texas Press, 1973.

Ministère de l'Instruction Publique. *Archives de la Commission Scientifique du Mexique*. Paris: Imprimerie Imperiale, 1865–1867.

Molina Montes, Augusto. "Archaeological Buildings: Restoration or Misrepresentation." In *Falsifications and Misreconstructions of Pre-Columbian Art: A Conference at Dumbarton Oaks, October 14th and 15th, 1978*, edited by Elizabeth Hill Boone, 125–41. Washington, DC: Dumbarton Oaks, 1982.

———. "Palenque: The Archaeological City Today." http://www.mesoweb.com/pari/publications/RT04/Palenque.pdf

Morales Moreno, Luis Gerardo. *Orígenes de la museología mexicana: Fuentes para el estudio histórico del Museo Nacional, 1780–1940*. Mexico City: Universidad Iberoamericana, 1994.

Moraña, Mabel, Enrique Dussel, and Carlos A. Jáuregui, eds. *Coloniality at Large: Latin America and the Postcolonial Debate*. Durham, NC: Duke University Press, 2008.

Mora-Torres, Juan. *The Making of the Mexican Border: The State, Capitalism, and Society in Nuevo León, 1848–1910*. Austin: University of Texas Press, 2001.

Nahmad, Salomón. "Las ideas sociales del positivismo en el indigenismo de la época pre-revolucionaria en México." *América Indígena* 33, no. 4 (1973): 1169–82.

Noguera, Eduardo. *Ruinas arqueológicas del norte de México: Casas Grandes (Chihuahua), La Quemada, Chalchihuites (Zacatecas)*. Mexico City: Publicaciones de la Secretaría de Educación Pública, 1930.

Nora, Pierre. "Between Memory and History: *Les Lieux de Mémoire*." *Representations* 26 (1989): 7–24.

Nuttall, Zelia. "The Island of Sacrificios." *American Anthropologist* 12, no. 2 (1910): 257–95.

Olivé Negrete, Julio César, and Augusto Urteaga Castro-Pozo. *INAH: Una historia*. Mexico City: INAH, 1988.

Orozco y Berra, Manuel. "Dedicación del Templo Mayor de México." *Anales del Museo Nacional* 1, ser. 1 (1877): 60–74.

Ortega y Medina, Juan A., ed. *Polémicas y ensayos mexicanos en torno a la historia*. México: UNAM, 1970.

Oyuela-Caycedo, Augusto. *History of Latin American Archaeology*. Aldershot, UK: Avebury, 1994.

Ozouf, Mona. *Festivals and the French Revolution.* Translated by Alan Sheridan. Cambridge, MA: Harvard University Press, 1988.

Peñafiel, Antonio. *Monumentos del arte mexicano antiguo.* 3 vols. Berlin: Asher, 1890.

———. *Teotihuacán: Estudio histórico y arqueológico.* Mexico City: Oficina Tipográfica de la Secretaría de Fomento, 1900.

Penny, H. Glenn. *Objects of Culture: Ethnology and Ethnographic Museums in Imperial Germany.* Chapel Hill: University of North Carolina Press, 2002.

Pick, Daniel. *Faces of Degeneration: A European Disorder, c. 1848– c. 1918.* Cambridge, UK: Cambridge University Press, 1989.

Pilcher, Jeffrey M. *¡Que vivan los tamales! Food and the Making of Mexican Identity.* Albuquerque: University of New Mexico Press, 1998.

Poole, Deborah. *Vision, Race, Modernity: A Visual Economy of the Andean Image World.* Princeton, NJ: Princeton University Press, 1997.

Price, Sally. *Primitive Art in Civilized Places.* 2nd ed. Chicago: University of Chicago Press, 2001.

Radnóti, Sándor. *The Fake: Forgery and Its Place in Art.* Translated by Ervin Dunai. New York: Rowan and Littlefield, 1999.

Ramírez Aznar, Luis. *El saqueo del cenote sagrado de Chichén Itzá.* Mexico City: Dante, 1990.

Rappaport, Joanne. *Cumbre Reborn: An Andean Ethnography of History.* Chicago: University of Chicago Press, 1994.

Read, Kay Almere, and Jason J. González. *Mesoamerican Mythology: A Guide to the Gods, Heroes, Rituals, and Beliefs of Mexico and Central America.* Oxford, UK: Oxford University Press, 2000.

Redfield, Robert. *Tepoztlán: A Mexican Village.* Chicago: University of Chicago Press, 1930.

Reis, Brian A. "The Nineteenth-Century Photographs of Désiré Charnay: Images and Interpretations of a Pre-Columbian Past." MA thesis, Northern Illinois University, 2005.

Rico Mansard, Luisa Fernanda Francisca. *Exhibir para educar: Objetos, colecciones y museos de la ciudad de México (1790–1910).* Barcelona: Pomares/Mexico City: Consejo Nacional para la Cultura y las Artes, 2004.

Ríos Meneses, Miriam Beatriz. "Museo regional de antropología de Yucatán." In vol. 7 of *La antropología en México,* 15 vols., edited by Carlos García Mora, 600–612. Mexico City: INAH, 1987.

Rius [Eduardo del Río García]. *Un siglo de caricatura en México.* Mexico City: Grijalbo, 1984.

Riva Palacio, Vicente, ed. *México a través de los siglos: Historia general y completa del desenvolvimiento social, político, religioso, militar, artístico, científico y literario de México desde la antigüedad más remota hasta la época actual.* Barcelona: Espasa, 1887–89.

Rivera Cambas, Manuel. *México pintoresco, artístico y monumental.* 3 vols. Mexico City: Editora Nacional, 1880.

Robelo, Cecilio. *Geografía del estado de Morelos.* Cuernavaca: Imprenta del Gobierno del Estado, 1885.

———. *Ruinas de Xochicalco.* Translated by Eugenio Le Baron. Cuernavaca: J. D. Rojas, 1902.

———. "Xochicalco." *La Semana* 1, no. 9 (1888).

Robles García, Nelly M. "Historia de la arqueología de Mesoamérica: Oaxaca." In *Descubridores del pasado en Mesoamérica,* edited by Eduardo Matos Mocte-zuma, 111–33. Mexico City: Océano, 2001.

Robles García, Nelly M., and Alfredo J. Moreira Quirós. *Proyecto Mitla: Restauración de la zona arqueológica en su contexto urbano.* Mexico City: INAH, 1990.

Robles García, Nelly M., Marcelo Leonardo Magadán, and Alfredo Moreira Quirós. *Reconstrucción colonial en Mitla, Oaxaca.* Mexico City: INAH, 1987.

Roldán Vera, Eugenia, and Marcelo Caruso. *Imported Modernity in Post-Colonial State Formation: The Appropriation of Political, Educational, and Cultural Models in Nineteenth-Century Latin America.* Frankfurt am Main, Germany: Peter Lang, 2007.

Romer, John. *The History of Archaeology.* New York: Checkmark Books, 2001.

Romero, Héctor Manuel. *Crónica mexicana del turismo.* Mexico City: Textos Universitarios, 1977.

Rosas, María. *Tepoztlán: Crónica de desacatos y resistencia.* Mexico City: Era, 1997.

Ruiz, Carmen. "Insiders and Outsiders in Mexican Archaeology, 1890–1930." PhD diss., University of Texas, 2003.

Ruiz Gutiérrez, Rosaura. *Positivismo y evolución: Introducción del darwinismo en México.* Mexico City: UNAM, 1987.

Ruiz Martínez, Apen. "La construcción del conocimiento en ruta: Expediciones antropológicas y arqueológicas en México a fines del siglo XIX." *Antípoda,* no. 11 (2010): 215–37.

Rutsch, Mechthild. *Entre el campo y el gabinete: Nacionales y extranjeros en la profe-sionalización de la antropología mexicana (1877–1920).* Mexico City: INAH/ UNAM, 2007.

———, ed. *La historia de la antropología en México: Fuentes y transmisión.* Mexico City: Universidad Iberoamericana, Instituto Nacional Indigenista, and Plaza y Valdes, 1996.

———. "Natural History, National Museum and Anthropology in Mexico: Some Reference Points in the Forging and Re-Forging of National Identity." *Perspectivas Latinoamericanas,* no. 1 (2004): 89–122.

Rydell, Robert W. *All the World's a Fair: Visions of Empire at American International Expositions, 1876–1916.* Chicago: University of Chicago Press, 1984.

Saldaña, Juan José, ed. *Science in Latin America: A History.* Translated by Bernabé Madrigal. Austin: University of Texas Press, 2006.

Sánchez, Jesús. "Estudio acerca de la estatua llamada Chac-Mool ó Rey Tigre." *Anales del Museo Nacional* 1, ser. 1 (1877): 270–78.

Sánchez Valdés, María Teresa, and Raul Reissner. "El despunte de la investigación científica (1862–1867)." In vol. 1 of *La antropología en México*, 15 vols., edited by Carlos Garcia Mora, 430–88. Mexico City: INAH, 1987.

Saville, Marshall H. *Bibliographic Notes on Palenque, Chiapas*. Indian Notes and Monographs 6, no. 5. New York: Museum of the American Indian, 1928.

———. *Bibliographic Notes on Xochicalco, Mexico*. Indian Notes and Monographs 6, no. 6. New York: Museum of the American Indian, 1928.

———. "The Cruciform Structures of Mitla and Vicinity." In *Anthropological Essays Presented to Frederic Ward Putnam in Honor of His Seventieth Birthday, April 16, 1909, by His Friends and Associates*, edited by Franz Boas, 151–90. New York: G. E. Stechert, 1909.

———. "The Temple of Tepoztlan, Mexico." *Bulletin of the American Museum of Natural History* 8 (1897): 221–26.

———. "The Work of the Loubat Expedition in Southern Mexico." Paris: privately printed, 1911.

Sax, Margaret, et al. "The Origins of Two Purportedly Pre-Columbian Mexican Crystal Skulls." *Journal of Archaeological Science* 35, no. 10 (2008): 2751–60.

Scarre, Geoffrey, and Chris Scarre, eds. *The Ethics of Archaeology: Philosophical Perspectives on the Practice of Archaeology*. Cambridge, UK: Cambridge University Press, 2006.

Schávelzon, Daniel. *Arte y falsificación en América Latina*. Buenos Aires: Fondo de Cultura Económica, 2009.

———. "Historia social de la restauración arquitectónica en México." *Vivienda* 6, no. 5 (1981): 434–37.

———. "La arqueología y el imperialismo: La invasión francesa a México (1864–1867)." *Mesoamérica* 15, no. 28 (1994): 321–35.

———. "La Comisión Científica Francesa a México (1864–1867) y el inicio de la arqueología en América." *Pacarina* 3, no. 3 (2003): 313–22.

———. "Saqueo y destrucción del patrimonio nacional (1821–1911)." http://www.daniel schavelzon.com.ar/?p-2919

Schele, Linda, and David Freidel. *A Forest of Kings: The Untold Story of the Ancient Maya*. New York: William Morrow, 1990.

Schiffman, Zachary Sayre. *The Birth of the Past*. Baltimore: Johns Hopkins University Press, 2011.

Scott, James C. *Seeing Like a State: How Certain Schemes to Improve the Human Condition Have Failed*. New Haven: Yale University Press, 1998.

Secretaría de Gobernación. *Crónica oficial de las fiestas del primer centenario de la independencia de México, publicada bajo la dirección de Genaro García por acuerdo de la Secretaría de Gobernación*. Mexico City: Talleres del Museo Nacional, 1911.

Sierra, Justo. *Epistolario y papeles privados.* Edited by Catalina Sierra de Peimbert. Mexico City: UNAM, 1949.

———. *Obras completas.* 14 Vols. Mexico: UNAM, 1984.

———. *Obras completas del maestro Justo Sierra.* Edited by Agustín Yáñez. 17 vols. Mexico City: UNAM, 1948.

———. *The Political Evolution of the Mexican People.* Translated by Charles Ramsdell. Austin: University of Texas Press, 1969.

Sierra Carrillo, Dora. *Cien Años de etnografía en el Museo.* Mexico: INAH, 1994.

Sigaux, Gilbert. *History of Tourism.* Translated by Joan White. London: Leisure Arts, 1966.

Smith, Claire, and H. Martin Wobst. *Indigenous Archaeologies: Decolonizing Theory and Practice.* New York: Routledge, 2005.

Smith, Valene L., and Maryann Brent. *Hosts and Guests Revisited: Tourism Issues of the 21st Century.* New York: Cognizant Communication Corporation, 2001.

Sotelo Santos, Laura Elena. *Yaxchilán.* Chiapas, Mexico: Espejo de Obsidiana, 1992.

Stabb, Martin S. "Indigenism and Racism in Mexican Thought, 1857–1911." *Journal of Inter-American Studies* 1, no. 4 (1959): 405–23.

Steinberg, William H., Jr. *Uncovering the Past: A History of Archaeology.* Amherst, New York: Prometheus, 1993.

Stewart, Susan. *On Longing: Narratives of the Miniature, the Gigantic, the Souvenir, the Collection.* Durham, NC: Duke University Press, 1993.

Suárez Cortés, Blanca Estela. "Las interpretaciones positivistas del pasado y el presente (1880–1910)." In vol. 2 of *La antropología en México*, 15 vols., edited by Carlos García Mora, 13–88. Mexico City: INAH, 1987.

Suarez-Potts, William J. *The Making of Law: The Supreme Court and Labor Legislation in Mexico, 1875–1931.* Stanford, CA: Stanford University Press, 2012.

Sumner, Jaclyn. "National Autocracy, Regional Governance: Tlaxcala, Mexico, 1885–1909." PhD diss., University of Chicago, 2014.

Tenenbaum, Barbara A. *Mexico and the Royal Indian: The Porfiriato and the National Past.* College Park: Latin American Studies Center, University of Maryland, 1994.

———. "Streetwise History: The Paseo de la Reforma and the Porfirian State, 1876–1910." In *Rituals of Rule, Rituals of Resistance: Public Celebrations and Popular Culture in Mexico,* edited by William H. Beezley, Cheryl English Martin, and William E. French, 127–50. Wilmington, DE: Scholarly Resources, 1994.

Tenorio-Trillo, Mauricio. *Mexico at the World's Fairs: Crafting a Modern Nation.* Berkeley: University of California Press, 1999.

———. "1910 Mexico City: Space and Nation in the City of the *Centenario.*" *Journal of Latin American Studies* 28, no. 1 (1996): 75–104.

Thompson, Edward H. "Forty Years of Research and Exploration in Yucatan." *Proceedings of the American Antiquarian Society* 39, no. 1 (1929): 41–42.

Thurner, Mark, and Andrés Guerrero. *After Spanish Rule: Postcolonial Predicaments of the Americas.* Durham, NC: Duke University Press, 2003.

Tovar de Teresa, Guillermo. *Ciudades de Luz: Désiré Charnay, Viollet-Le-Duc*. Mexico City: Grupo Financiero del Sureste, 1993.

Trigger, Bruce G. *A History of Archaeological Thought*. Cambridge, UK: Cambridge University Press, 1989.

———. "Writing the History of Archaeology: A Survey of Trends." In *Objects and Others: Essays on Museums and Material Culture*, edited by George W. Stocking Jr., 218–35. Madison: University of Wisconsin Press, 1985.

Vázquez León, Luis. *El leviatán arqueológico: antropología de una tradición científica en México*. Mexico City: Centro de Investigaciones y Estudios Superiores en Antropología Social, 2003.

———. "Mexico: The Institutionalization of Archaeology, 1885–1942." In *History of Latin American Archaeology*, edited by Augusto Oyuela-Caycedo, 69–89. Aldershot, UK: Avebury, 1994.

Vigil, José María. "Necesidad y conveniencia de estudiar la historia patria." In *Polémicas y ensayos mexicanos en torno a la historia*, edited by Juan A. Ortega y Medina, 257–78. Mexico City: UNAM, 1970.

Wells, Allen, and Gilbert M. Joseph. "Modernizing Visions, 'Chilango' Blueprints, and Provincial Growing Pains: Mérida at the Turn of the Century." *Mexican Studies/Estudios Mexicanos* 8, no. 2 (1992): 167–215.

Widdifield, Stacie G. *The Embodiment of the National in Late Nineteenth-Century Mexican Painting*. Tucson: University of Arizona Press, 1996.

Wiener, Charles, ed. *América pintoresca: Descripción de viajes al nuevo continente por los más modernos exploradores*. Barcelona: Montaner y Simon, 1884.

Willard, Theodore Arthur. *The City of the Sacred Well*. New York: Century, 1926.

Willey, Gordon R., and Jeremy A. Sabloff. *A History of American Archaeology*. London: Thames and Hudson, 1974.

Williams, Elizabeth A. "Art and Artifact at the Trocadero: *Ars Americana* and the Primitivist Revolution." In *Objects and Others: Essays on Museums and Material Culture*, edited by George W. Stocking Jr., 146–66. Madison: University of Wisconsin Press, 1985.

———. "The Science of Man: Anthropological Thought and Institutions in Nineteenth-Century France." PhD diss., Indiana University, 1983.

Zavala, Silvio. *Francisco del Paso y Troncoso, su misión en Europa, 1892–1916*. Mexico City: Departamento Autónomo de Prensa y Publicidad, 1938.

Ziff, Bruce, and Pratima V. Rao, eds. *Borrowed Power: Essays on Cultural Appropriation*. New Brunswick, NJ: Rutgers University Press, 1997.

Index

Page numbers in italic text indicate illustrations.